THE DREADFUL YEARS

Collected Interviews & Reflections - 2018 to 2021

JOSHUA MILLICAN

Encyclopocalypse Publications
www.encyclopocalypse.com

Contents

Foreword

Gigi Saul Guerrero

It was back in 2016 in Little Rock, Arkansas where we found ourselves accepting the Fantastic Cinema Emerging Filmmakers Award from the Film Society of Little Rock. A quaint and small local film festival with a great community, found us in love with the people and team hosting the event. The great thing about traveling around with your projects is that you get to meet so many new people in the industry, some come and go, and some, you build a long-time friendship. That's where we met Josh Millican, the former Director of Community for CryptTV. Almost instantly hitting it off the start, we were both just getting into our careers in film and entertainment, and our values, tastes in film aligned perfectly.

With his knowledge in the horror genre, we could see how fitting Josh's time at CryptTV was, helping it grow into a massive horror social platform that ultimately ended up into them producing original shorts, series, and much more. Josh was always keeping an eye on us at Luchagore, and becoming a huge fan and supporter of us. Reviewing our works with professionalism and understanding our type of stories, and what we've strived to tell. As a Journalist/Author, he has become a valuable asset to the horror community, and it's fitting that he landed over at Dread Central.

Josh is also very immersive and found himself visiting one of the sets for the **Into the Dark** feature horror anthology series, **Culture Shock**. It was one of the toughest days where the cast had a heavy scene to shoot, with of course, no time at all. He instantly knew what was going on, and observed us working fast to keep on schedule. Cheering us on and pumping us up, he got to witness one of the best episodes of that series in the making. He just knows when to show up at the right times apparently, and how to be a champion.

When we completed another movie in 2021 called **Bingo Hell** with Amazon and Blumhouse productions, Josh called us up to see if we wanted to do a **Dissecting Horror** episode with him, along with some of the creatives. We knew, never turn down an opportunity when Josh comes knocking, as we know how he carefully crafts his programs with lots of research, amazing questions, and most of all, making a fun environment and safe place to talk about your works.

Josh is our good friend, colleague, and overall, just an amazing individual. And most recently a new father. We're so proud to see his growth in his line of work, and always a fan in cheering him for what the future always holds.

#Luchagore4life

Gore is love, LUCHAGORE PRODUCTIONS

Gigi Saul Guerrero & Raynor Shima

Foreword

Heather Buckley

Fantastic Fest 2018, recreating the "lost" scene from Nightbreed

Joshua Millican writes in 3-cord punk rock style. He keeps the circle pit energy up. He has an eye for cinema. The dark stuff. The *wild* stuff. He has dreads and was the EIC of Dread Central.

He supports the independent voice. He is a Nightbreed as evident in our on-the-ground at Fantasia Fest selfie. Do not deny it; that Peloquin energy is real. But above all in Horrorweird USA; he is a champion of genre, the people who make it, and the fans. Joshua Millican is also my friend.

Within these pages are his collected works—years of interviews and insights. All horror. His insights, his passion, his twist-of-the-knife style of prose laid bare for you, the reader, to pour over. I would say "life's work," but this is just the beginning. There is so much more to do.

Now turn the page if you dare. There's really no turning back now.

Heather Buckley
Producer | President of Black Mansion

Introduction

Well, how did I get here?

For starters, yes, I absolutely was one of those freaky horror kids. 1986 was a formative year for me, as that summer saw the release of both **Aliens** and David Cronenberg's **The Fly**. Of course I was well under the age of 18, but thankfully I had and aunt and a dad who were cool enough to accompany me.

Aliens and **The Fly**: The first had me glued to my seat while that latter had me on its absolute edge, ready to flee into the aisle should the intensity prove more than I could withstand. (That maggot birth scene really fucked me up!). Here's the kicker: I loved them both immensely. My love of the genre was solidified and I'd go on to enjoy more horror/sci-fi, more body horror, and more of everything in between.

My love affair with horror waned during my college years. I was more interested in (obsessed with) music and women. And that extended into my post-college phase as well, when

I put all of my efforts into founding a hybrid punk/metal/electronica band. Still, I always had my ears to the ground for a good genre flick. No, I wasn't avid, but horror was always my favorite aisle at the video store, and I remember seeing **The Exorcist: The Version You've Never Seen** when it was re-released theatrically. I saw **The Blair Witch Project** in a theater too, because the buzz was simply impossible to ignore.

My genre love never disappeared completely; it was merely laying dormant, like a sleeping Lovecraftian elder god at the bottom of the cold murky sea.

And then came Netflix.

Some of you might not even be old enough to know this, but in the beginning, Netflix used to mail you DVDs. No seriously. Up to three at a time with return shipping envelopes and no late fees. This is when I finally began searching horror websites for suggestions on what to watch, films I had missed throughout the 1990s and the aughts. I was playing catch-up for all my years of horror hibernation. And then, sometime during the late 2000s, Netflix began streaming—and my life would never be the same again.

These were some gory Glory Days indeed. In the beginning, it seemed like the horror selection on Netflix was limitless. It wasn't like it is now, where movies of every breed are spread out over a half-dozen competing platforms. And it seemed like Netflix had everything—everything worth seeing at least. The classics, the hits, the obscure, the foreign, the extreme, the arthouse, and the bombs. I watch one, two, maybe three horror movies a day.

Now, the woman I was involved with at the time was no fan of horror, so all of these viewings were solitary occasions.

But that probably helped me immerse myself more completely into the movie-watching experience. I'd stay up late watching horror until the wee hours, falling asleep exhausted and (if I was lucky) pleasantly terrified.

Inevitably, I'd be anxious to tell my partner what I'd seen the night before. I never did the chatroom thing, so this was how I'd decompress and solidify my thoughts about movies. I'd give her extended plot summaries (sometimes including dramatic re-enactments), break down character arcs and symbolism, place the film in a historical context and wrap it up with concise summary.

"I'll still never watch a horror movie with you," she told me one day. "But I love the way you talk about them. You should start a blog." That was it. The moment.

Like a lot of Gen Xers in the 21st Century, I've always felt a little out of place and out of time. Had I been born 10 years earlier, I might have been poised to master industries that had been established before me. Had I been born 10 years later, I would have come of age in this current digital world where the Internet and computers are essential. Instead, I watched the world shift completely after I'd already graduated from college with degrees in Literature and Creative Writing. I hadn't given a bit of consideration to preparing myself for the massive shift in global technologies because I'm not fucking psychic. I didn't even get my first email address until I got my first post-college office job. (My 10-month-old son already has his first Gmail account, for comparison). Not a Boomer, not quite a Millennial. Always in Limbo.

So, yeah, I was late to the blogging game when I launched mine in the late 2000s, but I was nonetheless completely inspired. I snagged myself one of those free WordPress accounts, plugged in a pre-fabricated theme, and **Blood & Guts for Grown-Ups** was born.

It might seem like a lame title in retrospect, but back then, horror still wasn't mainstream, was still unrecognized as the entertainment juggernaut it would become by the late 2010s. This was before "elevated horror" and the genre still needed all of the proponents it could get. Most people still considered it gutter entertainment, the lowest rung, kid stuff. When most people heard "horror", they thought **Friday the 13th**. But of course, we all know it's so much more.

I'd review horror movies that weren't aimed at a teenage audience, horror movies that pushed boundaries and broke preconceived expectations. And it turned out that my litera-ture and writing degrees came in handy (along with some advanced journalism courses I'd taken one summer). I was able to identify themes, plumb subtexts, and present theo-ries and opinions with concise, structured expositions. In other words, I was a natural critic. I'd aspire to review one film a day on my blog. I set out to become more than just a horror fan, more than an aficionado even. I set out to become a horror expert!

I didn't get into horror journalism to get rich. I got into it for the love of it, for the joy of dissecting genre flicks and sharing my opinions with other interested parties. It wasn't long until I started getting recruited to write for more estab-lished horror outlets. None could afford to pay me, but this was back when "writing for exposure" wasn't as insulting as it is today. Soon after I began my foray into horror on the internet, it was clear who the major players were: **Bloody Disgusting** and **Dread Central**. I set my sites and began manifesting my destiny. "I will work for one of these outlets," I told myself. "And I will make my living as a professional horror journalist."

I think journalists are heroes. They're on the tip of the spearhead of history unfolding. Sure, war correspondents are more heroic than entertainment journalists, but everyone who writes with a desire to inform and a sense of urgency deserves praise for their efforts. And I took my job as a journalist seriously. Still, I was unprepared for this Internet world. I didn't fully understand these new cyber rules and mores. And I made mistakes along the way. I stumbled, I embarrassed myself, but I always picked up the pieces and moved forward. I realized fast that being the best journalist in the world was less important than being the best Joshua Millican in the world. And with this outlook, I would indeed achieve my wildest aspirations.

The site that launched me on this course was ***The Blood-Shed***. They couldn't pay me, but the then-owner actually gave me a stake in the "company" and the lofty title of Managing Editor. It was through my work at ***The Blood-Shed*** that I met Jack Davis, who had only recently launched ***Crypt TV***.

It's almost funny, because in those early days, no one really knew what Crypt TV was. I'm not even sure if Davis and his crew were sure at first. I knew that Crypt TV had been co-founded by Eli Roth, and, well, that's about it. But that's a testament to Jack's genius; he could get folks excited about something that was nebulous. He began inducting websites into a Crypt TV Network, and as soon as I saw who the other members were (every horror site of prominence plus the big boys at Dread Central). I knew The Blood-Shed had to be on board. Jack was very one-on-one with the folks who reached out to him. He liked my enthusiasm and agreed that The Blood-Shed was perfect for the Network. And, in turn, Jack inspired me. It wasn't long before I decided that I wanted to work at Crypt TV.

Crypt TV couldn't afford to pay me back then either, but the perks were awesome. All the swag a boy could hope for —and that was just for starters. I made a trip down from Oakland to Los Angeles just to meet the Crypt TV team in person. I begged Jack to let me add a news component CryptTV.com, but he wasn't interested. There were already dozens of horror news outlets on the net and he didn't want to come in as a new kid. He had higher aspirations for Crypt TV. But even though he shot me down, he kept me close. He gave me the title of Community Manager, put me in charge of The Crypt Family Facebook Group (a tribe of weird horror lovers that no longer exists). And it was as a brand ambassador of Crypt TV that I took all-expenses-paid trips to the Fantastic Cinema and Craft Beer Festival in Little Rock, Arkansas, and the first Monsterpalooza festival in Houston, Texas.

These were my first tastes of Festival Life and Convention Life respectively—and I fucking loved it. The travel, the hotels, the rabid fandom. It was bliss. And while, ultimately, my affiliation with Crypt TV would never manifest into a full-time paid gig, it did serve as a stepping stone to what would indeed be my first real horror job.

Horror Freak News was also a member of the Crypt TV network of websites. They had an enviable following, owing to the fact that it had been launched as **BestHorror-Movies.com** back in the long-long ago when all of the best domain names were still up for grabs. The owners identified me as a rising personae on the scene, agreed that I had an above average aptitude for producing great written content, and brought me aboard, first as a contributor and, eventually, as Managing Editor. And it was at Horror Freak News that I built my reputation as a recognizable (if not always lauded) name in the industry.

By the time Horror Freak News imploded and was forced into a brief hiatus (through absolutely no fault of mine, I promise!) I was poised to earn a subsistence living by working as a paid freelancer. It was during this period that I officially left my current day-job, never looking back.

While my first interview with Dread Central wouldn't be published until 2018, I'd been making brief appearances on the lauded site since 2016. My first article was a list of the best Bigfoot movies of the 21st Century. It was written in a heavy California vernacular, giving it a sense of geography and injecting some humor. And, for a while, I had a bi-monthly column at Dread called "Want to See Something Really Scary?" Obviously a shout-out to the intro of ***The Twilight Zone Movie***, my column explored the darkest, weirdest corners of YouTube, exposing something shocking, bizarre, and sometimes grotesque.

It was actually a misunderstanding on Twitter that put me into contact with Jonathan Barkan who, as Dread Central's Managing Editor, was the right-hand man of Steve Barton (aka Uncle Creepy). And it was Jonathan who "promoted" me from occasional contributor pitching ideas from time to time, to a bona fide Staff Writer. At weekly meetings, I was introduced to the other key writers, including the illustrious Uncle Creepy himself. And though my time actually working with Steve was somewhat brief, he left a huge impression on me. Even when he split from Dread Central, he always made himself available to me as a consummate mentor. I still consider him a friend to this day (and certainly hope he feels the same).

Me and Uncle Creepy himself, Steve Barton.

When Steve left, Jonathan became Editor-in-Chief and I became his right-hand man, (Managing Editor). And I realized that I was now living my dream. I was making enough money to live on working exclusively for Dread Central, so they became my exclusive focus. Not only did I become the primary reporter of daily news, I was first in line for interviews, screenings, and set visits. I had made it: I was a professional horror journalist. I was no longer simply Josh Millican, I was Josh from Dread Central.

When Jonathan Barkan resigned from Dread Central, I slid into a role I had previously never dreamed of obtaining: I became Editor-In-Chief. I had arrived at my apex. The line between who I was and what I did was completely obliterated. They say when you love your job you never work a day, and for me, this adage held true.

The entire world changed during my tenure at Dread Central, and I'm not being facetious or exaggerating. If you're reading this book, then you know it's true. I've watched horror go from the red-headed stepchild of the entertainment industry to one of the top dogs. I saw and welcomed an explosion of new voices on the scene. I saw horror being embraced like never before. I wrote throughout the #MeToo movement, through two Presidential regime changes. I wrote continuously through the pandemic, attempting to maintain a degree of normalcy during truly terrifying times. I wrote through the turbulent election of 2020 and the previously unimaginable events of January 6th. And I've witnessed the emergence of more new technologies, ones that enhance how news is distributed and consumed.

The pandemic created a new digital world where anyone with a Zoom account could record their conversations on video. This drastically changed how outlets release interviews. Less common now are the long-form, deep-dive, written interviews assembled in this tome. Now, it's video snippets designed to be consumed quickly, enhanced through hypnotic editing, and timed for fleeting attention spans. For these reasons, I'm exceptionally thrilled to have my work assembled here, physically, liberated from the computer screen. Even when the apocalypse arrives and the internet crashes forever, when an EMP fries everything with a circuit board, these interviews will have a chance to endure.

These interviews will not be lost, they will not evaporate into broken code. And, therefore, neither will I.

10 Years Behind the Mask

AN INTERVIEW WITH LESLIE VERNON ACTOR NATHAN BAESEL

Method: *Phone*

Reflections: My first interview from Dread Central! I had heard about a couple of 10th Anniversary events for **Behind the Mask,** and since Nathan Baesel and I were already friendly on the convention circuit, it seemed like a natural tie-in. I pitched Steve Barton, Dread Central's original Editor-in-Chief, an event recap/interview hybrid. He gave me the green light and, even though I was still living in Northern California at the time, I dipped down to L.A. on my own dime to be a part of it all.

Funny Story: I have a high-quality replica of Leslie Vernon's mask, so for the film screening, I wore it with a pair of overalls and carried a rusty antique scythe I had scored on eBay. I didn't even think about it at the time, but there was no way in Hell that Security was going to let me into a theater complex with what was, objectively, a dangerous weapon. I didn't want to miss the show, so I went outside intending to trash the banned cosplay accessory.

ANTrunning

But I was attending the event with one of my best friends, famous Los Angele poet Milo Martin, and he wouldn't hear of it. He stashed the scythe behind his back, handle tucked into his pants and blade curved across his back, and we went back inside. And even though Security searched our bags and frisked us, Milo managed to make it inside with the offensive object. Obviously, we kept it out of sight for the remainder of the night.

The irony of interviewing Nathan Baesel for this pair of **Behind the Mask** 10th Anniversary events is that he never actually made it out to Los Angeles. He had a family emergency. Still, it was a great event and, at the time of this interview, he genuinely intended to be a part of it.

————

ORIGINALLY PUBLISHED: **January 3, 2018**

If you live in the Los Angeles area, this weekend offers two unprecedented opportunities to meet and interact with the cast and creators of a legendary indie horror movie. **Behind the Mask: The Rise of Leslie Vernon**, directed by Scott Glosserman from a screenplay co-scribed by David Stieve, arrived in 2006 and quickly became a cult sensation. The film is notable for its meta presentation (creating an alternate reality where characters like Jason Voorhees and Freddy Krueger actually exist) while deftly mixing found footage and traditional methods of cinematic storytelling.

If you haven't experienced **Behind the Mask** for yourself, it's available to stream on Shudder. [**Behind the Mask** is no longer on Shudder at the time of publication.]

Synopsis: *Nice, normal-looking Leslie Vernon (Nathan Baesel) has an obsession with movie-style slashers like Michael Myers, Jason*

Voorhees and Freddy Krueger. Leslie decides to follow in the footsteps of his heroes, and, ever the self-promoter, invites a documentary filmmaker (Angela Goethals) and her crew to follow him around as he constructs his own grisly legacy.

This Friday (January 5th), **Behind the Mask** fans can pick up the first issue of the 6-part prequel comic **Before the Mask** at Dark Delicacies in Burbank. The signing will be attended by Nathan Baesel, Angela Goethals [Taylor Gentry in the film], David Stievve, and Scott Glosserman, along with illustrator Nathan Thomas Milliner. The event kicks off at 7 PM.

This Saturday (January 6th) promises to offer an event of epic proportions when **Behind the Mask** holds its 10th Anniversary screening at the LA Live Stadium 13. Everyone from the Dark Delicacies signing will be in attendance, along with cast members Ben Pace (Doug), Britain Spellings (Todd), Hart Turner (Shane), Bridgette Newton (Jamie) and **Behind the Mask** composer Gordy Haab.

The organizers have hinted that other celebrities will be in attendance, as well as a camera crew who'll be shooting footage for a **Behind the Mask** 10th Anniversary DVD re-release scheduled for March.

Dread Central was lucky enough to sit down with **Behind the Mask**'s leading slasher, Nathan Baesel, who's clearly excited for this weekend's festivities. We discussed the film's enduring legacy, unearthing some juicy bits of history along the way. And, of course, we just had to ask about the status of the long-gestating "Spreemake".

Dread Central: We understand that Scott Glosserman, David Stieve, Angela Goethals, Ben Pace, Britain Spellings, Hart Turner, and Bridgett

Newton will all be attending the screening on the 6th. Will this be the largest gathering of *Behind the Mask* alum since the wrap party? It's kind of like your guys' 10-year High School Reunion.

Nathan Baesel: It is and we're such a stupid group that get-togethers of two are an event. This thing is going to go south real fast. The police will be called in at some point. At least once.

DC: When you were making this film, did you have any idea you guys were making a future cult classic?

NB: We all believed if we did our jobs competently then the cleverness of the story and quality of the script would take care of everything. In the end we mostly managed to execute both extremely well and, in some cases, delivered really exceptional moments. We'd hoped people would respond to the qualities in BTM we loved and I think I can speak for everyone in saying we've been so gratified in seeing that people did.

DC: What was it like for you working with horror icons like Kane Hodder, Robert Englund, and Zelda Rubenstein?

NB: Yeah, no pressure, right? I was really lucky in that they were all extremely gracious people with a fantastic work ethic and were dedicated to the idea of telling our unique story as well as possible. They were great collaborators which made working with them so inviting. Robert was so supportive of the work I was doing, which was incredibly affirming of the direction we were going with Leslie. It's admittedly an unusual film but once I got his blessing, I committed even further to mining all the gems in it.

DC: I've seen you at a number of conventions in California over the past few years. Do you enjoy the convention experience and are you ever

surprised by the level of fandom *Behind the Mask* has inspired?

*NB: I never expect anyone to even recognize **Behind the Mask** let alone me and it never ceases to amaze me that people are happy to pay me money to sign my name on pictures of myself for them. That's a concept I hope I never get used to the idea of.*

DC: Of course, everyone wants to know about the sequel/prequel/remake/reboot. We're excited to follow the further adventures of Leslie Vernon in comics, but when can we expect to see you guys in another feature film?

NB: Fortunately, I'm not in that department. That's someone else's headache to work out. All I have to do is show up and say words. But I will say, I like the idea of there being such a gap in time between the original and future sequel. Frankly, I think the more time between them the more fun ideas we're playing with in the sequel will be highlighted.

DC: What was your most embarrassing moment on set? Give us the scoop on some Leslie Vernon bloopers!

*NB: Every camera setup was an opportunity for fresh lunacy and it came in high frequency. We had a ridiculous amount of fun shooting the movie and I'm so glad that gets across to people who've really responded to **Behind the Mask**.*

I like scented candles and I don't care who knows it. I lit my hotel room on fire one night when my candle burned to its base and popped out of the holder from the heat, spreading flammable wax everywhere. I woke up to my dresser in flames. The hotel was surprisingly under-standing. I was obviously not their first moron.

DC: How has your participation in *Behind the Mask* affected your life over the past 10 years?

NB: I've got unbreakable bonds with a group of people that I love, both folks from the film and around it. I've been able to support my family from it and leave behind something my children can appreciate when/if they're interested in seeing what dad did at his creative best. I've got a legacy. I feel honored to have that.

Winchester

Method: *Location Visit*

Reflections: Working for Dread Central allowed me to take my career as a horror journalist into new arenas, specifically, paranormal investigations. In advance of **Winchester**'s release in 2018, I got the idea to record a video investigation at the actual historical site of the Winchester Mystery House in San Jose, California. Thankfully, those curating the estate agreed and gave us unprecedented access, after hours, for what was a truly once-in-a-lifetime opportunity.

I put together a team of friends, acquaintances, and strangers. I reunited with an old college buddy (Go, Banana Slugs!) who agreed to film it all. Nothing was off limits, and the experience exceeded all of my expectations—even as a paranormal skeptic. I'm really proud of the end result and I hope that, after reading this recap, you'll seek it out on YouTube.

ORIGINALLY PUBLISHED: **January 31, 2018**

In just a few days **Winchester**, starring Helen Mirren arrives in theaters; the Oscar-winning actress plays an elusive heiress who spends the majority of her life surrounded by ghosts. One of the most intriguing aspects of the film (and a major hook) is that it's based on a true story.

Sarah Winchester was heiress to the Winchester Rifle fortune; she built a sprawling mansion in San Jose, California, that still stands today. Recently, Dread Central was given unprecedented access to what's been called "The House That Ghosts Built". Our goal: To determine if the estate deserves its reputation as one of the most haunted locations in America.

We assembled some of the country's most prominent paranormal investigators and mediums who employed a variety of techniques, all in an effort to detect the supernatural forces long rumored to roam these halls. Most importantly, we were joined by historian Janan Boehme, an expert on the life of Sarah Winchester and the mansion, who was able to immediately validate some of the details provided by our mediums.

Our group consisted of Tim Wood, founder of the TV series **In Search of the Paranormal** which launched in 2006; he was joined by team members Kristin Manning, a medium who uses her drawing talents to illustrate what she senses, and photographer Patrick Langdon who utilized specific camera techniques and film stocks to detect paranormal remnants.

Tim Meunier is the founder of American Paranormal Investigations as well as the founder of both the Sacramento Horror Film Festival and the bi-annual Sinister Creature Con. Michael B. Chochla is a medium and member of River City Paranormal; Michelle Goyette has been working as a professional spiritual medium for over 5 years, and Chloë Tatro is an empath and Reiki Master.

History: Sarah Winchester lived a long and sad life. The heiress to the Winchester Rifle fortune lost her infant daughter and husband very early into her marriage. Widowed and childless, she sought the aid of a spiritualist in Boston, something that wasn't uncommon in the 19th Century. And it was there, the story goes, that she received a message from the ghost of her husband, William.

"Move out west, start building a giant mansion, and never stop." Failure to oblige would result in terrifying consequences. What Sarah realized that day was that her wealth was a source of incredible luxury and privilege, but it was also a terrible curse.

The house was intended to hold thousands of guests—none of them alive. Sarah was charged with attending to the restless spirits of everyone who died by a Winchester rifle. From those who fell in the Civil War to Native Americans whose lands were stolen and anyone murdered in a crime of passion; they were all to be welcomed. And those spirits who couldn't be appeased by the mansion's many treasures? They'd be contained within an ever-changing labyrinth, trapped by numerological talisman and their own confusion.

Construction began in 1880 on a stately yet modest estate, but legends abound about teams of carpenters working non-stop for almost forty years, only ending their efforts on the morning of Sarah Winchester's death. What had started as an 8-room home had grown to over 160 rooms connected by miles of corridors and, at one point, towering seven stories tall.

The Investigation: The investigation exceeded all of my expectations; you can see much of what transpired in the video below, produced by Matthew Galvin of Active Matrix Networks. [You can find the video on Dread Central's YouTube channel by searching "Dread Central Investigates the Winchester Mansion".]

Highlights: A medium was overcome by the pervasive sadness of The Winchester Mansion; another felt compelled to speak the name Daisy—one of Sarah Winchester's favorite nieces who had her own bedroom in the estate.

On our initial walk-thru, two members of our team got lost. It's a testament to the labyrinthine nature of The Winchester Mansion, where a simple wrong turn can get you hopelessly confused.

One of our mediums saw a "shadow person", something supported by photographic evidence; another drew an image of an inhuman, dark entity she believed tormented Sarah, feeding off of her sadness.

An EVP experiment seemed to produce detectable responses.

Finally, we utilized an early 20th Century Ouija board in an attempt to contact Sarah Winchester herself. It included a ganzfeld experiment, a method of sensory deprivation utilized by psychic Elise Rainier (played by Lin Shaye) in the **Insidious** movie franchise.

Conclusions: I've always considered myself, objectively, a skeptic. But part of what draws me to horror movies is that question of "What if?" As long as humans have been able to express themselves, we've been obsessed with the afterlife. What happens when we die and are those who meet with violent ends somehow trapped in a realm just beyond our detection?

I approached this opportunity with a skeptical, yet opened mind, allowing myself to become immersed in the ambiance of The Winchester Mansion. While my core beliefs remain intact, there were moments that affected me deeply. Our investigation produced evidence that seems to support past reports of supernatural activity—provided you already believe such forces exist.

There's a profound sadness here, likely to infect anyone who visits the Winchester Mystery House. You can't help but hope that Sarah Winchester finally found happiness when she was reunited with her husband and daughter in the afterlife. After decades of attending to the dead, we hope she's finally at peace.

Be sure to check out ***Winchester*** when it arrives in theaters on Friday; we'll have a review here at Dread Central posted shortly!

Daeg Faerch

ON LIFE SINCE ROB ZOMBIE'S HALLOWEEN,
STARRING IN JOSIE & ANTI-BULLYING

Method: *Email*

Reflections: Look, the last thing I want to do is to stir up any weirdness—but this was a weird one. I had met Daeg Faerch at Sinister Creature Con in Stockton the previous summer. All grown up, he exuded a stoner vibe which I was instantly attracted to. I've always said that one of the quickest ways to start a genuine friendship with someone is to smoke a bowl with them—and Daeg and I smoked many bowls that weekend.

At a Dread Central writers' meeting, Steve Barton asked us all to think of exciting horror personalities to interview. Since everyone was already anticipating Blumhouse's ***Halloween*** reboot/sequel in October, it seemed like a good opportunity to talk to Daeg about his experiences on the set of Rob Zombie's ***Halloween***, and how playing young Michael Myers had affected his life. I knew that Daeg had a new film coming up as well (as well as budding careers as a hip-hop artist and a body builder), so I dropped him a line asking if he'd be interested in some primo publicity.

"What am I going to get for it?" was his response. It was a question I'd never gotten before from a potential interviewee. I mean, wouldn't anyone in the horror arena cherish an opportunity to be featured on Dread Central? Did he actually want money? The stoner friendship we'd established at Sinister Creature Con had evaporated.

I told him I could put together a package of swag for him; some shirts and some Dread Presents Blu-rays. He somewhat unenthusiastically agreed, so I emailed him a half dozen questions. All of my past interviewees had been really open and responsive to my questions, even when delivered via email. Not Daeg. His replies were rushed and minimal. One sentence tops, and sometimes not even a complete sentence. It was frustrating.

I mentioned to Steve that I'd be fine abandoning the interview, as Daeg had been weird from the get-go and I hadn't harvested anything really worth reporting—especially not on a prestigious website like Dread Central. But Steve, a true mentor, taught me a lesson instead. "See if you can get him to open up. Engage him with a few follow-up questions." I was up for the challenge and inspired by Steve's suggestions. And while this won't go down in history as one of my best interviews, it was at least something worthy of being published on Dread Central.

When the shirts I sent to Daeg eventually reached him, he emailed me to tell me that none of them fit since he was a body builder now. He implied that we should send him more free stuff. I never responded.

———

ORIGINALLY PUBLISHED: **March 14, 2018**

When Rob Zombie released his remake of *Halloween* in 2007, many John Carpenter fans were beyond apoplectic. Some even sought to turn the shock-rocker-turned-film-maker into a pariah, lambasting his approach to the horror classic's mythology along with his writing and directing skills. While fans can objectively make the case that Zombie's *Halloween* fails in ways that Carpenter's *Halloween* succeeds, no one deserves the level of abuse he suffered from online trolls and professional journalists alike.

While Zombie is known for his thick skin and don't-give-a-fuck attitude, the disproportionate negativity the film received couldn't have been easy on the cast and crew. Someone who probably took way more than his share of venomous bluster is Daeg Faerch, the actor who played young Michael Myers; he was only 12 when the film hit theaters.

The main difference between Carpenter's *Halloween* and Zombie's *Halloween* is that the latter spent an entire first act giving a backstory to a young psychopath who was left completely enigmatic in 1978. Whether you found Myers' extended backstory a success or a fumble, Daeg is blameless; he was a paid actor who did his job as instructed. If he wasn't able to accurately communicate Zombie's vision, he'd have been fired. So, whether you love or hate Rob Zombie's *Halloween*, Daeg did a damn fine job and deserves his due credit.

But Daeg isn't a kid anymore and he's building a solid legacy where *Halloween* is just a single chapter. Since working with Zombie, he's appeared in *Hancock*, *Run! Bitch Run!*, and *Ditch Party*. And he's not limiting himself to just film, having recently appeared in the Blondie video for "Fun"; he also models and spits hip-hop fire!

We were lucky enough to catch up with Daeg as his latest film, **Josie**, is set to arrive in theaters and VOD on March 16th. The film is directed by Eric England (**Contracted**, **Get the Girl**), and he stars as Gator opposite Dylan McDermott (**American Horror Story**) and Sophie Turner (**Game of Thrones**). Check out our interview below.

Dread Central: How did you land the role of young Michael Myers in Rob Zombie's *Halloween*?

Daeg Faerch: In a nutshell, I walked into a room full of brunette boys who were all smaller than me, and I booked it!

DC: Halloween received a lot of backlash from John Carpenter fans. How has playing young Michael Myers affect your life?

DF: Playing young Michael will always be part of my journey. The experience and opportunities have been a blessing.

DC: What have you been up to lately?

DF: I love making music; music production and film production for my rap music videos. Yeah, spending a lot of time there. I'm developing a fitness routine now that I'm a sponsored bodybuilder. I work out every day and I'm sponsored by INSANE LABZ; get 20% off using promo code "GreatDaeg."

DC: Let's talk about Josie! How did you get involved in the production? Can you tell us a bit about the character you play?

DF: Eric reached out to me to play Gator. Love me some Gator, but I'm vegan!

DC: What was it like working with Eric England? How would you describe his style versus other directors you've worked with?

DF: Eric is a cool, laid-back director. I may even compare him to Rob Zombie in that they understand that the actor brings his own talent to the project and they let me have fun with the roles.

DC: What was it like working with Sophie Turner and Dylan McDermott?

DF: Dylan was in character the entire time and that was awesome, but it didn't give me much of an opportunity to get to know him. Sophie is super cool with wild, awesome energy. At the point that I met her, I was just starting to make my music videos and she was very supportive and even did a little dance for the music video "GIGGIN" along with Jack Kilmer and Eric England.

DC: What's next for you in terms of movies and music?

DF: I played a necrophiliac recently in a film that's running the festival circuit. I've got other stuff in the works, but nothing I can talk about yet. Music-wise there is always another slap around the corner!

DC: Are you looking forward to Blumhouse's *Halloween*?

DF: It is really cool that they are bringing Jamie Lee [Curtis] back. I am happy the franchise is boomin'!

DC: Is there anything else you want to tell our readers?

DF: I have a message for the kids: Be better than you were yesterday, no holds barred. I'm now taking bookings for talks about anti-bullying because it's an important issue to me.

DC: That's awesome! Tell us more.

*DF: The message is especially important with the recent school shootings. My past includes playing young Michael Myers and being bullied, and there's a strong anti-bullying message in **Ditch Party**. I've recently accepted offers to speak at schools and locations with my message of being positive… being better than you were yesterday. I want to help the victims of bullying deal with their experiences in a positive way and bring hope to all.*

DC: Thanks so much for talking to us.

DF: Thanks, Josh! Ask your readers to follow GreatDaeg on Spotify!

Jen and Sylvia Soska

TALK RABID, DAVID CRONENBERG & TRANSHUMANISM

Method: *Video Conference*

Reflections: I began horror blogging in the early 2010s and Jen and Sylvia Soska caught my attention, back when young female genre directors were more of an anomaly. I heard about ***Dead Hooker in a Trunk***, but it was hard to find, so I officially became a fan following the release of ***American Mary*** in 2012. I was thoroughly impressed by their bold, unflinching methods of storytelling and have been an ardent supporter ever since.

And, likewise, Jen and Sylvia Soska (aka The Twisted Twins) have been consummate supporters of my work as a journalist. Every time I'd mention them in an article, one or both of them would reach out to thank me for the coverage (something that's surprisingly rare in this industry). And when I began covering film festivals and conventions for work, I was lucky enough to meet them in person—and they're wonderful.

Some of my best memories from my life in horror include times hanging out with Jen and Sylvia Soska. In addition to being talented artists, they're genuinely brilliant human beings. When their remake of David Cronenberg's *Rabid* was in pre-production, I was lucky enough to score some incredible in-depth interviews. And yes, I can definitely tell who is who.

Jen and Sylvia, thank you so much for your support and friendship. I can't wait to see what you guys come up with next!

ORIGINALLY PUBLISHED: **March 28, 2018**

Jen and Sylvia Soska are the first names genre aficionados think of whenever 21st Century body horror is the topic of conversation. Their breakout hit *American Mary* especially injected fresh elements into the subgenre popularized by David Cronenberg in the 1970s and 1980s.

It seems perfect, then, that the "Twisted Twins" are remaking Cronenberg's **Rabid** (originally released in 1977). It's been about a month since we reported that Shout! Factory had secured distribution rights to the remake, which is now neck-deep into pre-production.

We were lucky enough to sit down with the Soska Sisters as they prepare to descend on Toronto, where **Rabid**'s being filmed. We discussed their initial gravitation towards horror and how David Cronenberg has already been part of their lives for decades. They also revealed as much as possible about who will be playing Rose in their remake.

Dread Central: The term "body horror" gets thrown around a lot; just so we're all on the same page, what exactly is body horror? How would you explain it to a 20-year-old?

*Sylvia Soska: The most obvious associations are the works of David Cronenberg, like **Videodrome**. Today, we're looking at body horror as something that's going past what we medically know is possible. There's a theoretical aspect involving what we can do with medicine when we manipulated the body.*

Jen Soska: For me, the easy way to describe body horror is it's scientifically based, or medicine-based horror. David Cronenberg, for example, doesn't believe in an afterlife, he doesn't believe in that supernatural bullshit, so there's none of that in his films. The fear that we all have is when we see blood is that it's going to be our own blood; when you see someone getting hurt, you're thinking about your own flesh being hurt. That's something that's universal for everyone.

DC: How has body horror changed since the heyday of David Cronenberg? How has the subgenre evolved in the past couple decades?

JS: In the 1970s they were making fun of cosmetic surgery saying, "Oh, you'll get a new nose because you don't like the last one you got," like in David's original **Rabid***. These days, it's so accepted it's not far off to imagine extreme body modifications or extreme cosmetic surgery. It's just the norm. For me, I think the next levels are transhumanism and we're already seeing hybrid parts being harvested in labs. There was an article recently about a human/sheep fetus that was being raised to create these half-human/half-sheep parts for transplants. I think that's the direction body horror is going.*

SS: Back in the 20th Century, people were just discovering body horror was something you could do, so movies were weird and abstract. In Western culture right now, it's so disturbing because it's taking the self that you know and transforming it into something you would never imagine.

DC: Can you explain the importance of David Cronenberg's legacy, especially for our younger readers.

JS: I would say he's anti-Hollywood; he's the guys who's always done films his own way and he asks more questions than he gives answers. He encourages thought and encourages films to be art. He doesn't categorize himself as a horror filmmaker. He's a filmmaker and there are horrific elements in his different films. He has a lovely series of body horror films, but then he goes into real-life horror in things like **A History of Violence** *and it shows the horrific price of the human condition. Again, he doesn't believe in that supernatural bullshit; he's really fascinated by the darkness that we're capable of—not only in our minds but if we have no limits on our creativity with biology and science.*

*SS: He's so fascinating. I remember there was a point where they wanted to invite him to [participate in the Showtime series] **Masters of Horror**, but he refused to be categorized or placed into a specific group like that. No matter what's going on with David and his successes he always wants to maintain an outsider's sensibilities and he's not afraid to do things people don't readily accept. I remember hearing about how when he was doing **Rabid**, the press was saying "Marilyn Chambers is doing legitimate work" and David was like, "Since when has my work been considered legitimate?" He'd always been considered taboo or overtly sexual. Again, you're talking about a guy who wrote a movie about sex slugs! It was almost like he anticipated the kind of sexually transmitted diseases hysteria that was about to explode in the 1980s. And with Marilyn Chambers [in **Rabid**], here you have a biological vampire; it's a very sexualized role and she's a female aggressor.*

JS: Also, he's Canadian. He's one of us! We have David Cronenberg, Wolverine, and Deadpool.

SS: And we have Mary Heron!

JS: Maybe because David's Canadian is the reason Americans don't hear about him as much.

DC: How has David Cronenberg influenced your work and your lives growing up? You guys weren't even born when *Rabid* was originally released.

*JS: **Rabid** was released in 1977 and we were released in 1983.*

SS: Yeah but our parents did meet Marilyn Chambers! I'm trying to find the autograph they got so I can keep it on set as a blessing to the whole production.

JS: Our parents always let us watch horror movies, especially our mom. Every horror movie writer or director I know watched horror movies as kids—it was like mom/dad bonding time. With David, I didn't automatically consider him a horror director. **Dead Ringers** is the ultimate for my people…

SS: *Twins.*

JS: *…and I loved it. There are few directors that defy the genre they excel in. David is one of them, [Quentin] Tarantino is one of them. You go into their films specifically for what they bring to the table. Their films are larger than life.*

SS: *We were little kids when we discovered David. I missed the beginning of* **Shivers** *but it was on TV late at night. I didn't even ask my mom; I just knew I had to sneak a watch. I remember watching and being like, "What is even happening?" I remember years later I was watching* **Videodrome**, *and then we saw* **Rabid**, *and that's when I started connecting the dots. I was like, "Oh, this is the same guy! Oh my God, this is the same guy and this is his style!"*

JS: *I felt the same way about John Carpenter too. I was like, "He couldn't have made all these films!"*

DC: Have you guys met David Cronenberg?

SS: *We have never met David, but I know that he watched* **American Mary** *and we got an invite to meet with him but we couldn't leave our premiere. I know he knows of us and we've met his son Brandon.*

JS: *We ripped [Brandon's] heart up in "W is for Wish" in* **The ABCs of Death** 2.

SS: *We put a glowing crystal in it, so that was a great bonding experience. Canadian Horror Royalty! I tried to get David to do a cameo in* **Rabid** *and we wrote a role for him, but I heard they're also remaking* **The Fly** *and offered him a part in that and he was cameoed out at that point. But I heard through the grapevine that our remake is the only one he's looking forward to—and that's better than anything else. I consider that a blessing. I'm planning on not disappointing him.*

DC: I was hoping for a Cronenberg cameo.

JS: He's such an amazing actor.

DC: Absolutely. I'll always remember him as Dr. Decker in *Nightbreed*.

*SS: He killed it in **Nightbreed**!*

*JS: The first time I saw **Nightbreed** I remember hearing that David had a cameo role, but we weren't expecting that! He has such amazing energy.*

DC: Let's talk about *Rabid*: Where are you in the production process?

SS: We're in prep right now. We're about to go to Toronto where we're going to be doing the rest of the heavy prep. We're locking down our cast. We're locking down our locations. The monsters are about to be made. It's the most exciting phase of the project, but it's also the time where we're like, "Oh my God, how much time do we have before things start?"

JS: You're going to be learning more about who our cast is. Do we have our Rose? Yes, we do! It's a fan-favorite, great in the genre, and someone we've wanted to work with for a while. Fans are going to be really excited when they see who we cast.

*SS: David originally wanted Sissy Spacek for **Rabid** but went with Marylin Chambers. I think we've found someone who's in between. And (I hope this doesn't give it away, but) she looks a lot like Marilyn —like a lot!*

JS: People are going to read this over and over again trying to guess! I can say we've re-teamed with MastersFX again, so we're going to have some amazing practical effects. Because we want to be very true to David Cronenberg's work.

DC: So, how did you guys end up with *Rabid*? Was it a film you sought out specifically? Why not another Cronenberg remake?

JS: The project came to us. If you were to ask me what my favorite Cronenberg film is, you know, I love all of them, but it would be **Dead Ringers***, obviously. I've thought of remaking that one a million times.* **Rabid** *was actually brought to us, and I was very skeptical when I heard someone was remaking this film. But when I realized we'd be working with [John Serge] a real author, I was like, "Well, I hate remakes, but it's really important for someone who gives a shit about David's body of work, the fans of the original film, to revamp it." I thought, "Oh, God, what if it's just one of those soulless remakes?" I don't need to name any of them, but you know what I'm talking about. I was afraid this would be* **Rabid** *in title only with nothing to do with the original.*

SS: The cool thing is it forced us to go back to Cronenberg Film School. We read all of his interviews, watched all of his commentaries, read every book that he had—especially from around the 1970s and 1980s so we could build on that. It's almost like a companion piece to David's original. **Shivers** *is being remade too. I found that out. There are a few Cronenberg remakes in the works, but ours will be the first out of the gates. The Twins will win the race—with the support of the Canadian Government no less! So how 'bout that, eh?*

DC: I just re-watched *Rabid* to prepare for this interview. There are some pretty big, explosive car crashes. Are you guys going to go all-out Michael Bay style?

[Both Twins go silent, but raise pinkies to their lips impersonating Dr. Evil]

SS: We have one of the best effects team on the planet—and it starts with a car accident, so...

JS: The car accident is so important because it sets up the entire calamity of the misadventure.

SS: We do have Todd Masters who's known for his body horror, like in **Six Feet Under** *so… It's going to suck for Rose. It's going to suck for Rose until it gets better.*

DC: What other innovations do you have planned for *Rabid*, visually or thematically?

JS: Well I think the big difference between our **Rabid** *and David's* **Rabid** *is, firstly we're female, so it's going to be from a female gaze. As much as I feel in touch with the male side of myself it will be seen through the eyes of a lady. And I believe in life after death; I believe in spirituality and that's going to play into the themes as well. There are going to be moments where, maybe a guy will be watching and be like, "Wow! Do women really experience shit like this?" Unfortunately, yes. It's going to be a very timely piece in addition to going back to the original sensibilities of transhumanism in David's* **Rabid**.

SS: And there's going to be a TV component as well, so it's kind of fun to have these two pieces working at the same time. To date, I don't think there's ever been a twin creative force involved with this kind of endeavor, so I'm excited to see how that develops and impacts the movie.

JS: I'm really excited about creating people and maybe animals with rabies. I don't think that many people realize that zombies were inspired by rabies. And if you watch some video of people with rabies it's like—wow! It's very cinematic, fortunately for us. People should be afraid of catching rabies, which is incurable by the way.

SS: It looks like a demonic possession and by the time you get the symptoms you're a goner. So, they just tie you to a bed like Regan [from **The Exorcist**] *and hope for the best. It's scary!*

DC: You mentioned the timeliness of your version of *Rabid*, can you speak more to that?

JS: Absolutely. I think it's no secret that there's a rather large conversation going on right now between offenders and what is acceptable behavior. And the issues involved with people who have been abusing their power for so long. You're definitely going to see these issues explored in **Rabid***. It's just so prevalent in society now. And it's a film that's being set in 2017/2018/2019 whatever. It's not a 1970s film, it's very modern. So, you will see how Rose fits into this culture. As she gets stronger and as she evolves you'll see how her position shifts. I hope that's not being too vague.*

SS: I know what you're talking about, but I'm very well-versed with the script!

DC: Knowing your previous work and the potential for *Rabid*, it's easy to imagine a tentacle porn angle. Am I totally off base? Are you guys going there?

SS: You know I really like the tentacle that comes out of Rose's armpit, but my first suggestion was a tentacle coming out from between her legs. And then I found out that was David's original idea as well. Both of us got shot down. So, this is going to be… different than what you've seen but it's pretty disturbing.

JS: I don't think most people realize that **Rabid***, at its heart, is a story about a biological vampire. I was really excited to create someone who feeds on blood, human blood, but not in a supernatural way—in a scientific way. One of the original titles was actually* **Mosquito***, and that's why Rose had her thorn and her tentacle. That's also something explored in our version. There were parts that David had to cut out of his original and you can find it in his commentary where Rose loses part of her intestines in her car accident. That's also why she can't consume anything besides high-protein blood. That part of the film was edited out, so you never really get that explanation. We pick up where those aspects are missing.*

SS: It's interesting because the FDA just recently removed the sanctions they had on human/hybrid animal testing. The reason the restrictions were in place before is because they don't want animals with human intelligence. And so they came back and said, "Do you want us to not make smart animals?" and they were like, "Yeah, sure." So, they just started all these crazy experiments and testing again using the weirdest stuff right now. Again, David Cronenberg anticipated that back in **Rabid***. He was talking about fusing humans and animals together.*

DC: You guys are awesome. Is there anything else you want to tell our readers?

JS: This is going to be the widest theatrical release we've had for any of our films, so I really hope fans will go out and see this movie. It makes such a big difference, what you go to see and what you take your friends to see. And there's no better marketing than fans saying, "This is going to be a fucking good movie!" Come out and see it. Don't worry about Marvel and DC; they'll be fine! We need butts in seats.

SS: And also, we'll be connecting with our audience in some unique ways, so, keep an eye out for an announcement. There's going to be a lot of information from the set being made available so fans will feel like they're part of the movie. But we'll be keeping the big surprises behind a curtain so they won't be able to actually see it.

JS: It'll be very interactive.

Jordan Fields

Method: *Phone*

Originally Published: March 30, 2018

It's been over a month since we reported that Shout! Factory had secured distribution rights to the remake of David Cronenberg's ***Rabid***, currently neck-deep into pre-production. The project is being written and directed by Jen and Sylvia Soska (***American Mary***), considered masters and innovators of 21st Century body horror.

We recently brought you an exclusive interview with the "Twisted Twins" where we talked about Cronenberg, transhumanism, and everything they were at liberty to discuss about ***Rabid***. We also caught up with Jordan Fields, Vice President of Acquisitions at Shout! Factory, to discuss release plans for ***Rabid***, and what makes the Soskas the "only" filmmakers for the job.

Dread Central: As an avid collector and fan of obscure horror, I obviously know about Shout! Factory/Scream Factory, but can you give our

younger readers a brief history of your company?

Jordan Fields: Our entry into horror began when we started up our Scream Factory division. Scream Factory was established to be a home for the reissuing of classic horror on disc. For several years we tried to build a reputation for reissuing these beloved horror titles fans wanted. They were remastered beautifully and delivered with a new level of online fan engagement that the community wanted, loved, and responded to. Over the years, after we earned a certain level of credibility with the fans, we leveraged that credibility to position ourselves as curators for what's new and cool in horror. That's when we started acquiring new horror films. But we continue releasing classic titles in very fan-friendly ways.

DC: What are your plans for the future? Will you be doing more theatrical releases like *Rabid*?

*JF: Over the past few years, we've been acquiring films with an eye towards distributing them across all platforms, including theatrical and the various downstream windows: DVD, transaction, and television. A few years ago, we launched an initiative to get involved in original productions. It made sense to release it through Scream Factory since that's where we built our community, and our first original was **Fender Bender**. It had a contemporary setting but was a throwback to 1980s-era slasher films that we're fans of here, and that we've released successfully on disc. That was a great experience and making a film we enjoyed whetted our appetite to produce more original features. It was about this time that the opportunity to produce **Rabid** came along.*

DC: Perfect segue! How did *Rabid* end up at Shout! Factory?

JF: What happened was a couple years ago I contacted a guy named John Boudet who's the owner of Sommerville House which controls rights to a library that included **Rabid**. *I had just heard that a remake was in the works and, to be honest, I was more interested in acquiring the rights for the original film. We ended up licensing his library and releasing titles like* **Rabid** *and* **Black Christmas** *in collectors' editions. and a couple of months later the producer of the remake, Michael Walker, asked if we'd be interested in distributing the remake. Again, at that time our appetite for new features was growing and I read the script. It was super sharp, sexy, scary. I was already a big fan of the Soskas' previous work, especially* **American Mary**. *I knew the Scream Factory team would knock this one out of the park, so it just made sense to be the home for this movie.*

DC: What's it been like working with the Soskas so far?

JF: Those sisters are forces of nature. They're such an incredible team; they're really among the most horror-literate filmmakers I've ever met. They're a complete blast to hang out with. They have an enormous amount of creative energy that they're bringing to **Rabid**. *They're uniquely capable of bringing to* **Rabid** *the kind of detected intelligence and ferocious Id that made Cronenberg's films so disturbing. They're the only filmmakers for this film, in my opinion.*

DC: Your excitement it contagious—pun intended!

JF: One of the things that also attracted us to this project was the degree to which the Soskas are partners in the marketing and promotion of their work. They're online, they're engaged, they have a tremendous following and an insane amount of energy that will drive our marketing and PR campaign.

DC: Fantastic! Is there anything else you'd like to tell our readers?

JF: After I met the Soskas, I sent them this New York Times article about stem cell therapy. It was a cautionary tale about stem cell therapy gone horribly wrong. People went through treatment and suffered in some terrible ways when those cells mutated. So, **Rabid** *uses that premise as a launchpad into a truly worst-case scenario, and I think that's current, relevant, and going to be really exciting to fans. To borrow the title of another movie:* **There Will Be Blood**.

Justin Benson & Aaron Moorhead

DISCUSS THE ENDLESS, RESOLUTION & RED MARIJUANA

Method: *Phone*

Reflections: I love how open these filmmakers are about their interest in psychotropics.

———

ORIGINALLY PUBLISHED: **April 18, 2018**

If you read my recent 2018 Q1 State of Horror Report [published on Dread Central on April 13, 2018], you know that ***The Endless*** is one of my hot-picks for the second quarter of the year. It's the 3rd movie from filmmaking duo Justin Benson and Aaron Moorhead, who took the indie world by storm with their debut feature ***Resolution*** in 2012. Their sophomore offering, ***Spring***, was a potent mix of star-crossed romance and Lovecraftian body horror.

We recently had the opportunity to sit down with Benson and Moorhead to discuss ***The Endless***, now playing in

New York and Los Angeles with plans to expand to additional markets throughout the month.

This interview contains spoilers for *The Endless*, *Resolution*, and *Spring* so proceed with caution!

Synopsis: *Two brothers receive a cryptic video message inspiring them to revisit the UFO death cult they escaped a decade earlier. Hoping to find the closure that they couldn't find as young men, they're forced to reconsider the cult's beliefs when confronted with unexplainable phenomena surrounding the camp. As the members prepare for the coming of a mysterious event, the brothers race to unravel the seemingly impossible truth before their lives become permanently entangled with the cult.*

Dread Central: In all the information I found about you guys online, there's nothing about how the two of you met. What's the story?

*Aaron Moorhead: We met when I came to work at RSA Films, Ridley Scott's production company. It was my first day and Justin's last day. I came to LA convinced I was going to become Ridley Scott's protégé, not realized I'd never meet him, that I'd just be moving papers around and making coffee and stuff like that. So I was placed at a table with Justin and he quickly dissolved the notion that I was ever going to meet Ridley Scott in person, much less learn how to become a better film-maker from him. But he helped me out by talking about his own experiences as a director. So we kept in touch; we started working together more and more on low-budget commercials and that sort of thing. At a certain point, Justin throws the first draft of a film called **Resolution** at me and that was our first film which took off at the Tribeca Film Festival.*

*Justin Benson: I was thinking about going to medical school actually. Making **Resolution** was just something I wanted to do so I could* *check making a movie off my life's bucket list. Through the course of making* **Resolution** *with Aaron, it became obvious that I'd be much happy doing this with my life. I'm not sure I would have made a good doctor.*

DC: I know you have a lot of fans who are glad you chose filmmaking over medicine! I loved the fact that *The Endless* is a continuation of *Resolution*. Congratulations on keeping that fact kind of under wraps, by the way. But I'm curious: Since *The Endless* doesn't fit the traditional definition of a sequel or a prequel, how would you describe its relationship to *Resolution*?

JB: We actually spent a lot of time trying to figure out what the word is for that relationship because it's not necessary for you to have seen one before the other. We liked the idea of creating an indie micro-Universe; we hadn't seen anyone else who had done that. So actually, there's even more continuity between the film than most people realize. It'll probably take several viewings to catch all the little things. But ultimately, the two films can exist entirely independent of each other. You've obviously seen **Resolution** *and you find that connection interesting, but the thing is, most people haven't seen it and probably never will because it had such a tiny release. It's not something most people are even aware exists. But, man, we like the idea that* **Resolution** *might come on HBO in the middle of the night and someone who's seen* **The Endless** *will be, like, "I had no idea this whole world existed!" It'll be a surreal moment.*

DC: I had that surreal moment you're talking about and it was awesome! Well, what you just said explains my next question, which was why you guys didn't market *The Endless* as a follow-up to *Resolution*. It was a conscious decision on your part.

*AM: I wish I could say we were that dedicated to avoiding spoilers, but it has to do with the fact that almost nobody saw **Resolution**. So if **The Endless** was marketed as a sequel to a movie you haven't seen, you won't want to watch it. But besides the marketability reasons, it also has to do with our humility where we don't really want to rely on a past movie for the success of our current one. Anyone who liked **Resolution** will, of course, like **The Endless** (I think they absolutely have to). But we'd rather people just go in and discover it for themselves than to have someone coming in as a fan of something that already exists the way franchises use their characters.*

DC: The geography felt really important in *The Endless*. There were deserts and forests in close proximity. Can you speak a bit about the location and how it affected the tone and themes of the film?

*JB: The setting for **The Endless** started as a practical decision. **Resolution** takes place in the same place and, for lack of a better word, the same universe. So we had this location available to us basically for free, about an hour outside of San Diego in a high desert, rural area. When we filmed **Resolution** there, we realized there were areas available to us that we hadn't used, like where we housed the crew. We realized there was still a lot of interesting potentials there. So when it was time to shoot our 3rd micro-budget film, **The Endless**, the space was still available to us. At a certain point, though, we realized there was something special about this place. It's not a traditional setting for a horror or sci-fi movie. There's something very eerie about the landscape and the light in those places.*

DC: *The Endless* uses the idea of a UFO death cult as a hook, but the cult in the film turns out to be something much different than we first thought. Was this an attempt to demystify cults and

humanize their followers or was there another reason for toying with the audience's expectations?

*AM: Cults are destructive, period. They all are. Communes aren't, but you still have a hive-mind phenomenon. What we wanted was to make sure that people believed these brothers would actually want to return (well, one of them). So we had to create this cult that was genuinely attractive while still being dangerous. We did a lot of research. But ultimately, you realize around the halfway mark [in **The Endless**] that the cult isn't the actual danger, right? But we were still able to talk about things like conformity and rebellion and the virtues of breaking out of a cycle. Breaking out of cycles is kind of a rebellion against the self, and that's the conflict of Aaron in the film. The cult ends up being a construct for the themes of the movie.*

DC: The cult in *The Endless*, at least at first, had a lot of similarities to The Heaven's Gate cult, which was also active outside San Diego. I'm assuming that was a major inspiration?

*JB: Like most people, we're extremely fascinated by cults. I just watched **Wild Wild Country** on Netflix and it was fascinating. But, you're right, the group in the film is most similar to Heaven's Gate, in terms of a real-life counterpart. But then you find out the character Justin has been dishonest about their actual practices. You realize he lifted a lot of details from what we know about Heaven's Gate.*

DC: That's what I noticed. Like castration.

*JB: We actually created a website for **The Endless** modeled after Heaven's Gate's website, using the same platform they use. I'll send you the link to use as you see fit.*

DC: Please do! Anyone who sees *The Endless* will be struck by how personal the story feels, so I have

to ask: Have either of you been involved in cults or fringe groups?

AM: Not really. I grew up religious but that's not a cult. I think we realized when we were making the movie, though, that a cult was the perfect vehicle for a story about the virtues of rebellion. We were really attracted to the idea of a story about a person who thinks they know it all and wants to lead the world to a better place. But then it all goes wrong because it's based on terrible things.

DC: Okay, so I've been dying to ask: Where did the idea for red marijuana come from?

*JB: Let me try to remember... I know that I've always been fascinated by the odd relationship between homo sapiens and the plants that are available to them on the planet, especially those that have a hallucinogenic or psycho-active effect. Whether that be marijuana or mushrooms or ayahuasca or whatever. There are these plants available to human beings that cause perceptional shifts that do affect the material world and influence behavior, giving them insights they wouldn't have otherwise had. Now, do I do any of these drugs? I actually don't, to be totally honest. But I'm fascinated by that relationship and what it provides. I've also done research into ceremonial magic where drugs are used in rituals in order to come to certain spiritual conclusions. People think they can actually commune with God, or a higher power, or an otherworldly entity. So I just had the idea, like, what if in this particular region [where **Resolution** and **The Endless** take place] produced something unique, this red plant. And the affect would depend on the person. Some would see this entity, this "God" or whatever it is.*

DC: I bet there are tons of stoners out there Googling "Red Weed".

JB: It would be a huge compliment if, years from now, somebody was inspired to grow something similar. Or just for people to know about it and talk about it.

DC: You might end up with a strain of weed named after *The Endless*—something with bright orange hairs and rusty undertones. It's too bad you couldn't have created a tie-in product for theaters in California and Colorado. You could have given out dime-bags of red weed!

JB: We actually investigated that, but the producers didn't go for it. I don't understand.

DC: So after I realized *Resolution* and *The Endless* were closely related, I went back and re-watched *Spring* [your 2nd film] in order to see if that was also part of the same universe. It fits, but I couldn't find any direct connections. Did I miss anything?

*AM: More than anything, there are tonal similarities. **Spring** is more about external danger than relationships. The greatest tension at the end of **Spring** is whether or not these lovers will become a couple. In **Resolution** and **The Endless** there's tension, but the internal struggles are more prominent. However, if you look closely, to be totally honest, there are crossovers with **Spring**.*

DC: Really?

*AM: Shitty Carl is mentioned in **Spring** and then you actually meet him in **The Endless** [played by James Jordan]. Also, take a good look at the t-shirt Vinny Curran [who plays Mike in Spring] is wearing.*

DC: Fantastic! Is there anything else you want to let our readers know about before I let you go?

AM: We have a ton of stuff we're working on but nothing we can talk about just yet.

JB: Just because we can't say anything now doesn't mean we're retiring or going into construction contracting or anything.

DC: Good to know!

Clifton Collins, Jr.

TALKS DIVERSITY IN HOLLYWOOD, WESTWORLD & FREDDY'S NIGHTMARES

Method: *Phone*

Reflection: My interview with Clifton Collins, Jr. took place over the phone, but it was part of a more extensive ***Westwood*** Season 2 press junket that included face-to-face roundtable Q&As with cast members.

At the most recent staff writers' meeting, Steve Barton asked if anyone would be interested and able to attend. The junket was taking place at this swanky hotel in Hollywood. It amazed me that Dread Central, one of the flagship horror websites on the internet, didn't have a regular correspondent in Los Angeles. Steve himself was living in San Diego at the time. So no one complained when I enthusiastically volunteered.

By the way, I wasn't living in Los Angeles at the time either. I was still wrapping up my former life in Northern California. But I was so gung-ho to do as much work for Dread Central as possible that I was willing to make the drive. I left at 3 AM that morning knowing that would get me there with time to spare. It was my first junket!

As expected, I arrived late morning in plenty of time. In the months until my ultimate relocation to Los Angeles, approximately 15 of them, I'd drive to LA and back so often I thought about writing a book: ***Zen and the Art of Getting from Oakland to Los Angeles in Five Hours Flat***. And when I say five hours, I don't mean five hours and one minute. But I also don't mean four hours and 59 minutes. That's the Zen part of it all: By accepting that face that you can't make it to Los Angeles in under five hours, your mind and body are cleared to arrive unencumbered in five hours flat. Am I saying it's impossible to make it from Oakland to Los Angeles in under five hours? Of course not. But that's just being stupid. You're likely to get a ticket (or three), ultimately losing time. And you're likely driving like an asshole, and that's not Zen. I had about 200 rules and equations that seemed almost scientifically infallible. Maybe I will write that damn book one day. But now I'm getting off topic.

The morning of my first press junket, I was all jacked up on Red Bull and lack of sleep, but also really excited to be there. Excited to be at a real Hollywood press junket representing an established outlet. ***Westwood*** isn't even technically horror, rather it uses elements of horror (more on that later)—but I didn't care.

I was directed to onc of several rooms in a large suite inside the hotel. The place had hot coffee and pastries and other delectable (fruit, muffins) that seemed fancy to me at the time. And it was here that I was joined by other journalists from other outlets. There was someone from The Mary Sue and someone from Comic Book Universe (I think), and maybe someone else.

It was an interesting crew to be assigned to, as none of their sites were horror-specific. Maybe they keep horror journalists separated on purpose, I might have thought. Maybe they worried that a fight might break out if they put someone from Dread Central in the same room as someone from Bloody Disgusting. And, truthfully, who knows? But the diversity of outlets brought home how genre-defying **Westwood** was, I struck up a conversation about it, asking each of them how they were planning to present the show's coverage to their particular niche audiences.

Just then, someone I absolutely recognized entered the room. She was one of the biggest names in horror journalism, representing a very big player in the horror space. While I was still trying (and failing) to gain an audience on Twitter, she was well-established as a no-nonsense, unflappable voice in the "community". She had recently released a non-fiction book and I recall it being very well received. I even bought a copy (although I admit I never got around to reading it). I was excited to introduce myself, maybe even pop a selfie (if I could pull it off without being a blatant fan boy).

But she was completely withdrawn. She took a seat that put her as far away from every other person in the room as possible and buried her nose in her cellphone. Maybe she was working out a personal issue, or maybe she was doing something work-related. She wasn't just a correspondent, she was an Editor. Nonetheless the conversation about how to classify **Westwood** continued around her until, at one point, we were deep into the show's science fiction aspects.

"Science fiction is horror's sister genre," I remember saying nonchalantly. And I remember, because it was this moment that finally got the journalist I admired to look up from her phone. I smiled and tipped my head, hoping she'd feel compelled to join the conversation. But almost as quickly as she looked up, she looked back down at her cell phone. I began to think that she must be very shy. I wondered if she was powerful online, but perhaps agoraphobic in real life. But whatever I thought, ultimately, I didn't think too much about it.

The cast members came in, endured our questions, and left. I shook hands with the journalists I had passed the time with, but the one I admired most packed up the quickest and was out the door while my formal goodbyes were still in progress. I felt lucky when I finally caught up with her at the elevator.

"I'm such a big fan," I told her, probably sounding way too goofy. "I follow you on Twitter. Congratulations on your book! It's so great to meet you in person!" We shared the elevator down and said our polite goodbyes. And then just as quickly and singularly as I had driven to Los Angeles a few hours earlier, I set my sites back to Oakland, and made it back in five hours flat.

It wasn't until that night, or maybe even the next day, that I caught up with her twitter feed. "I'm at a press junket," she wrote, "and someone who obviously doesn't realize who I am just told me 'Science Fiction is the sister genre to Horror.' I love it when guys just assume that chicks can't be horror writers."

Obviously I was shocked. Shocked to realize her complete misinterpretation and misrepresentation of the incident. I was embarrassed. The tweet had gotten lots of attention and some people wanted to know the identity of the offending idiot. "I'll DM you," she told a few of her friends.

Of course she made that tweet as soon as I had said it, and clearly she was doing some creative editing. That comment was made to everyone else in the room, the ones who weren't horror centric. When she looked up, for a brief moment I hoped it might have been to agree with me—and what a validation that would have been, from someone I respected so much. That's why I looked at her and smiled. Clearly it was no attempt to "horror-splain" to someone at the top of the game.

So, okay, she has a laugh at my expense in the snark of the moment, but she left the tweet in place after I had finally introduced myself at the elevator, after I made it clear that I knew exactly who she was. After I informed her that I was a fan who had purchased her book. She made no effort to undo it.

And it hurts. All these years later, I have nothing but respect for this woman. Over the years, I've congratulated her on her fabulous writing and/or accolades. She's never replied or even acknowledged me. And it still hurts, because it proved what I didn't want to believe. Something I still struggle with. That even though we were all (mostly) attracted to horror as outcasts and rejects, the scene is already big enough to have its own cliques of cool kids. And just like I was never able to break into one of those in high school, I was never truly considered one of the cool kids on social media. Not for my entire career in horror. Not by my closest peers at least.

But journalism is supposed to be selfless, isn't it? As the reporter of truth on the spear-head of history unfolding, a journalist is supposed to be invisible. Especially in entertainment journalist. Critics can espouse on strengths and weaknesses, but journalists use their voices to elevate the creative endeavors of others. And maybe that's why I've never been successful at mastering social media. Because it's not about me. It's about the horror, man.

————

ORIGINALLY PUBLISHED: **April 27, 2018**

You may not immediately recognize the name Clifton Collins, Jr. but chances are you've seen his face. The character actor has delivered impactful performances in films helmed by today's most prestigious directors, starring alongside a who's-who of A-List Actors.

These days, most people will recognize Collins as the host Lawrence on HBO's *Westworld* (which just kicked off season 2). He comes from a multicultural background and was deeply inspired by his grandfather, who worked as a contract player for John Wayne. To honor the man who inspired and encouraged him, Collins briefly changed his name to Clifton Gonzalez-Gonzalez in loving tribute.

He soon learned that the Gonzalez moniker came with unexpected hurdles, specifically the preconceived notions of casting directors auditioning an actor with a Mexican surname. But like anyone with true passion, he turned his obstacles into stepping stones, steadily rising in both prestige and prominence.

Dread Central was lucky enough to sit down with Collins to discuss the current state of multiculturalism in Hollywood, the intersection of horror and procedurals, and a retrospective of some of his best genre performances. Oh yeah, we also talked about ***Westworld***! Have a read and let us know what you think!

Synopsis: *Westworld isn't your typical amusement park. Intended for rich vacationers, the futuristic park — which is looked after by robotic "hosts" — allows its visitors to live out their fantasies through artificial consciousness. No matter how illicit the fantasy may be, there are no consequences for the park's guests, allowing for any wish to be indulged. Westworld — which is based on the 1973 Michael Crichton movie of the same name — features an all-star cast that includes Oscar winner Anthony Hopkins and Golden Globe winner Ed Harris.*

Dread Central: Can you introduce yourself to some of our newer readers? Specifically, we'd love to hear about your upbringing and what inspired you to become an actor.

Clifton Collins, Jr.: My grandfather was a contract player for John Wayne; he was in a lot of westerns in the early 1950s. He started me tap dancing at the age of 7 which, coincidentally, was the same age he started performing—which is why he couldn't read. In 1932, they didn't really care about performers and their education. He was doing more vaudevillian type of theater, coming from a family of nine brothers and sisters.

So, he couldn't read, but he became a contract player for the biggest star of his time. Still, he was adamant about his grandchildren having an academic education as well as a creative one (like playing a musical instrument, tap dancing, doing jazz, or ballet or any of those things). So around when I was 17, honestly, I heard my grandfather complaining how his job wasn't worthy of anyone following in his footsteps. He was all, "Seven grandkids and not one of them is following in my footsteps! What I've done is nothing." I felt bad for him and, at that time my cousin and I were teaching martial arts. I was watching a bunch of Bruce Lee movies. During the next month, I had so many little signs, like people coming up to me and comparing me to this actor or that actor. It felt like my grandfather had gone out and told people to say these things to me.

So I started thinking about it, like, sheesh, this is my grandfather's thing and if it's something I'm going to do, I'm really going to do it, not just try. Do it or don't do it. You have to have a passion for it, because if you do it for the money or the fame you're going to end up being bitter because that has nothing to do with what's behind a real character. I think the core of any decent actor is great empathy and that doesn't come from seeking fame. It comes from passion.

My mom didn't believe in me; my stepdad told me to get a "real job" and my mom laughed telling me not to call her when I needed money. But my grandfather was the one voice of encouragement. He said, "No, son, listen to me: You can do it." We all need that one voice. So as soon as I heard him say it, that was it.

DC: I'd love to hear your thoughts about the current state of diversity in Hollywood and your own personal experiences overcoming Latino stereotypes.

CCJ: Things are certainly opening up. It's interesting because I really had to ramp up my own work ethic. My grandfather instilled an incredible work ethic in us, but I had to really ramp it up when I changed my name to Clifton Gonzalez-Gonzales honor him.

Casting directors can be so quick to judge by a name vs talent. I expected to be judged for my talent, not my name. So I found I had to work harder just to get in the room. I had to work harder just to get the opportunity to audition. But it was good for me because it forced me to expand my capacity as an artist by doing more research and things of that nature.

But, again, when I went by Gonzalez-Gonzalez it was like The Spanish Inquisition all over again, except it was The Mexican Inquisition. I was like, "Oh my God, I had no idea they were gunning for

*me!" I'm actually Mexican, German, and Apache, but [casting direc-
tors] would be like, "What's your background Clifton Mexican-
Mexican?"*

A big break for me came when the Mali Finn, the casting director for
Tigerland*, saw me and recommended me for the third lead, and it
was a southern character from Louisiana. It was very important to
have the opportunity to do a film with Joel Schumacher, playing one of
the three leads, and it's a southern role. So she had to go to Joel Schumacher and then he had to go to the writers and ask if they were okay
with this talented Latino actor [playing Pvt. Miter].*

*That was a big breakthrough for me and having the odds stacked
against me and having the stigma of Gonzalez not just once but twice,
made me work harder and research harder. It made me more impas-
sioned for what I was doing. My grandfather believed in me, so I was
going to make these people believe in me. And I was driven by that and
the fact that my mother said I'd never make it. ("Don't call me when
you need a check").*

*Now all of that negative fuel has turned into a pure passion for and a
love for the craft. And the exploring of other cultures is beautiful for me
too because when am I ever going to delve into playing a Cajun character like I did in* **Little Chenier** *or prepare a German monologue
to audition for* **Saving Private Ryan***, you know what I mean?
It's a beautiful way to study other cultures and humanity because I do
work so hard to play diverse characters.*

My goal isn't to not play Latinos or to only play white characters. My goal is to play complicated, interesting characters that can inspire thought and emotion, that can help
people grow and, at the end of the day, entertain. My joy
comes from creating characters I haven't been able to do
before. Like, in **Traffic**, there are so many great roles, but I
wanted to play Franky Flowers because he was complicated:
He was gay, he was a cocaine addict, his character was

based on an actual assassin. They wanted me to read for all these Latino roles, and I get it. Steven Soderbergh is a huge hero of mine, but I told him I want to play this character because he's complex.

DC: I was looking at your bio on IMDB and had to do a double take when I saw your very first acting gig. I know it's something our readers will get a kick out of. You know what I'm talking about...

CCJ: Freddy's Nightmares?

DC: Hell yeah! Not only did you get your start in horror, you're affiliated with one of its most enduring franchises!

CCJ: I don't know if I'd say I got my start in horror, necessarily. In the beginning, you take whatever they give you just to get your feet wet because you're still learning how to act. I'm still growing, thankfully, but those first 5-10 years of trial and error—it's pretty horrific!

DC: Tell me some of your memories about that first gig on *Freddy's Nightmares*.

CCJ: Oh my God, I mean, Robert Englund? Jesus Christ! It's like, "That's Freddy Krueger!"

DC: So, you were an *Elm Street* fan to begin with?

*CCJ: A huge fan! **Elm Street**, **Friday the 13th**, **Halloween**: These are the movies I grew up with as a kid. So even being a day-player was fantastic. And, you know, you start out as a day-player and eventually you slide into a weekly gig. And then it's like, "Wow, I'm blowing up! I'm on set for a whole week!" You just celebrate every victory and having a chance to work with Robert Englund, who I was such a big fan of, was a beautiful thing.*

DC: You've also done a lot of crime thrillers. I've always maintained there's a clear relationship between these police procedurals (hunting down serial killers, etc.) and horror movies. Agree or disagree?

*CCJ: It depends on the film. Like **Seven** is clearly a procedural and a horror movie and you can play a detective in a movie like **Halloween**. In terms of authenticity, it's really up to the filmmaker. Personally, I strive for extreme authenticity and I'm kind of a research whore because I want to bring truth to it. If the people involved don't want that kind of authenticity, then it's not a film for me. I probably could be a private detective because of all the research I've done preparing for roles.*

I love reading about police scandals because they're not very good storytellers. So when you read these police reports from the backwoods, it's pretty hilarious! It's like a really terrible Hollywood script that will never get made. But I do love procedurals! And I have police in my family, so anytime I can speak from a place of truth, it's important to me.

DC: One of your recent films that really blurred the lines between horror and procedurals was *M.F.A.* I really wish more people knew about that movie!

CCJ: It was tough! Francesca [Eastwood] shines, doesn't she?

DC: She sure does!

CCJ: She destroys it! I had already studied a lot of these rape cases you've been hearing about on college campuses—and even high school cases with football players in Ohio and how their victim was shunned, and I was livid! I didn't know what to do. I couldn't believe that football meant more to these people than a young woman who got raped.

The value system, or rather lack of values in these supposedly God-fearing communities is just so wrong. And this was a couple years before the film.

So when Francesca told me [she was doing **M.F.A.**] *I was like, "This is great!" and I was excited about the detective role. But the detective role was a bit lacking. The writer and the director had some experiences with the subject matter [campus rape] so their focus was on that.*

This was the first movie I ever did for love vs career because I loved the social message, and I wish I had time beforehand to sit down with the director to discuss the detective role. But I was doing **A Crooked Somebody** *with Rich Sommer and Ed Harris and we had been shooting all night long until sun-up. So Francesca called me up and said, "Hey, the detective role [in* **M.F.A.**] *opened up because the actor dropped out! Do you want that role?" I said, "Oh hell yeah! I'd love to play that role!"*

So they called me saying, "Oh, Mr. Collins welcome to the production! We're so happy to have you! Your call time is tomorrow at 7 AM." This was an email, actually, so I replied, "Ha-ha, very funny. I'm happy to be part of the show. So what's the actual date that I'm shooting?" They replied, "No really. You're shooting tomorrow."

I was like, damn, I'm working all night in Elysian Park [in Los Angeles] tonight and they want me in Orange County at 7 AM? I'm not even sure I can make it! Plus, I'd just had half my skull blown off! So I've got half my skull blown off and I'm driving to Orange County in rush hour traffic—and I was actually studying my lines along the way. I had to go to this frat house to wash all the blood off of myself and get into wardrobe. No sleep, mind you. And that was my first day on **M.F.A.** *You never know what you can actually do until you do it, right?*

DC: I guess so!

CCJ: So I never really had time to connect with the director, which is a relationship I really would have loved to have had, because one of the joys of filmmaking is collaboration. But, thankfully, because of all my experience on procedurals, there were things I already knew how to do. But when a director asks you if you know how to run with a gun, it kind of makes you question who you're working with. But it was an important film and Francesca did an amazing job. But truth told: I would have liked to develop my character more.

DC: It's still an important film and I'm glad you were a part of it. Switching gears now: *Stung* [2015] is a film I always mention when people ask me for a great horror comedy or an underrated horror movie. What was it like being in a madcap monster movie compared to the films you've made that are more grounded in reality?

*CCJ: **Stung** was kind of like a nostalgic shoot for me because it took me back to the days of puppeteering. Remember Them with the giant ants?*

DC: Absolutely.

CCJ: It took me back to that. And to have the opportunity to work in that medium was a unique experience. There was a lot of downtime but, hey, I was in Berlin for six weeks with Matt O'Leary who's a fantastic actor and, of course, Lance Henricksen. And not many people are doing puppeteering anymore. With CGI it's becoming a lost art. So it was a rare opportunity to take a dip into this medium.

Related Article [on DreadCentral.com]: The Cast of WESTWORLD Explains Why the Show Is a Must-Watch for Horror Fans

DC: I have a feeling some of our readers would appreciate it if we discussed a little show called *Westworld*. Since our site is horror-oriented, I

posed this same question to your co-stars Luke Hemsworth (Ashley Stubbs) and Angela Sarafyan (Clementine Pennyfeather). How would you convince someone who loves horror that Westworld is something they should watch? Complete this sentence: "If you love horror movies, you should watch *Westworld* because…"

*CCJ: If you love horror movies, you should watch **Westworld** because the same rushes you get from scares in a horror movie, those thrilling and suspenseful events happen in the show. Just from reading it I can tell Season 2 is really cranked-up compared to Season 1. You're going to have those moments where your heart palpitates or skips a beat and a lot of "Oh my gosh!" moments. There are some serious white-knuckle moments this season. It's the same thrill you get from watching a horror film!*

DC: *Westworld* is such a complex story and it's been over a year since the conclusion of Season 1. Can you sort of give our readers a recap of where we left your character, Lawrence?

CCJ: That's a really good question because they haven't even given me the backstory. Lawrence is a family man you see in town and The Man in Black [Ed Harris] picks him up, and… needs his help. They end up forging a bond and friendship by having to rely on one another. It represents the duality of humanity and many of the issues we're facing today. So many people just want to stay among themselves but we really need one another. And that's revealed in the interactions between The Man in Black and Lawrence.

DC: *Westworld* is so unique for its intelligence, nuance, and brilliant ensemble cast. How does this experience compare with some of the other productions you've worked on?

CCJ: Everyone is always on their A Game. There's such a high standard for quality and a passion for excellence. These people care so much: The cast, the crew, the showrunners. And I'm working with actors who I'm huge fans of. I'm so familiar with the work of the majority of the cast and being among them is humbling.

The first takes are amazing. In the past, I'd dream of being part of a team that could get takes this good on the 10th try! Everyone comes swinging their bats to knock that ball out of the park. We sometimes have to battle the elements. We had fires and rain. We muscle through it and shoot through it with smiles. We're so passionate about the gift of **Westworld***. Honestly, I think the actors are just as excited about the show as the fans because we love the show too.*

DC: Is there anything else you'd like to tell our readers before I let you go?

CCJ: I'm so excited for this season of **Westworld** *to come out. We've been blessed with incredible fans and 22 Emmy nominations. People have been waiting a while for* **Westworld** *to return and it'll be worth the wait. It's been an honor and I already miss it since the season wrapped. Now I want to buy a horse and learn some of my grandfather's gun tricks so I'll be ready for Season 3. They might not need me to do tricks in Season 3, but I'd still like to learn some. You've got to get ready to stay ready!*

DC: It's been an absolute pleasure speaking with you!

Angela Sarafyan

TALKS CLEMENTINE'S REVENGE & TED BUNDY BIOPIC EXTREMELY WICKED, SHOCKINGLY EVIL AND VILE

Method: *Junket/Roundtable*

Originally Published: May 10, 2018

Westworld recently kicked off its 2nd Season after a hiatus of more than a year and, by all accounts, it's been worth the wait. Dread Central recently had the opportunity to sit down with several cast members of HBO's hit sci-fi series, including Angela Sarafyan, who fans will immediately recognize as the hypnotic seductress, Clementine Pennyfeather.

Those in the know can attest to the fact that *Westworld* is extremely brutal, certainly not what one might expect from a show that's (basically) about robot cowboys. *Westworld*'s female "hosts" specifically are often subjected to cruel atrocities. And while no one takes more punishment than Delores Abernathy (Evan Rachel Wood) and Maeve Millay (Thandie Newton), Clementine's suffering in Season 1 is legendary.

Describing her character to a group of journalists, Sarafyan explained: "The tragedy of Clementine is what brings her strength out. She was framed, in a way, and then put down. But there was an innocence to Clementine before that; she was always looking for a connection beyond sex."

Portraying a thoroughly victimized character must be hard on thespians tasked with bringing them to life. But when Sarafyan talks about the catharsis of Clementine's revenge, we can celebrate it as a victory for both the character and the actress. In addition to jawing about **Westworld**, we got Sarafyan to discuss her participation in the upcoming Ted Bundy biopic, **Extremely Wicked, Shockingly Evil and Vile**.

Synopsis: *Westworld isn't your typical amusement park. Intended for rich vacationers, the futuristic park — which is looked after by robotic "hosts" — allows its visitors to live out their fantasies through artificial consciousness. No matter how illicit the fantasy may be, there are no consequences for the park's guests, allowing for any wish to be indulged. Westworld — which is based on the 1973 Michael Crichton movie of the same name — features an all-star cast that includes Oscar winner Anthony Hopkins and Golden Globe winner Ed Harris.*

Dread Central: Since Dread Central is a horror website, tell us how you'd convince a horror fan that Westworld is worthy of their time. Complete this sentence: "If you love horror movies, you should watch Westworld because..."

*Angela Sarafyan: You should definitely watch **Westworld** because it makes you face death. It's a show that questions your mortality. The show not only projects these feelings but makes you think about the boundlessness of human destruction and how far we can take our reality. Meaning: Will technology eventually be our destruction? And it's poetic too!*

DC: Can you tell us a bit about your part in the Ted Bundy biopic *Extremely Wicked, Shockingly Evil and Vile*?

AS: It's not a typical Ted Bundy movie because it's not about the atrocities. It's not about nasty killings. It's more about the psychological element of it. It's a different perspective. Imagine having a friend getting arrested and being like, "What? Why? What's going on?" And then all these things start to come out and you're thinking, "That's insane! How can this person that I love have done that?"

And what was crazy about doing that movie is I actually met one of Ted Bundy's girlfriends on set. She was there and we had dinner together.

DC: And that's the character you play?

AS: I actually play the girlfriend's best friend who tries to convince her that something's wrong. She has an addiction to alcohol and becomes very self-destructive and I have to convince her that there's something wrong with [Ted Bundy]: "You can not talk to him or be in touch with him." And this happened in real life. I found some articles about [my character, Joanna] telling her best friend, "This cannot continue," and they actually called the cops on Ted. And the way the film is made, I don't want to reveal too much about it, but you understand why.

DC: We're excited to see it!

AS: Yeah, I hope you like it. The director is Joe Berlinger and he's a documentary filmmaker, so his whole approach reflected that. He wanted to document the story as it was happening, which made things a little trickier than regular filmmaking.

DC: On *Westworld*, your character takes so much abuse. Besides Delores and Maeve, I can't think of anyone who takes the kind of brutality Clementine's subjected to. As an actress, did that ever

weigh on you? Did you ever go back to your trailer feeling depressed, like you'd actually been abused?

AS: I found that everything led to that scene [of Clementine's revenge] and I thought, "Yes!" That is the moment where she found her strength, even though she was the victim of someone else's agenda and that led to her being put down. But that moment was when the character's evolution really began. It shows that, sometimes, you find your strength during the most difficult moments.

And I was grateful for that because I think it was also a reflection of a lot of what we're going through in the world today. When I participated in The Women's March in Los Angeles, I was so amazed at the way millions of people came together. Women and men are finally being believed. And I personally know women who have been abused and even women who are still in abusive relationships. They don't believe they have a voice.

And at that moment [snaps fingers] I think Clementine represented that voice. Her beating was very much like a domestic violence situation and she broke him; she killed him—and that was awesome! I loved it! And I love doing my own stunts, too.

Bear McCreary

SHOWERS LOVE ON OINGO BOINGO ON THE EVE
OF DANNY ELFMAN'S BIRTHDAY

Method: *Phone*

Reflections: I've never been a music journalist because I've never been a musician. And while music alone has never been as striking to me as cinema in its entirety, I loved it. Who doesn't love music? More importantly, who says, "I'll do it!" any time Steve Barton asks, "Is anyone interested in interviewing…" I think you know the answer.

I did my homework and researched Bear McCreary in the days leading up to our skype interview. There wasn't a ton of stuff about him. He had a Wikipedia page, but it didn't reveal much. But he was the composer of ***The Walking Dead***, and ***The Walking Dead*** fans were bringing a lot of traffic to Dread Central.

So I saw how many awesome movies he's scored when I scoped his IMDB. Some horror, mostly sci-fi; both film and TV. I don't remember where I heard that he was a fan of Danny Elfman, but I'm also a huge fan of Danny Elfman and Oingo Boingo. I figured it might be a cool topic for us to riff on. Our interview lasted over an hour.

Ironically, Bear and I would meet in person a few years later at the home of Richard Elfman, (Danny's big brother and founder of The Mystic Knights of the Oingo Boingo). But that's a tawdry tale for another time.

———

ORIGINALLY PUBLISHED: **May 21, 2018**

Fans of today's best horror and sci-fi know the name Bear McCreary. The composer has built up an enviable resume working on popular shows like *The Walking Dead* and *Battlestar Galactica* and recent films like *The Cloverfield Paradox* and *Happy Death Day*.

Although he rarely gives interviews, we were able to snag Bear for a sit-down when he heard our main topic of conversation would be his idol, Danny Elfman (who turns 65 later this month). What transpired was more than can be absorbed in a single read, so we'll be bringing you our conversation with Bear in 2 parts.

Read about Bear's connections to the post-farewell reincarnation of Oingo Boingo and the roots of his appreciation for the music of Danny Elfman below. Come back next week to hear him weigh in on *The Walking Dead*'s dwindling viewership.

Dread Central: Let's talk about our mutual love for Danny Elfman since his birthday is coming up on May 29th.

Bear McCreary: Where do you want to start?

DC: Are you an Oingo Boingo fan?

BM: [Long pause] Yes. That's the short answer.

DC: I read your blog post where you said at age 10, you were watching a movie and as soon as you heard the score, you immediately knew it was done by Danny Elfman even before his name came up in the credits.

BM: That was the first time my mom looked at me and thought, "Who is this kid?"

DC: Did you already know Danny Elfman from Oingo Boingo or was your first introduction to him through movies?

BM: I found out about Danny through films. When I was a kid all I listened to were film scores. From age five until about age 15, I didn't listen to pop music—at all. It was only when I found out that my favorite film composer had a rock band that I thought I would check them out. For a lot of people, Danny Elfman is their gateway from popular music to film music. For me it was the other way around: Through Danny Elfman's film music, I found out about popular music. Once I got into Oingo Boingo, I started listening to Pink Floyd and Guns 'n Roses and Rage Against the Machine and Queen. I was like, "Oh wow! Popular music has a lot of great stuff!". It all started with my discovery of Oingo Boingo (who I adore) which came from my appreciation of Danny's film music.

DC: That's exactly right. I'm from Southern California and Oingo Boingo were local legends in the 1980s, and it was my love of Oingo Boingo that led to my love of Danny Elfman's film music. Danny Elfman has such a unique sound, it wasn't long before I could instantly identify his film music too. What's your favorite Oingo Boingo album?

BM: Man, Josh! That's a tough one!

DC: I know!

BM: I don't know that I can pick. Let me give you a few: What I always appreciate about Danny and Oingo Boingo is the way they explore new frontiers and new sounds. So there's a number of gear-shifts in their output where we go from one gear to another, and those tend to be the records I really like. First of all, you have to start with **Only a Lad** *which is where they're transitioning from The Mystic Knights of the Oingo Boingo and* **Forbidden Zone***; from being a weird performance art troupe in Venice Beach to being an actual rock band. There's a lot in that record that's pulled over from that more theatrical era but being shoved into this New Wave mentality.*

I love **Nothing to Fear***, I love* **Good for Your Soul***.* **Dead Man's Party** *is another gear-shift for the band where they're starting to explore some new sounds. For me, if I had to pick a favorite, I really might go with* **Dark at the End of the Tunnel** *or their final album,* **Boingo***. This is probably because I got my first intro-duction to Danny Elfman through his film music, and those last two records, you could tell his film music was really influencing Oingo Boingo and not the other way around. I think there's a maturity and sophistication and a narrative musicality in those two records that, for me, is super appealing.*

It almost feels sacrilegious to say **Dark at the End of the Tunnel** *is a better record than* **Good for Your Soul***—I'm not saying that. I'm saying that for me personally, those last two Oingo Boingo records mean the most to me.*

DC: I love your reverence for the band. I had no idea you were a true Oingo Boingo expert.

BM: Do you want me to blow your mind?

DC: Um—of course!

*BM: Here's something you don't know about me: In 2005, Johnny Vatos Hernandez put the vast majority of Oingo Boingo together to do a concert. It was John Avila, Steve Bartek, Sluggo [Sam Phipps], Doug Lacy, and I was the MD. I did all the arrangements, I played keys. My brother [Brendan] sang lead vocals and so we reunited Oingo Boingo under the Johnny Vatos banner, and we did shows for three or four years in that configuration. We had strings and backing vocalists. My wife Raya [Yarbrough] was in there. And that ensemble is continuing today as The Johnny Vatos Oingo Boingo Dance Party. My brother is still the lead singer and they're still playing a lot of my arrangements. And I worked with the Oingo Boingo guys when they played in **Battlestar Galactica**. They play on a lot of my film scores. Steve Bartek was a groomsman at my wedding. I've known these guys since I moved to LA. They're my family.*

DC: Mind. Fucking. Blown. I was excited to interview you from the get-go, but I had no idea I'd be talking to a bona fide member of Oingo Boingo! This stuff isn't on your Wikipedia page, man!

BM: Not only were Oingo Boingo a huge part of my life growing up, they are my family. I don't know Danny that well, but Steve and Johnny and John and Sam and Doug: These are some of the closest people in my life and I talk to them all the time.

DC: Amazing.

BM: I'm a fan for sure, and all those guys influenced me immensely. In this post-1995 era, the band and associated musicians have all gone on to do their own things, but my brother and my wife and I have been able to be part of that post-farewell afterlife of Oingo Boingo. Steve Bartek told me that the first time he and Vatos and Avila played together since the last Oingo Boingo concert was when I reunited them to score a short film. I had met them all and was like, [nervous voice] "Will you play on my student film score?" They said "Sure" and from there, they did a few more scores on student films. So when

Battlestar Galactica *came up, it was my first job and I needed a guitar player. So I brought in Steve and brought in John and Johnny. And when I played the music of **Battlestar Galactic** in concert, Bartek, Vatos, and Avila all played on stage with me. So I've been on stage with these guys doing Oingo Boingo music and my own music.*

DC: You said you were going to blow my mind and you did. Thank you!

BM: You're welcome. That's why when you asked, "Are you a fan of Oingo Boingo?" I had a feeling this would go well. I was like, "Where do I begin?"

DC: With Danny Elfman's birthday coming up, I think this discussion about Oingo Boingo and the band's legacy will be really interesting for our readers.

BM: It's interesting though because, despite the fact that I know the rest of the band very well, I don't know Danny that well. I've met him a couple of times and he's a sweet guy. But to me, Danny Elfman is probably a lot like what he is to you. He's this mythic figure. He is the person who created all this music that I adore. And, I think for the purpose of honoring him, as opposed to talking about all this shit I've done with his friends, it's important to know that Danny inspires me. Even to this day, when I'm writing music and I'm thinking about the music I loved.

*Like, when I was doing **The Cloverfield Paradox**, I thought, "What kind of music would I have wanted to hear at age 15? What would have made me go, 'Oh my God, that was amazing!'?" And that's what I want to write. And I think about Danny at these times, what he meant to me and still means to me and his inventiveness. I don't think it can be overstated what a profound creative impact he's had on me. I'd like to think I'm taking that energy and paying it forward.*

DC: Hopefully he'll read this and appreciate your appreciation.

BM: That would be nice, but at the same time, he's inspired millions of people. I don't think there's anything special about me in that regard. He's created such an incredible body of work spanning all these genres. And it's like you said, you always recognize his sound. To me, that's the ultimate sign of musical genius. Maybe more than just genius. It really gets into craftsmanship. This is a guy who's worked really hard. And that makes me admire him more. There are lots of people in life who are really talented and can get by on talent alone, but Danny Elfman is talented and he works his ass off. Every few years he's reinventing himself and trying something new. He strikes me as the kind person who isn't satisfied doing things he's already wildly successful at because he wants to do something challenging, you know what I mean?

*I admire that. In many ways, I've modeled my career in that way. When I really established myself in television, especially science fiction television, that became a world that was available to me. And I think, taking a cue from Danny Elfman, I thought, "Okay, what else is there for me out there?" Because I want to challenge myself. I want to do something I'm not known for. I want to do something that people don't associate with my name. Like when **Good Will Hunting** came out, that came out of nowhere. And in hindsight, the same can be said about the first **Mission Impossible** movie. These were scores that you would not think, at that time, would be something Danny Elfman would be doing. And he did. He redefined himself. And that's the artist I want to be. I'd also throw in Jerry Goldsmith and Elmer Bernstein as examples of musicians who would constantly strive to do new things.*

Bear McCreary

TALKS DANNY ELFMAN'S INFLUENCE & WEIGHS IN ON THE WALKING DEAD'S DWINDLING VIEWERSHIP

Method: *Phone*

Originally Published: May 28, 2018

Last week, we began our conversation with lauded composer Bear McCreary, known for his work on shows like ***Battlestar Galactica*** and ***The Walking Dead***, along with recent films ***The Cloverfield Paradox*** and ***Happy Death Day***.

Since Danny Elfman has been a constant source of influence and inspiration for Bear, and since the composer's birthday is coming up on May 29th, he's been a reoccurring theme throughout our conversation. In this conclusion of our interview, we also discuss Bear's appreciation of horror and his thoughts regarding ***The Walking Dead***'s dwindling viewership (even as the show begins production on its 9th Season).

Dread Central: We've talked about how Danny Elfman's sound is instantly recognizable. It's circus-like, it's jaunty, it's whimsical. There's also

a Bear McCreary sound. By comparison, it's atmospheric, it's moody, it's surreal. How would you describe the Bear McCreary sound, and what elements can listeners tune into in order to recognize your work without even seeing your name?

Bear McCreary: That's a fascinating question, and I've got to say, Josh: I'm utterly unqualified to answer. You're more qualified than I am because I'm inside my brain. Even when I'm trying to reinvent myself, even when I'm trying to not sound like myself, I am myself! I make my version of whatever I'm doing. So I don't know. I will say, I certainly hope that there's no specific musical thing I can point to and say, "Well, you know, I always use the C minor chord in 4×4…" you know what I mean? I'm striving to not be known for using a specific bag of tricks. But I think that what I strive to do, and what Danny Elfman very frequently does, is write music with personality. That is a word that has stuck with me for just about 20 years now.

*The first time I heard that word pertaining to music was when I was working with Elmer Bernstein, one of my other heroes. I was a protégé of his for a few years. When I was just out of high school, I was sitting in on his film scoring class at USC (which I wasn't even allowed to attend). But I did the assignment, which was to score a scene from **Sudden Fear**, one of the films Elmer scored back in, I think it was 1952. He gave it to the class and said, "Okay everybody, write a cue."*

*So I wrote this cue and I remember thinking vividly, "This feels like a Danny Elfman cue". It had big tribal drums and low woodwinds. It reminded me of **Nightbreed** (one of my favorite Danny Elfman scores). And, of course, looking back on it, it was way too big and aggressive. It was steamrolling over this black and white scene from the 1950s. But Elmer smiled and he said, "This cue has a lot of personality."*

And I remember realizing I wasn't thinking about it that way. I was just trying to make the most awesome thing I could. And as I've gotten into this business, as I've written music and listened to music that's out there, I've realized: Music with personality is consistently the music I enjoy. It's the music that stands out to me. And I really picked that up from Danny Elfman. His music has so much personality we immediately identify it with him. But even his scores that don't immediately jump out as being a Danny Elfman score still have personality and that's an incredibly valuable thing.

DC: You've built a very diverse body of work, including scoring horror for *The Walking Dead* and dark sci-fi for the last two *Cloverfield* movies. How does it compare to other genres and what do you like best about scoring horror?

*BM: I have a blast with horror films. To me horror isn't even a genre —it's a medium. Like, **The Cloverfield Paradox** is this epic science fiction body horror psychological thriller, and **Happy Death Day** is like a charming comedy, but they're both horror films! And they allow me to explore completely different moods and textures. I think one of the things I love most about horror films is they really lean on music, perhaps more than other genres, to really help pull in the audience. It doesn't just mean the music is bigger and louder all the time. It's actually quite the opposite. The music needs to be expertly delivered, so when it is big and bombastic you can really scare people—which is the hardest thing to do and one of the things I love the most.*

I grew up on horror movies and I think horror audiences are massively sophisticated. When people go to see a comedy, even if they've already seen thousands of them, they're still going to laugh—if it's funny. Horror audiences like me, when you've seen a thousand horror movies, you have to work hard to scare me. I know all the tricks, I know all the clichés, I know where the plot is going, which is why it can be fun for me because it's a challenge.

That's why I think movies like **Get Out** *and, in its own way, Happy Death Day are so effective. Because even if you've seen a million horror films, you're still disarmed by something in those films that's new. And music can really be a big part of that and it's an absolute thrill for me.*

DC: Complete this sentence: "A movie I wish they'd remake so I could do the score the new version would be…"

BM: **The Great Escape**.

DC: Let's dish about The Walking Dead. Of course, we know you have nothing to do with the decision-making involved in producing the show, but as someone with a stake in it, I think your insights will be interesting. Cool?

BM: Totally cool.

DC: Are you a fan of the comic books?

BM: Yes.

DC: How would you explain the show's dwindling viewership?

BM: As a fan of the show, I think there's a natural exhaustion that kicks in when you go beyond Season 3 of anything. I mean, name me a show where Season 8 had the highest ratings. I wonder if there's even an example in the history of television where that's the case. So I look at it differently. I'm like, "Hey, this show is in Season 8 and look at how many people watching it!" Think of all the shows that never made it this far. **Buffy** *never got there; I don't remember if* **The Next Generation** *got there, but whatever. My point is, it's a juggernaut that's lasted a long time and it's continuing strong with its core demographic.*

*Personally, I think that since the time that the comics were written in and the era that we exist in now, the politics and national conversation has changed to the degree that it's altered what makes **The Walking Dead** appealing to a lot of people. The escapist fantasy has changed. It posed the question: "Can you imagine if our country was a devastated hell-scape?" In the early 2000s until 2016, that was really an escapist fantasy. It was a fun world. I love **I Am Legend**. I love these kinds of stories.*

DC: The idea of starting over from scratch.

*BM: Exactly! But I think the ratings started to go down around the time of the election, around the time of the campaign. And I think there was really a sense of unease, no matter what side of the political spectrum you're on. Things are just a little less known, and things that we all took for granted suddenly we're thinking about. And then you turn on your TV and you see Negan... Now, five years ago when I first met this guy in the comic, I loved him because he represented this escapist fantasy. I really think that some of the viewership that has left **The Walking Dead** might be because, nationally, we're more scared than we were. And it's not as much fun to turn on the TV every Sunday and get that kind of hyper-violence.*

DC: You're saying it's hitting too close to home these days.

*BM: Exactly. You can weave politics and satire more in into fantasy and sci-fi but there needs to be a sense of detachment. As a contrary example, we did an arch on **Battlestar Galactica** that was, in my estimation, a very thinly-veiled allegory for the war in Iraq. It had our heroes strapping themselves in with suicide bombs, going in to blow up a police station of the occupying force. And the audience was like, "Yeah, go do that." It really had a lot to say about what was happening, but it was buried under the surface enough that people just enjoyed it as a science fiction show. Not to mention, for most Americans, the war in Iraq is far away. So **The Walking Dead** hits closer to* *home literally and geographically. So I don't know, but I do wonder if that has something to do with it.*

DC: I never thought about it like that and I think our readers will find your input illuminating. If you've still got a couple minutes, we'd love to hear about what you're working on next.

*BM: I'm very excited about **God of War**, for Sony PlayStation. I don't do video games very often but this one is just epic and I think it's going to be fantastic. And I have a number of horror and science fiction films around the corner, but it's a little early to say what they are just yet. There's a lot of cool stuff coming up in the next year, so I'd just say stay tuned!*

And please include, from me, a hearty Happy Birthday to Danny Elfman and thanks for all the years of inspiration.

Adam Rifkin

TALKS DIRECTOR'S CUT, THE DARK BACKWARD & HIS LAST CONVERSATION WITH BILL PAXTON

Method: *Phone*

Reflections: I'm not a shill. Despite the persistent myth, critics and journalists don't get paid for writing favorable press. Anyone making a living as a journalist knows how absurd that concept is. But, there can be a gray area when an outlet is owned by a horror distributor, as is the case with Dread Central, which was acquired by Epic Pictures in 2017. That's why Dread Central never reviews films released by Dread (formerly Dread Central Presents) Epic's horror distribution arm. But that doesn't mean we can't promote these films.

Back when I did this interview, I was still just a contributor —but a scrappy one. At our weekly writers' meetings, Steve Barton used to make me wait 10 seconds before accepting an assignment. It wasn't to give me time to think, it was to give other writers a chance to throw their hats in the ring. It was a given that I'd do anything to write for Dread, at the drop of a hat, no matter who what where or when.

The first head of distribution for Dread had complete autonomy when it came to deciding what the label would produce and release. There was a submission committee, but this dude had the ultimate say (barring extreme interventions from above in the form of a greenlight from a Chief Executive). While quite a few of Dread's flagship releases were stellar, some were below par for a brand affiliated with Dread Central. A couple were excellent, except they weren't even horror movies.

One of these awesome-but-not-really-horror flicks released in the early days of Dread is **Director's Cut**. You can make a case for it being horror-adjacent if you're adamant and micro-focused on nomenclature. Still, **Director's Cut** is fucking brilliant. At the time, I never sought to present **Director's Cut** as anything besides a great film, a funny film; a black comedy that could induce laughs big enough to knock you off your couch. And, of course, the film afforded me the opportunity to speak with Adam Rifkin.

Horror fans still may not be instantly familiar with Rifkin, but Josh Millican was already a fan. Anyone who's seen me in person, my left hand specifically, knows that I've tattooed my affiliation with the KISS Army. So a chance to interview the director of **Detroit Rock City**? Yes, please! And the KISS flick wasn't the only Rifkin joint I'd enjoyed.

In 1991, he wrote and directed **The Dark Backwards**, another film that perfectly straddles the line between horror and something as yet undefinable. I didn't see this sleeper until the early aughts, but it blew my mind. It was so hilarious and utterly nightmarish with subtle hints of David Cronenberg and David Lynch.

What he told me about Bill Paxton still gives me shivers to this day: That he was nervous about the upcoming surgery that ended up killing him. That he had bad vibes. I'm surprised none of the trades or other genre sites picked up on it.

My interview with Adam Rifkin turned out to go beyond anything that I might have imagined. And we've kept in touch ever since. I suspect I'll be interviewing him again sometime soon.

———

ORIGINALLY PUBLISHED JUNE 1, **2018**

Long-time Dread friends know we've radically reshaped ourselves over the past year. In addition to maintaining our mission to curate, educate, and entertain horror fans, we launched Dread Central Presents, the genre-distribution arm of Epic Pictures.

We've been proud to bring you a quality catalog of diverse horror offerings like **The Lodgers**, **Imitation Girl**, **Terrifier**, and **#Screamers**. Our latest release, available on VOD since May 29th, is **Director's Cut**. The film is directed by Adam Rifkin and stars Missi Pyle, Penn Jillette, Harry Hamlin, and Hayes MacArthur.

Despite building an enviable filmography, this is one of Rifkin's rare forays into horror. It's also one of the rare occasions when he's directed a film he didn't write. We were lucky enough to sit down with Rifkin recently, where we discussed **Director's Cut**, his cult **sleeper The Dark Backward**, and his final conversation with Bill Paxton, who tragically passed away in 2017.

As our sit-down was extensive, and probably too much to consume in a single dose, we're presenting it in 2 parts. Give the synopsis for **Director's Cut** a look-see below, followed by Part 1 of our interview with Adam Rifkin. Be sure to check back next week for Part 2!

Synopsis: *The ultimate "meta movie",* **Director's Cut** *is an insane, cinematic sleight of hand trick that reflects on itself, much like the stage persona of its co-star and creator, world famous illusionist Penn Jillette. Here, teamed with acclaimed Director Adam Rifkin, Jillette conjures a mind bending, genre defying movie-within-a-movie-mash-up that's part narrative thriller, part docu-mental-case.*

Herbert Blount (Jillette) is a crowdfunding contributor for the new Adam Rifkin feature **Knocked Off**. *Unhappy with the film, he steals the footage and kidnaps actress Missi Pyle to star in his own "director's cut!"*

Dread Central: Can you introduce yourself to some of our younger readers?

Adam Rifkin: Yeah, I'm Adam Rifkin; I'm a writer and a director and, sometimes, I act. But I would definitely not consider myself an actor. I would never besmirch the fine people who take the profession seriously and devote their life to the craft. I just like to ham it up every once in a while. But, I'm definitely not a professional actor.

DC: Your filmography is kind of all over the place. You've done some family-friendly flicks for Disney and Pixar, as well as some high drama. As a true Renaissance filmmaker, how does writing and directing horror compare to other genres?

AR: Well my first love of movies from the time I was a little kid was the love of monster movies. When I was about four or five years old, I remember vividly my grandfather bought me an issue of **Famous Monsters of Filmland Magazine**. *I was absolutely fascinated by the pictures of all the classic monsters: Dracula, Frankenstein,*

The Wolfman, The Creature from the Black Lagoon. And that got me started on this obsession with monster movies.

I got my first film education in Chicago, which is where I'm from, watching all the classic horror movies on a show called Svengoolie. And he's still doing it. In those days, every regional market had its own local horror show host: LA had Elvira, New York had [John] Zacherle, and Chicago has Svengoolie. This was the era of local television and so a monster show host would introduce this week's movie and during the commercials they'd do some little schtick about the movie and some trivia. So, on Svengoolie, I saw all the classic Universal monster movies, I watched all the Hammer horror films from England, I saw all the AIP Drive In movies, I saw all the Japanese giant monster movies. It was a real cinematic education.

*But I've never really made a horror movie [before **Director's Cut**] in my professional career—and, actually, I'd say that still holds true. I know **Director's Cut** is sort of a horror film, but it's more of a very black comedy or horror comedy. So, I still have yet to make a genuine, genuinely scary horror film.*

DC: Your first film that I saw was *The Dark Backward* [released in 1991]. That one also kind of straddles the line between horror and deadpan, black comedy. I just read on IMDB that it's now considered a bona fide cult classic.

AR: I am very happy about that. I'm grateful for that.

DC: It's been almost a year since the passing of Bill Paxton, one of the stars of *The Dark Backward*. Can you talk about what it was like working with him back when he was just a young actor cutting his teeth?

*AR: Sure. To back up just a bit further, **The Dark Backward** was the first screenplay that I ever wrote. It definitely has horror* elements, specifically body horror, but it absolutely is a very black comedy as well. At the time when I wrote it, I was trying to get my first movie made, and I knew that no one was going to give me a lot of money to direct. I was young and just out of the gate.

So, in lieu of explosions and big special effects, I tried to create some-thing unusual enough that its offbeat nature would get it some attention. I didn't think I'd get attention for it in any other way. I didn't think I'd be able to have stars or big special effects or anything really. But if it's unusual enough, I figured, maybe it will stand out.

What ultimately did end up happening is we did get stars in it. Judd Nelson, at the time, was a big enough name to carry the whole movie. And Bill Paxton was just coming off of **Aliens** and **Near Dark** and **Weird Science**, and he was very funny. A very hot young actor. Wayne Newton has always been an icon. James Caan was just coming off of **Misery** so he was flying high. Rob Lowe has always been a big star. So, the fact that I got these stars was a shock to me. But, really, the reason we got them was because the script was so left of center. They'd never been offered anything like it before, which is why they all signed on to do it.

Working with Bill was absolutely one of the greatest joys of my life. We became very close friends on that movie and remained friends for all these years. In fact, a week before he tragically passed, I had just gone over to his place to show him a rough cut of the film I'd just done with Burt Reynolds called **The Last Movie Star**. I showed him the rough cut and he really liked it. We had lunch that day and he actually told me that he had to go into surgery and he was nervous about it. Those words will haunt me forever.

The fact that Bill Paxton isn't around anymore is one of the great losses of our time.

DC: Wow, Adam, I had no idea you guys were so close. I know our readers will appreciate your emotional recollections.

AR: Anyone who's a Bill Paxton fan should know: He was as great in real life as he was on screen. He was just a great guy, a funny guy. A really generous and wonderful person.

DC: That's great to hear, because he was one of those actors who always seemed to bring a bit of himself to the roles he played. After watching a few of his films, you feel like you actually know him. Thanks again for sharing your memories. Let's jump back to *Director's Cut*: How did it all come to fruition?

*AR: I'll tell you how it came to me. As you may know, I didn't write **Director's Cut**. I usually write what I direct, but in this instance, the screenplay was written by Penn Jillette, of **Penn and Teller** fame. I had made a film called **Look** that was a drama shot entirely on surveillance cameras. And **Look** had done well on the arthouse scene and spawned a TV series on Showtime. When Penn Jillette saw the movie, unbeknownst to me, it had already been out and gone and was only available on video.*

*One day, late on a Friday night I get a Facebook message from Penn Jillette. Of course, I was home on a Friday night because I have no life! He said some very complimentary things about **Look**, which he had just watched with a group of friends. He had reached out to his manager and agent and said, "I want to get in touch with Adam Rifkin," and they said, "We'll look into it first thing Monday morning." Well, instead of waiting, he found me on Facebook and saw that we had mutual friends. He sent me a direct message saying, "I loved **Look**, I want to talk to you about it, here's my phone number."*

Since it was getting late, I didn't want to call him on the phone; I'd never met him before, you know? So, I wrote him back on Facebook saying, "Thank you so much. I'm a fan of yours. I'd love to discuss the movie with you. I know it's late, so here's my phone number. Feel free to call me anytime over the weekend." Two seconds after I hit "Send" my phone was ringing, and it was Penn.

Adam Rifkin

TALKS DIRECTOR'S CUT, THE PITFALLS OF
CROWDFUNDING & THE INCOMPARABLE MISSI PYLE

Method: *Phone*

Originally Published: June 8, 2018

Last week, we brought you Part 1 of our extensive interview
with Rifkin. In addition to dishing about how ***Director's
Cut*** got rolling, we discussed his directorial debut, ***The
Dark Backward***, and his resulting friendship with Bill
Paxton. Today, we continue talking about ***Director's Cut***
with specific attention given to the cast and the potential
perils of crowdfunding.

**Dread Central: You were telling us about your first
conversation with [*Director's Cut* writer/star]
Penn Jillette. Please continue.**

*Adam Rifkin: After talking about my movie **Look** for a while, he said
he had written a script that he had been working on for a number of
years called **Director's Cut**. One of the things that stood out to me
most was he said he wanted to use the concept of the director's
commentary as a narrative device. I'd never heard of that before so I
was immediately intrigued.*

So he said, "Would you be interested in possibly directing it?" I told him I'd love to read it, even though I usually only direct films I write. I was very open, because he's legendarily brilliant, so anything he came up with would be worth checking out.

So he sent me the script right then. I read it immediately and by 3:30 am we were back on the phone together. I thought it was so unusual and so unique, the opportunity was impossible to pass up. I could not see myself saying "No" to something this rare. So I said, "I'm in!" Still, even then, we both knew it would be a difficult film to get funded.

We went back and forth for a while and Penn was the first one to come up with the idea of crowdfunding. He said, "Look, I'm somewhat well known. I have 2M+ Twitter followers. I'll be the face of the campaign. If we make the money, great! If we don't and it's embarrassing, I'll take the hit." I said, "Great, let's go for it!"

So we mounted an aggressive crowdfunding campaign and we both worked really hard. We ended up raising more money than we were looking for, and it worked great! So we were able to make the movie exactly the way we wanted without any compromise.

DC: Since it's impossible to talk about *Director's Cut* without using the term "meta-film", can you explain to some of our younger viewers, in your own words, exactly what that means?

AR: Meta is a pop term that means something is self-referential. **Scream** *is a great example of a meta-film because it's a movie about slasher movies and it's acutely aware of all the tropes, rules, and conventions of this subgenre to the point where it comments on them blatantly, yet still uses them for dramatic effect.*

We wanted to take meta to even more extreme levels, so we've got all kinds of tropes and conventions that we're sending up and deconstructing with **Director's Cut**. *The thing about* **Director's Cut** *is that it's hard to explain but absolutely easy as hell to under-*

stand when you're watching it is: It's a movie about a crowd-funder but the movie is also crowdfunded.

We premiered **Director's Cut** opening night of Slamdance 2016 and all the distributors who saw the movie loved it. But none of them wanted to distribute it because they said, "We don't know how to sell it. It's an impossible movie to explain." That's why Dread Central Presents and Epic Pictures are such saviors because they said, "We don't care that it's tough to sell. We love the movie. We're putting it out no matter what."

DC: Those guys are awesome.

AR: They're the best! So basically, to boil it down, **Director's Cut** is a movie about a film obsessed stalker who gains access to a movie set by being one of that film's crowd-funders. Since he's not happy with the way the film is unfolding, and because he's obsessed with the lead actress, he steals all the footage from the movie while it's being made, kidnaps the lead actress, re-shoots scenes in his basement studio, and re-casts himself as the lead. He then takes footage from the movie and the movie he's created in his basement and he cuts them both together into what he believes is the perfect "Director's Cut".

The rules we set up for ourselves were that the movie you're watching is what our lead character Herbert Blount [Penn] created. The footage he uses, the footage he shoots, the access he had—everything you see has to be something he actually could have created. You couldn't have made this film 10 years ago because the technology didn't exist yet, specifically being able to steal a film's footage by hacking into an FTP site where all the raw footage exists. There was no such thing as a mash-up or a fan-edit in those days. Now that they're common place, we're taking full advantage of the ideas and conventions that exists now to make fun of (and have fun with) this bizarro **Director's Cut**.

DC: Herbert Blount is such a fascinating character. While I was watching *Director's Cut*, I

wondered if there actually was an adversarial relationship between you two on set? Were there times when, as a director, you felt you had to give up control of the creative process to accommodate this huge, irrational character?

AR: No. Penn is a consummate show business professional. He loved this idea and handed it off to me. He doesn't fancy himself a director in real-life at all. He entrusted me with the entire production. So everything you see involving Herbert Blount's character taking over the set of the movie I'm directing, and the chaos that ensues, is completely crafted by the two of us together.

DC: Since crowdfunding is at the crux of the film, can you talk a bit about how the practice of crowdfunding is changing the industry?

AR: Getting independent movies made is hard no matter what, because they're expensive. Getting any movie made is hard because even small movies are expensive. So if there are alternative opportunities for getting films funded, it's good for everybody. The things that's great about crowdfunding is you're going directly to the fans of this would-be movie and saying, "Instead of buying a ticket when the movie's done, why don't you buy in now, so your support actually gets the movie made?" It's a roll of the dice for everybody because you might get a ticket and a t-shirt for a movie you eventually hate. But, really, you could say the same thing about any movie. So, I think it's a great opportunity to get movies made that might otherwise never come to fruition. And it's a great opportunity for fans of a particular film-maker, actor, or idea to get a movie made that they want to see, something that otherwise might never have the opportunity to see the light of day.

DC: *Director's Cut* is so funny, but it suggests there might be some legitimate pitfalls to crowdfunding. I'm curious if you or Penn actually had some relat-

able experiences with these potential crowd-funding perils?

AR: Any time you raise money to make a movie there are always challenges involved with those unique circumstances. So, yes, crowdfunding has a unique set of challenges as well. We had over 6,000 supporters who we wanted to keep happy and fulfill our promises to. That's a lot of t-shirts and grab bags and DVDs to get out. That's a lot of money that doesn't go on screen, you know? But we know that going in, that a certain percentage of the money goes back to the crowd-funders, and that's cool. I have no problem with that.

Because we've been making movies for a long time, we understand how slowly the gears turn, how nearly impossible it is to get a film made, much less seen. But sometimes the crowd-funders get frustrated that things take so long, and I wish I had foreseen this going into the crowd-funding arena. I wish I had been clearer [with crowd-funders] that we hope the film will get made and released as soon as possible, but it doesn't always work that way.

*For example, we opened the 2016 Slamdance Film Festival. Now, we would have loved to have sold it to a big studio and seen it released a few months later, but it didn't happen that way. So we spent two years looking for a way to get the film released, and the crowd-funders spend that whole time wondering what the hell is taking so long. Most everybody understood and we did our best to keep everyone informed with updates, but unless you're in "the business" and have been for a while, it's hard to fathom that it really does take this long. But it does. And so, now that we do have these fabulous distributors and **Director's Cut** is finally being released the crowd-funders have been fantastic. The response has been tremendous with everyone saying it was worth the wait.*

Still, I wish I had prepared them from the beginning about how long this could take.

DC: With crowdfunding becoming such a popular, even necessary component of indie filmmaking, I know a lot of aspiring up-and-comers will appreciate your insights.

AR: I would definitely crowdfund a movie again. I would just be clear going in about every possible scenario.

DC: The cast of *Director's Cut* was absolutely fantastic! Do you have any fun stories about what it was like working with Missi Pyle, Penn Jillette, Harry Hamlin, Hayes MacArthur, and Lin Shaye?

*AR: Absolutely. I will say that Missi Pyle changed the whole tone and tenor of the movie just by accepting the role. The first draft of the script was more of a straight-up horror film. The character Hebert was more meanspirited. He kidnapped someone and tortured them and it was a much more brutal story. We pursued several other actresses for the role and fully intended to go in that direction. But when Missi Pyle accepted the role and we met her, she was just so funny. She's so sweet and exudes this lighthearted sweetness, we decided it just wouldn't be fun watching her being brutalized. We felt instead it would be much more fitting to have Herbert be madly in love with her. He's stalking her because he loves her and really wants to star in a movie with her, as opposed to wanting to destroy her. Herbert changed from a brutal killer to something of an oafish Phantom of the Opera, madly in love with his Christine. Missi changed the style, feel, and in many ways the entire genre of **Director's Cut**, and working with her was an absolute blast. And she did something I can't imagine any other actress doing: She played so many different versions of herself in one movie and they all are distinct. Even when she's about to die, it's totally believable and she's still doing it in a way that's funny.*

Hayes MacArthur is an actor I've worked with several times before and I think he's super charming and super funny. I can't believe he's not a bigger star at this moment. I think he way out Ryan-Reynolds Ryan Reynolds in my opinion. He was a blast and I'm so glad he came on.

*Harry Hamlin is an icon. I mean, **Clash of the Titan**—come on! And, by the way, he's so good looking still it's a joke. You look at him and it's like he's been Photoshopped into your field of vision. You can't believe this is a real person in his 60s.*

And Lin Shaye I've worked with before; she's just absolutely the coolest. She loves cool projects and I'm so glad she's enjoying a career Renaissance right now.

Everyone was game for something unusual. Everyone knew it was something of a risk and had no idea how it would turn out. Everyone was a total sport and trusted that, no matter what, it was going to be fun to do. I can't tell you how much I appreciate their trust in me and Penn. And I will tell you, working with Penn has been a dream. He's brilliant and funny and a blast just to hang with and now, we've become really good friends.

DC: Do you have any other upcoming projects you'd like to tell our readers about before I let you go?

*AR: I'd love for people to check out **The Last Movie Star** with Burt Reynolds that just came out thanks to A24. It's as polar opposite to **Director's Cut** as a movie could possibly be, so I'd say they'd make a perfect double feature.*

Matt from VOWWS

Method: *Phone*

Reflections: While I'm not a trained musician in any capacity, music has been a huge component in my life and an absolute artistic joy. Had I not gone the film journalism route, I absolutely might have gone the Cameron Crowe route and aspired to write for **Rolling Stone**. So, when offered the opportunity to interview a member of a new dark-wave duo, I was eager to give it a go.

And while I never turned down an assignment from Steve Barton, it's important to note that this interview coincides with a major shift at Dread Central. Over a decade after starting the company, Steve retired from Dread Central. His Managing Editor, Jonathan Barkan, took over his role. So, this was my first Barkan assignment.

Literally days later another key figure left Epic Pictures. He had been the driving force for Epic's acquisition of Dread Central, seeing the site's value to the company. His co-founder at Epic, Patrick Ewald, had been less gung-ho about the merger initially. And, now, the success or failure of Dread Central Presents fell directly on his shoulders.

While I didn't know a lot of details at the time (and there are still major information gaps in my understanding of the situation), it definitely marked a new chapter in the saga of Dread Central. And though I had no idea at the time, I'd actually be promoted to Editor-in-Chief in less than two years' time.

This was the Barkan Era, and I became his Managing Editor.

As for the article itself, Matt never gave me an identifier beyond his first name.

———

ORIGINALLY PUBLISHED: **June 28, 2018**

The Los Angeles-based, Australian-born "Death Pop" duo VOWWS have been touring in support of their sophomore LP, *Under the World*, since last March, with additional gigs set throughout the summer. The synth outfit is making a name for themselves with a unique sound and an aesthetic that defies easy classification--not to mention cinematic live shows where the band leaves everything on the stage.

Here's how Costa Rican-born Rizz, one half of VOWWS, describes their latest album: "The theme of isolation is strong in a lot of the stuff surrounding this release. ['Structure of Love', specifically] is about paranoid love, obsession, idealization and the hopelessness it can bring."

Dread Central was lucky enough to sit down with the other half of VOWWS, the single-monikered Matt, to discuss the band's past, present, and future.

About *Under the World*: *With their new album,* **Under the World***, VOWWS craft their dark pop masterpiece — a cinematic, stylish and menacing statement of intent. Drawing upon influences as diverse as classic western, electronica, surf rock, metal, and film music, the enigmatic duo weaves disparate threads of cultural influence together into a tapestry of drama, imagination and surprising warmth — only to deconstruct them again in front of your ears.*

Dread Central: Tell us about VOWWS! How did you and Rizz meet?

Matt: We met at college in Australia. We were both playing in a bunch of bands and neither of us was really happy with what we were doing and where we were going and the music we were playing. We were part of a music performance program and everything felt forced. We were playing a bunch of types of music we weren't interested in, just for the experience or whatever. But we met at an end-of-the-year party after our first year. We got drunk and decided to form a metal covers band; I would play drums and Rizz would sing (and scream and all that sort of stuff). We just hit it off. She joined a band I was in with some high school friends and it just went from there.

DC: I'm curious about the significance of the name VOWWS and the use of the extra "W". Can you illuminate me?

M: VOWWS signifies heaviness and commitment—everything we wanted to come through in the music. It conveys permanence. Also, you don't want a name that tells people what you're not, if that makes sense. We didn't want to say anything that would detract from the music. There's a neutrality about the name that we liked. The extra "W" is just a stylization, something that gives a bit of weird neutrality and takes it away from having a direct meaning. It becomes sort of a blank canvas for our music.

DC: It's definitely effective. Now, I've seen VOWWS described as "Darkwave", "Goth Rock", and, my personal favorite, "Death Pop". How would you guys describe the band?

M: That's a tough one. We both sort of tend to steer clear of describing VOWWS. If we do describe it to a casual music listener or a stranger or something, we'll just start by comparing ourselves to the usual suspects. The 80s bands: Depeche Mode, Joy Division and the like. If they don't know much about 80s music we'll start to reference the bigger acts like The Cure. You sort of work backward from a reference point. But that's not really how we write our music, so it can be difficult to describe. We're also inside it, so it's hard sometimes to see how other people see it. It's always been tricky describing our music. I think it always is [for musicians] but I feel it's especially so for us because we side-step genres deliberately.

But having said all that, we described our first record as "Depeche Mode on steroids". But we've moved on from that direction too. I just tend to let the music speak for itself—if possible.

DC: I read that *Under the World* was inspired, in part, by film music. Since Dread Central is a horror website, I'm especially curious to know if you guys were inspired by horror in general or any horror movies specifically?

M: Rizz might have been, so I can't name any specific titles on her behalf. But we do take a lot from cinema, and not just the visual or artistic elements, but also from the soundtracks. We're fans of Phillip Glass who is a big inspiration for us. But also, some movies that aren't necessarily horror. Like, John Barry [who scored 11 James Bond movies] has been a formative influence for us. Generally speaking, we always want to have a cinematic element to our music and deliver some of that same drama—if we can. But there is a general influence from horror movies and dark films specifically.

DC: This leads perfectly into what I was going to bring up next: Since your sound is so cinematic, do you employ any theatrical elements when performing live? Props, projections, pyrotechnics, etc.?

M: Not really. We put everything we have into our live performances in terms of putting our full presence and our full bodies into it. But, again, we like to let the music speak for itself. We just get up there and play the stuff, but we put everything into it. No special theatrics because, to us, theatrics would just take away from the music, which is the important thing.

DC: I'm always curious about the set-ups synth-based bands use to perform live. What kind of equipment do you guys use on stage?

M: Rizz has a sampler she uses. She used to sample and hit triggers for the entire show, but now we have a drummer who holds down a strong backbone. She also has an LP-16 [standalone audio player] which is a new piece of equipment we really like because it's really stable. Besides that, there's nothing too unusual. We both sing and Rizz plays synths and I play guitar. There's definitely more of a rock element to our live shows now, which we really like. When you're a synth-based band I think it's easy to come across as somewhat karaoke, and that's something we've run a million miles from since the moment we existed. Having the live-drummer now is a good way to make sure that never happens.

DC: You guys recently performed at the SXSW Festival in Austin. How did those gigs go?

M: They went really well. The experience was totally chaotic with all these bands and fans trying to jam into the same venues at the same time, and you can't park near the venues… But it was the start of a tour for our new album, so it was good because we got all the hard stuff out of the way to begin with and it toughened us up for the rest of the tour. It was all around good and fun, but completely chaotic.

DC: Let's get creative: If you could design your own music festival featuring VOWWS, what other acts would you want on the bill? And they have to be bands that currently exists, so no Nirvana or The Beatles.

M: Wow. That's a tricky one. I'm not good at this kind of thing. But I can tell you one thing: I wouldn't want it to consist of a bunch of other bands like us. We'd want a variety of genres with a lot of different tastes on display. As for actual bands, there's a Russian band called Messer Chups we really like. They use a lot of kitschy horror samples that are really cool. We've actually wanted to play with them for a long time. Then, maybe a big headlining rock band. We've always liked Tomahawk. No matter what, we'd want our festival to be something different.

DC: Your vision reminds me a lot of the original Lollapalooza Festival [launched by Perry Ferrell in 1991]. It wasn't about a single band or a single genre. It was the diversity that filled the seats and gave the event a unique personality.

M: That's how it should be. If the music is all good, it doesn't need to be the same.

DC: The video for "Structure of Love" is awesome. I read you filmed out at Bombay Beach and The Salton Sea while doing mushrooms. Can you talk more about the shoot?

M: [Laughs] It was really fucking amazing. I don't want to sound like I'm talking shit, because I'm not, but it's pretty sad actually. There are ghosts of the past there, you know? It used to be this bustling, celebrity-driven tourist town and all of a sudden, nature hit back. The entire place turned into a wasteland. The lake was polluted by industrial runoff… The place is a legitimate ghost town and we wanted to capture that vibe. We're drawn to places that have flickers and shadows of the past, especially when there's a significant darkness. Even though there isn't a direct storyline, we just basically wanted to convey the feelings of that place. With Bombay Beach, in particular, there's a feeling that the world completely left this place behind. We wanted to get inside it and bring that feeling across so we just went in a tiny little camper van and got as close to living there as we could.

DC: Mission accomplished. The video is definitely haunting and arresting. So, are psychedelics a component of your creative process?

M: Yeah. I wouldn't say they're essential to it. But we like to alter our minds in different ways. I don't think we could do what we do if we were in a single state of consciousness the whole time. They tend to play a role in unlocking things that are already there as opposed to the drugs writing music for you, if that makes sense.

DC: As a "psychonaut" myself, it makes perfect sense! It's all about the journey.

M: Right, and sometimes you take the journey and write about those experiences at a later date.

DC: VOWWS is a truly international band. You're both from Australia and Rizz has a multicultural background. How does this worldview influence your music and do you think it sets you apart from your Los Angeles-based contemporaries?

M: That's a good question. Our background definitely does set us apart and gives us a unique perspective. Things are hyper-charged in Amer-

ica. There's a tendency in the "Industry" to pigeonhole bands into specific genres and if you haven't gotten it exactly right, you're doing something wrong. We take influence from places other bands in our genres probably wouldn't. And we definitely bring something that's a little left field to the table.

Australia can be a very inward-looking country, which can be a good thing and a bad thing. But there's a lot of incubating you can do there, time you can spend experimenting—and we did that. Having our formative years in Australia allowed us to build something unique before we came here.

DC: There's definitely a sonic quality to VOWWS that refuses to be pigeonholed. Now, **Under the World** *is a striking album. It exudes isolation and paranoia, but it's sonically warm and melodic. The juxtaposition is shocking, in part because it all works so well. Are these dichotomies intentional or is it just the organic nature of your collaborative process?*

M: I think it's largely organic now because we've spent so much time fine-tuning how everything works. We've laid a strong foundation to the point that it can be organic. But those choices are definitely intentional. There might have been times in the past when it was less organic because we were still experimenting. But we feel now, we've done enough of that work that things happen organically even though they are intentional.

DC: Any crazy stories from the road?

M: You're putting me on the spot again! Well, we've had people strip at shows, but that's not really that crazy. We're pretty low-key when we're on the road.

DC: No trashed hotel rooms or blood orgies?

M: I'll email you if something comes to mind.

DC: Is there anything else you want to tell our readers before I let you off the hook?

M: We've got a show on July 27th at The Resident in LA. We've got an exciting collaboration coming up, but we can't say who it is at the moment. But it's exciting and people are really going to like it. And be sure to check out the record!

Taissa Farmiga

Method: *Junket/Roundtable*

Reflections: One of the absolute high points of my career in horror journalism was attending the press junket for ***The Nun***. It was an international affair, one that saw me spending over three days in Mexico City. There were dozens of journalists from all over the world. We were treated to gourmet meals, roundtable interviews, and a screening of **The Nun** that took place in an actual deserted convent in the jungle.

But some of my favorite moments happened on our "day off" when I explored Mexico City with Meagan Navarro from **Bloody Disgusting** and Jonathan James from **Daily Dead**. There's this notion that reporters from competing outlets are adversarial towards one another, but nothing could be farther from the truth.

ORIGINALLY PUBLISHED: **August 31, 2018**

As Demonologist Lorraine Warren, Vera Farmiga anchors James Wan's **The Conjuring** franchise, along with Patrick Wilson who plays her husband Ed. Even the **Annabelle** spinoffs trace their roots to the Warren's basement/museum where they house cursed objects acquired throughout their career as eminent paranormal investigators. When **The Nun** hits theaters on September 7th, **The Conjuring** universe won't just be expanding in terms of featured characters, it will include another member of the Farmiga family.

Vera Farmiga first faced-off against Valak in 2016's **The Conjuring 2**, but when we learn the demon nun's origin story (set in Romania in the 1950s) it'll be her younger sister Taissa Farmiga who'll wage a fearsome battle. Horror fans will recognize Taissa from her prominent roles in several seasons of **American Horror Story**, not to mention 2015's indie crowd-pleaser **The Final Girls**.

At a recent press junket for **The Nun** in Mexico City, a journalist asked Taissa if her sister gave any important advice before filming, as she'd clearly have many valuable insights into The Conjuring's core mythologies. Instead, Vera suggested a different approach to achieving success in Wan's wicked domain; in a nutshell: Leave your work on the set!

Taissa Farmiga: I think the main thing she told me was, "Don't bring work home with you," because you don't want to bring home any spirits or demons or anything of the sort. Lucky for me, a lot of Vera's research was with demonology and exorcisms, which luckily, I didn't have to do. I got to look at more of the holy side of it. You know, what it takes to be a nun. So, I didn't have to delve too deep into that dark world. So, I took her advice and I did not bring home Bonnie Aarons, the demon nun with me at all, because I didn't want to. I didn't need that in my life!

The set, in this case, however, was more inherently terrifying than most. Not only was **The Nun** filmed in an actual abandoned fortress in Romania, director Corin Hardy told folks at San Diego Comic-Con that he had an actual paranormal experience in between shooting scenes. So, did

Taissa have any similarly spooky encounters before heading back to the safety of her hotel room?

*TF: I did not have any supernatural experiences. I've had [an experience] on Season 3 of American Horror Story. But I went into **The Nun** adamantly telling myself, "Okay, you're gonna come home, you're gonna be in Romania, you're gonna be in the hotel alone at night. You are not gonna let anything in…" Just, you know, you need the mental strength! And it worked. I mean, I had to do a whole lot of meditating and focus on breathing, and not letting the little demon that's like knocking on my head in. But I'm really happy I didn't have any [supernatural] experience because I probably would have wanted to go home!*

When I asked Taissa to elaborate on her scary experience while shooting **American Horror Story: Coven**, she happily obliged.

TF: Okay, so we're filming in New Orleans, which has such … there's so much voodoo and spirits and soul down there. I'm living in this old warehouse that's been turned into loft apartments. And I'm filming this scene, episode two. We have to put Evan Peter's character back together, Frankenstein. So I didn't think anything of it. We have to chant in Latin again. And Emma Roberts turns to me in the hair and makeup trailer and she's like, "So are you … are you scared? Like of something … do you think that we're going to like draw something out?" I was like, "What do you mean? No, like I know my lines, I'm good." She's like, "No, no, no. We're chanting Latin." So she's the one who opened me up to it. I blame her.

*We finish shooting, I get home, it's a little after 2, and also, to point out, Vera, my sister, just recently told me she was doing research for **The Conjuring**. She told me that witching hours are around 3 am. So I was excited to go to bed before that. So I'm lying in bed to go to sleep. I'm passing out, [but] it's like when you lay in bed and you can't fall asleep. So I'm like, just so close to being in dreamland and all of a* *sudden I'm wide awake. My eyes aren't open but I feel wide awake and I hear some walking. You know, on the wood floors, you hear it creak. I'm like, "Okay, that's bullshit."*

I'm sleeping on the left side of the bed. All of a sudden, I feel someone grab the covers... Someone's grabbing and starts pulling.

Oh man, you guys. I jump up. I freak out, turn the light on. There's nothing there, I don't see anything. But I can't sleep. I can't sleep for the rest of the night.

When another reporter asked if her covers had actually moved, she insisted:

TF: Yeah. The covers were moving. I mean, it was dark, so it was based on feeling it. But you can feel if someone's pulling the covers down. And that was the only time I ever experienced anything [super-natural]. But, I don't know. I let it go, I guess. But the next night I slept downstairs!

Back to **The Nun**: Although intense at times, Taissa clearly enjoyed working with Bonnie Aarons, who's reprising the role she made iconic in **The Conjuring 2**:

TF: Oh my gosh. I have such a strong affection for Bonnie because she's so passionate about the characters and the creatures that she plays and creates. I mean, one of her favorite pastimes on set was scaring me. And she would just be sitting out on the cast chair across from me, and she would just be like, [smiling] "Hmhmhm." And I'm like, "What?! Why are you laughing?" But honestly, it was a blast. It's fun working with people who are so excited by it, you know?

Synopsis: *When a young nun at a cloistered abbey in Romania takes her own life, a priest with a haunted past and a novitiate on the threshold of her final vows are sent by the Vatican to investigate. Together, they uncover the order's unholy secret. Risking not only their* *lives but their faith and their very souls, they confront a malevolent force in the form of a demonic nun.*

We'll be featuring additional articles featuring ***The Nun*** (including a review) so check back often as we march towards the film's release on Friday, September 7th!

Life After Charlie

A CONVERSATION WITH HERIDITARY'S MILLY SHAPIRO

Method: *Phone*

Reflections: Hype can be a double-edged sword. Hype can help build anticipation for a film to a fever pitch. Sometimes, though, moviegoers establish unrealistic expectations that won't be met. And maybe had these particular moviegoers gone in blind, they would have been blown away. ***Hereditary*** definitely benefited and suffered for its pre-release hype.

When I saw ***Hereditary*** at SXSW 2018 (only its second screening ever after premiering at Sundance), I picked my jaw up off the floor and shouted to the masses: "It's the scariest movie I've ever seen." It was true then, and it's still true today. It sits as part of an elite fear trifecta also comprised of ***The Exorcist*** and ***The Conjuring***.

And over the weeks leading up to its theatrical release, I simply couldn't shut up about ***Hereditary***—and I wasn't the only one. And while ***Hereditary*** was indeed as well-received as I predicted (instantly identifying Ari Aster as a

21st Century Master of Horror), there were some who found the film disappointing. It's not that it didn't live up to the hype per se. It just didn't meet some folks' expectations.

What I consider the scariest movies in the world might be different from your top three. So when I say, "scariest movie ever," you might be thinking of something deeply personal and traumatizing—and that might be quite different than the horrors of a specific film. Hype man, it can be a double-edged sword.

Still, I was hella stoked to get a chance to interview Milly Shapiro who was amazing and incomparable as Charlie.

———

ORIGINALLY PUBLISHED SEPTEMBER 1, **2018**

Unless you've been living under a rock, you can't possibly have missed the buzz surrounding the extreme shocker **Hereditary**, the debut feature film from writer/director Ari Aster. Dubbed this generation's *The Exorcist*, the film exudes trauma-inducing levels of relentless terror and emotional devastation.

The film's success was bolstered by knock-out performances from the core cast members. Toni Collette's performance is nothing short of Oscar-worthy juxtaposed against Gabriel Byrne's subdued yet harrowing portrayal of a man trying to keep his family from disintegrating. Of course, young actors Alex Wolff and Milly Shapiro excelled as the Graham siblings, delivering performances that were arresting and instantly iconic.

Dread Central was lucky enough to sit down with Shapiro, who played the clucking Charlie, for an in-depth conversation about **Hereditary** and how her life has changed since becoming a bona fide phenomenon. Be warned: This interview goes deep into Spoiler Territory.

If you missed **Hereditary** when it was released in Theaters last June, you'll be able to purchase the Blu-ray/DVD on Tuesday, September 4th. (It's also available to own digitally and/or view On Demand). Skip down to the synopsis at the bottom of the article and bookmark this interview for later.

Dread Central: *Hereditary* is your first film, but you've been acting for quite some time. In fact, you have a very impressive theater career most horror fans don't know about. Can you tell us about your creative career before *Hereditary* and how you made the transition to film?

*Milly Shapiro: Yeah! My first part ever was Matilda in **Matilda: The Musical** on Broadway, which was very exciting for me because it was actually my first audition. That almost never happens, so that was very incredible. I got to originate the role on Broadway and I got to perform in the Macy's Day parade, and at the Tonys. We got a Grammy nomination for our cast recording and the four girls who played the role of Matilda, including myself, we all got Honorary Tony Awards for Excellence in Theater. Then I had a dry stretch for a while, and the next big project I got was **Hereditary**.*

DC: Here's something I've always been curious about: Besides potentially being a vessel for evil, what's wrong with Charlie? She has ticks, food allergies, and seems emotionally disconnected, but she goes to a regular school with normal kids. Is she just really weird or does she have a diagnosed condition like autism that was never revealed in the film?

MS: [Director] Ari [Aster] and I actually talked about that for quite a bit. We came to the conclusion that there really never was a "Charlie". Paimon had always been in control since the grandmother put the demon in her body when she was a baby. So, it made her a little different. Everyone around her thinks she has mental disabilities, but she's really just a demon technically.

DC: Very insightful. So, what was it like for you to see *Hereditary* on the big screen for the first time?

MS: It was really exciting because I hadn't seen any of it at all during the production process. I make it a habit that, when I'm filming something, I don't watch it, because then I could change something based on how I work with one of the producers, and that could actually change the character. So, I had no idea what I was actually doing until I saw it. And I hate watching myself! The first time, I was like, "Oh my God, I'm so awkward! Uhg!" It's just a character but I was really weirded out watching myself. I hate it! But then I was watching all the other actors, who are all incredibly amazing, and I was totally blown away. I was there for a lot of the filming, but getting to see the final product with the music and the sound and the coloring and all the amazing actors… it was so cool!

DC: Awesome! So, what was it like for your parents to see you in *Hereditary*? I imagine it must have been somewhat traumatic for them?

MS: Kind of. They both read the script and my mom was with me when I was filming. It's funny, though, because when I see the film with someone I know, after the big decapitation scene, they always want to touch my head just to make sure I'm okay! They'll be like, "Okay, she's still alive!" and then they're usually fine with it.

DC: When I saw Ari Aster at the Q&A for *Hereditary* at SXSW, I was surprised at how young he is. *Hereditary* seems like a movie filmed by a

seasoned veteran with gray hair, but it's his first feature film and he seems like, you know, a regular dude. How was he as a director and what was your relationship with him like on set?

MS: I love Ari. He's got an incredible mind and he's a great person. We got along very well. The first time we talked after the audition we just spent hours talking about horror movies. And he spent five years working on the script for the film, which is incredible to me because it's such a long time to sit with one project. And he was really great as a director. He worked with each actor in a way that was different, because everyone has a different acting style. He wasn't trying to force any actors into doing something they didn't feel comfortable doing which was really great. And he was just so kind. Since we were working on something so dark he always wanted to make sure everyone was okay. It really helped us get the best results possible. He was really great to work with.

DC: One of the things that makes *Hereditary* so impactful is that the entire core cast (yourself included, obviously) was fantastic. Can you talk a bit about working with Toni [Collette], Gabriel [Byrne], and Alex [Wolff]? Did you guys feel an intense connection?

MS: Alex and I knew each other before **Hereditary**. *We actually started practicing before we even started filming where we would go out in public as our characters, just to develop their relationship more. So, when we were filming, there was already something there between us. But everyone was really nice and welcoming. I was nervous about meeting Toni and Gabriel because they're amazing actors who have done so many great films, and I'd never been in a film before at all. But they were both so kind and welcoming. The first time I was on set with Gabe we actually talked about tea for about an hour, which is a really random thing to talk about! And Toni is just amazing. Being able to* *watch her act up close was so cool! It was a really amazing experience and I'm so lucky to have done something with such an amazing cast.*

DC: That's awesome. So, did you say that you and Gabriel talked about tea, as in the hot beverage?

MS: Yes! He's Irish, so he was telling me how all American tea is really bad (which is very true) and how to make a proper cup of tea. It was very fascinating because I drink way too much tea, so it was cool to hear about it from someone who comes from a place where it's something that people do more often. In America, people run on coffee whereas Ireland and England are more tea-centric places.

DC: What a fun detail. Thanks for sharing that! Have you kept in touch with the cast much? Do you guys discuss the incredible reactions fans and critics are having to *Hereditary*?

MS: I haven't really seen them much. I usually see them at press events and interviews. Ari and I saw a bunch of plays with my mom when he was in New York. It was cool because of my involvement with theater I was like, "You should come to a bunch of shows with us because we know a lot of people and can get you backstage." I see Alex all the time in interviews and he's really great.

DC: What was the most difficult scene for you to film in *Hereditary*?

MS: The most difficult scene for me was the pigeon beheading. It was a real taxidermized pigeon and the idea of hurting an animal is worse for me than the idea of hurting a person.

DC: I think a lot of horror fans also feel that way!

MS: Yeah, because animals are such a pure form of life and it was a taxidermized pigeon so it was once alive. They had already cut the head off and reattached it with toothpicks, so that kind of weirded me out. Everyone was concerned, asking, "Are you sure you're okay with this?" And I was, like, "Yeah, I'm sure. As long as I can wash my hands afterward, I'm good!"

DC: Ari Aster told the audience at SXSW that the original cut of Hereditary was over three hours long. Can you tell us about some of your scenes that were cut and whether we'll see any of these deleted scenes when the DVD comes out on Tuesday?

MS: I'm not sure if we'll see [all the deleted scenes]. There's a longer version of the scene when Alex comes homes from school. There was another scene of me in the treehouse where you got to see more of my head collection that was cut. And there was another scene where Toni came to me in the treehouse. But I'm not sure what's going to be included on the DVD. I'm excited to see what is there because, whatever it is, I think it will be really interesting.

DC: Yeah, we're all excited to see what the DVD has in store for us! So, I recently spoke to Felissa Rose who, as a young actress, played Angela in *Sleepaway Camp*. We discussed how her life changed after the film was released and, while most of her classmates thought it was cool, others were kind of freaked out by her. How has your life changed since *Hereditary*'s been released? Do your peers treat you differently?

MS: Most of my friends knew me before I had made anything, so they haven't really changed. But some people do treat me differently. It's all part of being a famous actress. You can really see who your true friends are. You have to be careful with making new friends in order to make sure they're not just offering friendship because of what you do. But I have a wonderful, really close-knit group of great friends. I've known my oldest friend since we were both three and she makes fun of me because she's also a horror fan. We both do, like, an insane asylum laugh at things that are supposed to be scary! So, when she saw **Hereditary** *for the first time, she was just laughing the entire way through! It was really funny!*

DC: So now that you've become this famous horror character, do you ever sneak up behind people and do the Charlie "cluck" just to freak them out?

MS: I haven't. I've wanted to, but I don't want someone to turn around and sucker punch me! I think that's a lot of people's reflexive scared reaction: To just turn around and punch someone!

DC: What are you working on next?

MS: I just filmed a part for a TV show called **Splitting Up Together** *that was really fun. It's a comedy, so it's very different from* **Hereditary**. *Now I'm just waiting to hear back about my next gig and I'm excited about what might come next.*

DC: Is there anything else you'd like to tell our readers?

MS: I'm not scary in real life, I promise!

DC: Can I get you to give me a quick Charlie "cluck" before I let you go?

MS: [Cluck]

DC: [Scream]

Synopsis: *When the matriarch of the Graham family passes away, her daughter and grandchildren begin to unravel cryptic and increasingly terrifying secrets about their ancestry, trying to outrun the sinister fate they have inherited.*

Jake Busey

SAYS STUDIO EXECS NEED TO GET HEADS OUT OF "BEAN-COUNTER BUTTS"

Method: *Phone*

Originally Published: September 10, 2018

Normally, I kick off interviews by asking my subjects for a brief bio, but Jake Busey needs no introduction. After some choice roles in *Contact* and *The Frighteners*, he broke out in a big way with *Starship Troopers* in 1997 and has been working nonstop ever since. Still, 2018 and 2019 are shaping up to be red-letter years for the actor.

In addition to Shane Black's *The Predator*, which finally invades US theaters nationwide this weekend, Busey has prominent parts in the upcoming seasons of *Stranger Things* and Marvel's Agents of S.H.I.E.L.D.

Dread Central was lucky enough to catch up with Busey for an exclusive sit down, where we discussed his past successes and future prospects. Check it out below, followed by the synopsis for *The Predator*, arriving Friday, September 14th, at the bottom of the article.

Dread Central: Back in November 2016, we heard rumors of a *Starship Troopers* reboot brewing at Columbia with Paul Verhoeven directing from a script penned by Mark Swift and Damian Shannon. Do you know anything about it?

*Jake Busey: I heard a little bit about something brewing as well. I saw Casper [Van Dien] and [screenwriter] Edward Neumeier at the 20-Year reunion last summer. I believe they've already done it and it turned into an animated thing like **Johnny Rico Goes to Mars** or something.*

DC: I remember that. *Starship Troopers: Traitor of Mars* came out in 2017, but I didn't realize that was the reboot they were talking about. That's pretty disappointing, actually. So, there aren't any plans for a live-action reboot?

JB: I don't know. I certainly haven't been invited. Although I did tell them that if they're planning on doing that to let me know, that I'd love to come back and be Ace Levy, the old general or something.

DC: I think we all want to know what Ace has been up to. That guy was such a kooky character!

*JB: When the movie first came out, we really hoped it would become a powerhouse franchise. But all the sequels were kind of like low budget, independent film… experiments with the theme of **Starship Troopers**. Nothing like the original which had a $125 million budget and Paul Verhoeven directing it. For me, I still feel like there's only been one real **Starship Troopers** film, because not only was the narrative changed, but the characters who survived the first film didn't return, with the exception of Casper.*

DC: Do you feel like *Starship Troopers* didn't take off like it should have because people didn't get it? I mean, I feel like viewers over the age of 21 could

see that it was blistering political satire, but even today I think a lot of fans just don't get what the director was doing.

JB: That was a big thing. I'll be the first one to admit that it took Paul telling me during the film, "This is communism vs fascism." His earliest years were during World War II in the Netherlands, and the Nazis had bombs going off all around him. He was just a scared kid at the time and it made a big impact on him. So, the film had these undertones where you had to know world history in order to put it all together. If you were just a young person looking to see a fun movie like **Transformers** *or something, you missed the irony. There's a bigger message being conveyed and Paul is really a genius. But you're absolutely right, for a lot of people, it just went over their heads. I read a review article just last year by a movie critic who finally got it after 20 years. It was a great article and went in depth about all the political undertones in the film.*

I think the biggest thing that really hurt the film was that the studio really wanted a teen-friendly movie, something that would have 14-year-old boys flocking to the theaters. But you've got the director who made **RoboCop** *and* **Total Recall** *and very violent films, so we had a ton of gore and blood in* **Starship Troopers** *too. Because we were dealing with giant bugs and everything was tongue-in-cheek, though, it didn't seem that violent to those of us working on the film. It was almost comedic in that sense.*

When the film came out, I was working on **Enemy of the State** *in Baltimore. I was with my girlfriend at the time (who's now my wife), she and I saw that* **Starship Troopers** *was playing nearby and we were excited to see it. But the sad part was, right on the glass in front of the theater they had these fliers taped up all over, maybe 20 or 30 fliers all along the length of the building, saying: "ID Required to see* **Starship Troopers**".

DC: What a bummer.

JB: So, nobody could sneak in and the box office numbers were bad. There was a whole line of toys but they were only on the shelves at Toys 'r Us for a week. I really wish I had bought a bunch of them. I only ever picked up, like, $100 worth. They'd probably be worth something today!

DC: Maybe when people see you in *The Predator* and read this article, it'll start *some Starship Troopers* reboot buzz again. I mean, I'd just love to see Rico and Ace back together again, ripping shit up with Carmen Ibanez (Denise Richards) and Sgt. Zim (Clancy Brown) and Carl Jenkins (Neil Patrick Harris)—and I know I'm not the only one!

*JB: That would be amazing. A lot of us have gone on to do other projects, like Neil, and to come back to the world of **Starship Troopers** after all this time, 20-22 years, would be awesome.*

DC: Maybe we can get someone to launch a petition!

*JB: One of the big issues is that the studio now isn't run by the same people who were in charge when we made **Starship Troopers**. It's a new, younger group of individuals who might not get the gist of what it was all about and what a cult hit it's become. They just look at what the opening week box office numbers were. I think **Starship Troopers** made $70 million its opening weekend, but they spent $125 million, so they regarded it as a loss. They need get their heads out of their bean-counter butts and look at the tenure of the film and how it's stood the test of time. It's always on cable somewhere!*

DC: It really is one of those movies you can watch ten times and enjoy just as much the eleventh time.

JB: People tell me all that time that whenever it's on, they just have to watch it.

DC: I think it's the closest thing to a "feel good" horror movie ever made.

JB: [Laughs] I suppose it is.

DC: I think our readers would probably revolt if I didn't ask you a few questions about a little film called *The Predator*. What can you tell us in terms of whether we'll be seeing a reboot or a sequel?

*JB: The film definitely carries the spirit and tone of the first two movies. Shane Black told me this movie isn't so much a reboot as it is a return to the original narrative, something lateral to the **Alien vs Predator** movies and **Predators** [released in 2010]. So, Shane considers the first two movies to be the original narrative, but he didn't talk about the one with Adrien Brody [**Predators**]. I don't know if he considers it **Predator 3** or **Predator 4**, honestly. And **The Predator** doesn't hit you over the head with a specific time or date or place.*

But I think it'll reach a broader audience than the original film. This one will be more accessible to women and kids. One of the leads driving the movie is Olivia Munn and she has a huge fanbase. Back in the day, Schwarzenegger holding a fifty-caliber machine gun in the middle of the jungle wasn't exactly something most women wanted to see. This will be a far better date movie.

DC: And, of course, you're playing the son of Peter Keyes from *Predator 2*, who was played by your real-life father [Gary Busey].

*JB: Yeah, I'm playing Sean Keyes, which really makes a point for **The Predator** being part of the original narrative. I was very fortunate that Shane asked me to participate. It's the first part I got where it was 100% nepotism! I was delighted when he asked me to be involved. I thought it was a great idea and it was really fortunate timing. I only hope I did a good enough job!*

DC: Can I ask you about *Stranger Things* before I let you go?

JB: Sure!

DC: How will Season 3 compare to the first two seasons of *Stranger Things*?

JB: It's going to be fantastic! It's going to be edge-of-your-seat entertainment that fans will want to binge-watch in a single sitting. I think the first season was a bit of an introduction to that world and the people of Hawkins. In the second season, we got to see these characters get completely immersed in this "Upside Down" world where they faced really daunting odds. I think Season 3 is more like a nonstop roller coaster and it's going to be big. That's why it's not coming out until 2019 because it's going to be the best season yet.

DC: On IMDB it looks like you've got some great projects in pre-production. Is there anything you're especially excited to plug?

*JB: I'm just really excited to be part of **Stranger Things** Season 3 and **The Predator**. I'm also really looking forward to playing Tony Caine again in the next season of **Marvel's Agents of S.H.I.E.L.D**. which started filming in July. Marvel is so secretive you never know what's going to happen to your character-or when or how! So, it's almost like a birthday present when they call and say, "Okay, we need you next week". All of these projects are dreams come true.*

DC: It sounds like you're having a career renaissance.

JB: I'm trying, man. I've been knocking on doors for a long time now!

DC: Anyone who's followed your work knows that you've been making films and TV since you

started, but it's great to see you getting these bigger, high-profile parts. Congratulations!

JB: Thank you for that. I appreciate it!

Synopsis: *From the outer reaches of space to the small-town streets of suburbia, the hunt comes home. The universe's most lethal hunters are stronger, smarter and deadlier than ever before, having genetically upgraded themselves with DNA from other species. When a boy accidentally triggers their return to Earth, only a ragtag crew of ex-soldiers and an evolutionary biologist can prevent the end of the human race.*

Mandy's Cheddar Goblin

THE HOTTEST RISING STAR IN HORROR! [DELETED PARODY INTERVIEW]

Reflections: In general, Dread Central has always had a policy against deleting articles once they have been published. Deleted articles lead to dead links, and too many of them can negatively affect a site's SEO. If an article is disputed or contains inaccurate information, it can be updated; if elements are redacted there will be a note from the editor explaining why. During my tenure at Dread, I'd only ever seen one article completely removed—an infamous snafu that has not been forgotten by those with long memories.

But there is another. My parody interview with Cheddar Goblin for *Mandy*, one of the best lauded indie releases on 2018. So, what happened in this case? First, let me set the scene.

Fantastic Fest, held annually in Austin, Texas each September, is the most amazing genre film festival on the planet. Before my employment at Dread Central, I'd only attended small horror film festivals, all in my immediate geography. But working for a top-rated industry organization upped my game. The previous March, Dread brought me out to cover SXSW, an experience I found as overwhelming as it was awesome.

But Fantastic Fest is just perfect and The Alamo Drafthouse on South Lamar, where the entire festival takes place, is a Mecca for horror fans. Opening weekend of 2018 was completely off the chain. I met peers from other outlets, stars from mainstream and independent horror—and I met Cheddar Goblin on the red-carpet.

A woman representing Legion M, the company that distributed *Mandy*, was walking around with an exact replica of the grotesque imp known as Chaddar Goblin. Shit, maybe it was the actual puppet used in the film—I didn't ask. Mandy wasn't screening at the festival, but it was currently playing in select theaters and streaming on VOD, thus generating quite a buzz. So, of course I jumped at the chance for a "selfie", knowing it would light up my social media accounts.

The picture was brilliant and gave me an idea. Instead of just posting it on my personal accounts, what if I made it the featured image of an article for Dread Central? What if I whipped up a funny, tongue-in-cheek, parody interview with Cheddar Goblin? Something that straddled the line between fan-fiction and editorial? I stayed up late that night writing and it was published around noon the next day.

I wanted to make sure the folks at Legion M and *Mandy* writer/director Panos Cosmatos saw the article. Hopefully, they'd re-tweet it, giving it some legs. Maybe it would even go viral! I sent the film's rep a link and went to The Alamo Drafthouse to begin another block of horror movies. No sooner had I seated myself for the day's first offering when my cell-phone started blowing up.

There was a call I didn't recognize, so I sent it a voicemail. Then I started getting "Urgent" text messages. They were from Panos Cosmatos's rep. She "needed" to speak to me "immediately." I excused myself from the theater and called her, assuming it had something to do with the article. A typo, perhaps, or a link they wanted included. But no, it was much worse.

"Panos is furious," she told me, clearly somewhat rattled herself. "He had no idea that this was being published." Of course he had no idea, I remember thinking but not saying. He's not a psychic. That's why I sent you the link! "He's demanding that you pull it down immediately."

Okay, I'm not sure if she actually said he was "demanding" it, but that was the vibe conveyed. It blew my mind, actually. I knew that, as an obvious work of parody fiction, I hadn't broken any laws. I knew that we weren't beholden to anyone's "demands". And, look, the Cheddar Goblin interview wasn't high art (just a lark) but it was still a positive promotion of the film **Mandy**. So why did Panos have such a problem with it?

But, ultimately, it was a no-brainer, and the article was obliterated after only existing online for a few measly hours. I was still reeling from the "Myersgate" fiasco (you'll read more about that soon), and the last thing I wanted was to end up as fodder on Film Twitter again for pissing off yet another horror director. Still, I'm pleased that my interview with Cheddar Goblin is finally seeing the light of day. Sorry, Panos!

––––––

ORIGINALLY PUBLISHED **& Deleted: September 23, 2018**

When we talk about this 2018's breakout stars of the horror genre, three names will rise to the top of any list: Andi Matichak from **Halloween**, Milly Shapiro from **Hereditary**, and Cheddar Goblin from Mandy. We had the distinct honor of meeting and chatting it up the latter on the red carpet at this year's Fantastic Fest, currently in full swing in Austin, Texas.

While **Mandy** (now playing in select theaters and on VOD) isn't part of the program, Cheddar Goblin made the rounds, chatting it up with fans, press, and industry insiders.

Cheddar Goblin proves there really are no small parts in horror and, no, that's not a comment on his height. (The diminutive imp stands about two feet tall). Though his time onscreen is brief, his impact in **Mandy** is immense. But we wanted to know: Who is Cheddar Goblin really, and how's he dealing with his sudden fame? Is he prepared to become the next great horror icon of the 21st Century? Find out in our exclusive interview below.

Dread Central: Have you always been a Cheddar Goblin, or did you become affiliated with the dairy product later in life?

CG: I come from a long line of Cheese Goblins. My father's a Havarti Goblin and my mom's a Brie Goblin. My grandparents were Swiss all Goblins, and my cousins are Jack, Munster, Blue, and American

Cheese Goblins. We have a huge family reunion about once a year—it's a fondue party.

DC: What do you think about the reaction folks are having to your performance in Mandy? Did you have any idea you'd be such a hit?

*CG: You know, I put my heart and soul into the part, but I had no idea people would react so favorably to me. Since **Mandy** hit theaters and VOD, I get recognized everywhere I go. It's really heartening, you know, considering the amazing cast I was working with. I'm just completely humbled—which is a rare emotion for a goblin.*

DC: Can we look forward to Cheddar Goblin t-shirts, action figure, playsets and the like?

CG: You know, we'll have to see. [Writer/director] Panos Cosmatos worked so hard on this film, and it's really important to him. He wants to keep the focus on Nicholas Cage, Andrea Riseborough, and the rest of the amazing cast, not to mention the exploration of blind religious devotion and revenge, not some goofy side-character.

DC: So, can you vomit macaroni and cheese on command or what?

*CG: Yeah, I can magically summon up a gut full of extra-cheesy macaroni whenever I want. It's a blessing, actually. My gift to the world. I'm just happy my unique talent got Panos's attention, because being in **Mandy** was such an honor.*

DC: What's next for Cheddar Goblin? Do you have any other projects in the works?

CG: I'm trying to branch out, so I just auditioned for a rom-com opposite Katherine Heigl.

DC: Good luck with that, and thanks for giving us a few minutes of your time.

CG: My pleasure.

You can follow Cheddar Goblin on Twitter at @Cheddar-Goblin. If you have yet to experience **Mandy** for yourself, give the synopsis a look-see below.

Synopsis: *In the Pacific Northwest in 1983, outsiders Red Miller and Mandy Bloom lead a loving and peaceful existence. When their pine-scented haven is savagely destroyed by a cult led by the sadistic Jeremiah Sand, Red is catapulted into a phantasmagoric journey filled with bloody vengeance and laced with deadly fire.*

"Ghoulish" Gary Pullin

AN INTERVIEW WITH THE RENOWNED HORROR ARTIST

Method: *Phone*

Originally Published: October 16, 2018

We recently gave our readers an exclusive sneak peek at Gary Pullin's limited edition ***Halloween*** poster that he created for last weekend's 40 Years of Terror Convention in Pasadena. It was just a piece of a longer interview we conducted with the legendary horror artist. Our conversation spanned the entirety of his storied career, from his beginnings ***at Rue Morgue Magazine*** to his recent work with ***Fangoria*** and ***Mad Magazine***.

The interview includes some important advice for up-and-coming genre artists, along with his thoughts on modern horror and where he'd like to go next.

Dread Central: Do you have any fine arts training?

Gary Pullin: Yeah, I do. Basically, I went to an art school in London, Ontario where I grew up. It was for grades 13 and 14 but for all art. It was cool, because we did a little bit of painting, a little bit of draw-

ing, a little bit of printmaking—you name it. Anything creative. They had courses in animation and photography. I did that for two years. Then I went to Conestoga College in Kitchener. I moved out of the city and lived there. I took graphics design and advertising courses. They didn't really teach illustration or how to draw, so you had to have the basic know-how already. It was a three-year program and, after that, I went to Toronto and got a job at a graphics design and packaging firm doing labels for beer and cereal boxes and stuff like that. Commercial design packaging.

DC: You think it's important for today's up-and-coming artists to have some sort of fine arts training and, if so, what would you recommend for folks who don't have access to colleges and universities or institutions where they can take classes?

GP: You can teach yourself by observing others and taking online tutorials. If you have a natural ability, you'll stick with it. It's playing guitar: You practice and learn the tools and if you have a passion, you'll stick with it and excel. I do think it's important, though. Courses will sharpen you up for sure and I'm glad I did it. There was a time before college where I thought, "Do I really need to spend all this money?" But I'm glad I did. It focused my talent and opened my eyes to the jobs available to me. Even beer labels today are frameable. And I like to find ways to sneak my horror elements into commercial design. My love of horror was always seeping into it. I'd be like, "Can I do monster eyes for this chocolate bar?" and "Can I do the artwork for Halloween boxes?"

DC: Since you brought it up, let's talk about your love of horror and how you became immersed in the genre.

*GP: It came from watching Godzilla as a kid and reading Fangoria in the 1980s. I was mesmerized by VHS cover art. And I really liked heavy metal music. I was like one of **The Musters**. I just had a* *love for everything creepy as a kid. I loved* **Famous Monsters of Filmland** *and* **Deep Red Magazine**. *All these things were around me growing up. And I had a friend in Jr. High and we used to watch a bunch of movies in his basement while literally trying to scare the shit out of each other. And everyone knew I loved horror because I was always wearing creepy t-shirts and stuff.*

Before your next question, I just want to add that working for **Rue Morgue** *for 15 years was a huge part of my training as an artist and where I got a lot of my passion. When I got the job, I was still at that design firm doing packaging artwork. I met them at a film festival and knew I had to get involved. Before I knew it, I was their art director and, before I knew it the magazine took off and I was on their covers. And then, before I knew it I quit to start [my company] Ghoulish. It's been insane but awesome. It's been a crazy ride! And I still write my column for* **Rue Morgue** *but now I'm working for* **Fangoria** *as well. As a horror fan, I really couldn't be happier. You know what it's like to contribute to the things that you love, right?*

DC: Absolutely, man. I feel like I'm living the dream!

GP: And I love going to conventions and meeting people, too. People who I can just talk about old VHS covers with, you know?

DC: One of the best parts of the job is being able to meet and interact with fans.

GP: Absolutely. I love to travel and see North America. I get to exhibit my work and meet my idols and I get to work with them sometimes. Like, I can't even believe I'm talking to Dread Central right now.

DC: We're honored to be talking to you! Tell our readers about your column at *Rue Morgue* and what, specifically, you're doing for *Fango*?

*GP: I do an art column for **Rue Morgue** where every month I feature a new artist. It's always good to give up-and-comers a spotlight and I feature established artists too. For **Fangoria**, they've hired me to do illustrations and I did two big illustrations for their new issue and I'm really excited to be a part of that.*

DC: It's currently hitting mailboxes worldwide. I'm waiting for mine to arrive.

*GP: I'm waiting for mine too. I saw the "unboxing" on **Shock-waves** and it was really exciting. I was like, "Wow this is really cool!" So, hopefully, I'll be contributing more work for future issues. It's been great, you know, getting that email asking me to be a part of the relaunch. It's crazy and it's been really good to see that happen. It's just a really good time for horror right now, not just in films, but in music as well. Just look at John Carpenter: He's not directing right now but he's performing. He's up there on stage—he's a fucking rock star! We saw the Toronto show. It was like a family reunion, kind of, with half the horror fans in Canada in attendance. We're all walking out of the show and everybody was just floating. That's exciting considering his age. And he's doing the new **Halloween** and it's supposedly really good. And if you're a filmmaker or a writer or an artist, it's a great time to be in horror too, because the horror genre is supporting it. It feels like things are growing and getting better.*

DC: I want to give you props for another recent achievement: Your cover of *Mad Magazine*'s recent Halloween issue. How'd you get that gig?

*GP: Yeah. I just got an email and there it was! They had an idea for the cover, Alfred E. Newman as the twins from **The Shining**, and they wanted to see what I could do with that. So, we just went from there. If you look closely, the tongues on the Converse say "Room 237" and "Redrum". It's so cool to be working for a magazine that I grew up with. It's like playing baseball as a kid and growing up to play for* *the Yankees when you grow up. It's such a trip! I'd love to do another cover.*

DC: I wanted to get your opinion on enamel pins since they're really popular right now. Is that something you do as well?

GP: They're fun to do. It's not the focus of what I'm doing but I like doing them. It's like wearing a little piece of artwork. They're clever and cool and the demand is insane. I try to do ones that are different, totally original pins. People want pins and posters and soundtrack artwork and I'm happy to do it all. I even enjoy stepping out of the horror genre from time to time. I've done posters for comedies and documentaries as well.

DC: Just don't step outside the horror genre for too long. You're a treasure of our community and we love you!

GP: I'm just so happy being part of the horror genre. There are so many amazing artists right now, I'm just happy to be on the field with them.

DC: Since you brought it up, who are some artists who you appreciate or are inspired by?

*GP: Oh man, as far as contemporary artists, there Jason Edmiston, Phantom City Creative, a lot of the screen-print artists are awesome. I also love Alex Pardee, I love Joe Coleman, Charles Burns (**Black Hole**)—and all these artists are still working today.*

DC: Some good names for our readers to check out if they aren't already familiar with them. One of the companies you're most associated with is Mondo. You've been doing amazing work with them for a while and I'm curious if those limited-edition prints are becoming valuable?

GP: Yeah, they do. It's created a whole collector's market. Some people buy them to display and exhibit, but others buy them just to flip them. I make artwork for walls. I want people to want to hang them. But if they want to flip them, there's nothing I can do and they end up on eBay. With Mondo, those posters are inducted into the Motion Picture Association of America as official historical prints, which is pretty amazing. Mondo has obviously helped my career a lot too. Art director Rob Jones and Mitch Putnam—I love those guys. Rob Jones wrote the forward in my book. Then there's Larry Fessenden who also did a forward and introduction in **Ghoulish**. *It's awesome hearing them talk about my contributions to horror.*

DC: Yeah, talk about some serious validation!

GP: It is, and it's crazy to think about! Back in the **Rue Morgue** *days, I got a letter from Chas Balun, who was the editor of* **Deep Red** *back then and he also wrote for* **Gorezone** *and* **Fangoria**. *He's passed on, but he sent me an awesome letter telling me that he really loved my artwork. I was like, "Wow, this guy has his finger on the pulse of horror and he likes my work!" It blew me away. Another time I was at a Chiller convention in New Jersey maybe 20 years ago and Forrest Ackerman was sitting in the lobby. I nervously went up to him and told him I was a big fan and he was like, "Oh you work at Rue Morgue? What a fantastic looking magazine!" I was just like, "Whoa!" I walked away from that meeting feeling like the magazine was really going places.*

DC: You're clearly in love with genre films of the 1980s and with so many reissues and re-releases coming out these days, you get to revisit them fairly often. But how do you feel about modern horror films? Do you have the same love for genre movies being produced today?

GP: Absolutely. Certain ones, for sure. Like Martyrs and **The Decent** *and* **Get Out** *are all great. I still watch horror movies and* *often think I'd like to do posters for them as well, like **Hereditary** or something. If it's a strong film, it will stand on its own. A lot of people say horror's making a comeback, but for me, it's never gone away.*

DC: Don't call it a comeback! You mentioned that you would have liked to have done a poster for *Hereditary*. What are some other films that you would have loved to do artwork for, but never got the opportunity or couldn't get the rights?

*GP: **The Texas Chain Saw Massacre**. That would be great! Anything by Quentin Tarantino would be awesome too. **Jaws**, even though that's a tough one. I have to consider if I can bring something new to the property too. Sometimes, it can be hard to reinvent the same things over and over again.*

DC: You've built an incredible, immense body of work over your career. What are some of your personal favorites from your own library?

*GP: What does Freddy Say? "You're all my children now!" I don't know, it's hard to pick favorites. I did a **Psycho** print for a gallery in 1988. My Mondo **Vertigo**. **Re-Animator**, **My Bloody Valentine**, and **Creepshow** for Waxwork [Records]. **The Monster Squad** soundtrack is right up there!*

DC: Since it's been about a year since you released *Ghoulish*, let's talk about your book for a bit. How has it performed and do you have plans for a follow-up?

GP: The book's been great. It met my expectations and then some! We were looking into the possibility of special editions, and my publisher asked me for my wish-list of album covers I'd like to do the artwork for. I was like, Alice Cooper, Goblin, John Carpenter, and The Misfits. We reached out to all these guys and Goblin bit back! So, we used these live tracks from Austin, and I'd already done the merch and gig posters for the band. So, I did that and it was really cool. We released a special edition with Goblin. I also did some exclusives for Amazon that came with 3D glasses and they sold out.

DC: What are you working on next? Anything especially titillating?

GP: Nothing I can really talk about, but more stuff with Mondo and Waxwork. I'm just doing cool posters including a documentary poster. And I'd love to do some more covers, so we'll see!

Javier Botet

TALKS MAMA PART 2, IT: CHAPTER TWO & THE ENIGMATIC SLENDER MAN

Method: *Video Conference*

Originally Published: October 30, 2018

Since breaking out on the international horror scene for playing the uber-creepy, possessed Niña Medeiros in *[REC]* (2007), Javier Botet has become a sought-after body actor of enviable esteem. A permanent condition called Marfan Syndrome gives Botet his lanky frame and elongated limbs and fingers, but he's parlayed this genetic obstacle into a career bringing terrifying manifestations to life.

In the past few years, genre fans have seen Botet in major studio releases including *Alien: Covenant*, *IT: Chapter One*, *The Conjuring 2*, and *The Mummy*. He's also the actor who brought the titular *Mama* to life in Andy Muschietti's 2013 horror hit. Dread Central was lucky enough to sit down with Botet for an in-depth conversation about his most iconic roles as well as his future plans and aspirations.

We spent a significant portion of our conversation discussing *Slender Man*, which arrives on Blu-ray and DVD today (October 30th). Give the interview a read below and let us know what you think!

Dread Central: I'm a huge fan of your work. I've been following your career since *[REC]* and every time I see your name attached to a film, I know I'm in for something amazing.

Javier Botet: Thank you!

DC: What was the most difficult role you've had to play, either in terms of the appliances you had to wear or the filming conditions, or even on an emotional level?

JB: It's hard to choose because most of the creatures I play can be difficult with the weight of the makeup and prosthetics. But perhaps the most challenging in terms of physical weight was the alien in **Devil's Gate** *[2017]. The makeup was very heavy and tight. When every part of you is covered, the skin can't breathe so I was sweating a lot. Slender Man [in* **Slender Man**] *is similar in that it was heavy, but the costume was easy to wear and could be put on quickly. But the alien in* **Devil's Gate** *took about five or six hours to create.*

But the **Slender Man** *costume made it hard to breathe, because the character has a blank, white face. The mask covered every bit of my face, so I sometimes had to have an assistant put a tube in my mouth just so I could breathe. In terms of acting,* **Slender Man** *was also more difficult than many roles I've had. like* **Mama**, *for example, it took a lot of time for me to get made up, but I could be very expressive. With* **Slender Man**, *I couldn't see or hear and I could barely breathe. I was like a piece of white paper that the viewers write their own fears upon. So, I didn't want to express anything specific, rather I kept things more general. You know that actors try to express everything* *they can, but in the case of **Slender Man**, I didn't express too much so the audience could fill in the blank places with their own fears.*

DC: As far as *Slender Man* goes, there are a lot of theories presented in the film about what the entity actually is and his motivations and origins, but we never got a concrete explanation. I'm curious what your motivations were as an actor playing that role. In your own mind, who or what is Slender Man? Why does he do what he does and where does he come from?

JB: Slender Man first appeared in 2009 with the original creepypasta, but after he became popular, other writers and filmmakers put their own unique spins on the mythology. It became a collaborative process and I think that's why Slender Man became so popular and went viral, because everyone wanted to be a part of this phenomenon and this general fear. So, I read a lot about Slender Man and the characters in his world, but then I also met with Victor Surge [who invented the original creepypasta]. After speaking to him, I tried to forget about all of the collaborations and get back to the root of the character. Like I explained before, he wanted something very general and static, something not very expressive so that everybody who sees him can attribute their own fears to him. So, it wasn't like finding a motivation for the character, it was more like forgetting everything I had learned and returning to nothing.

DC: I thought I spotted you out of costume in Slender Man. Did you have a cameo as the doctor walking down the dark hallway in the hospital?

*JB: Yes! Everybody that knows me can see that easily. It's something I enjoy doing for the serious movie lovers who enjoy finding Easter Eggs. I try to do it in all the movies I can. I also appear out of makeup in **Mara** and a new film I'm shooting now.*

DC: It's kind of like how Alfred Hitchcock made cameos in his film. A little signature. I think if I hadn't seen you without makeup in *Witching and Bitching*, I probably wouldn't have noticed. It was a neat trick, in *Slender Man*, with your silhouette coming out of the shadows. It was a meta moment. Very clever.

JB: Exactly, and it's something that only a small group of people can detect. Only the serious movie fans will notice.

DC: We've been hearing rumors about a sequel to *Mama* (2013) for years. Was there ever really a plan to make *Mama 2* and, if so, what's the current status of that project?

JB: Well, there was a screenplay a few years ago. It was always a project that could be done, but I don't know anything about it at this point.

DC: *Mama* has so much finality in its conclusion, on the one hand, it's hard to imagine where the story would go next. On the other hand, Mama is such a brilliant, iconic, terrifying character, we really want to see more of her.

*JB: Yeah, we thought there might be more story to tell, especially in the first year or so after **Mama** came out. But now that it's been five years, I think that window has closed. So, I don't know. I'm more certain about sequels to other films, like a **Crooked Man** movie from **The Conjuring** franchise.*

DC: Is that definitely happening?

*JB: I think it's happening. I'm not sure, but it's definitely more likely than a **Mama** sequel at this point.*

DC: Good to know. So, you'll be returning in *IT: Chapter Two*, correct?

JB: Yes, yes. We'll finish filming up in Toronto by the end of October. I have an amazing feeling about what we're accomplishing.

DC: Since the budget for *IT: Chapter Two* is reportedly much bigger than 2017's *IT*, are there changes to the way your character is being made up and presented?

*JB: Well, there are definitely changes. In **IT: Chapter One**, I played the leper in just a few scenes. But in **IT: Chapter Two**, I'm doing... more. I can't say too much about it yet.*

DC: Well that's certainly titillating! So, when I was checking out your IMDB page, I noticed that you write and direct short films in addition to acting. Do you aspire to make a feature film someday?

*JB: Yes! I've written a movie called **Amigo** that we shot last year. I'm not the director, but I wrote the screenplay. But I've got other projects, stories that I've written and want to make into feature films in the future. But there's no rush because I'm currently so busy being an actor. But I'll get there one day! I love every aspect of filmmaking and I want to do everything.*

DC: Right on. You're a true Renaissance Man! So, of all the characters you've played, who would you most like to play again and see on the big screen again?

*JB: There's the **Crooked Man** spinoff that I already mentioned. The character's part in **The Conjuring 2** was really small, but there were incredible design elements and I loved the costume. I was, like, "I want to do more!" The producers told me they genuinely have the intention of making this spinoff, so I hope it happens.*

JOSHUA MILLICAN

DC: We do too! We only got a taste of the _Crooked Man_ in _The Conjuring 2_. There's a lot more to be fleshed out there.

JB: I agree.

DC: Is there a fiction character from film or literature or even mythology that you'd like to play? Is there anything on your Wish List?

JB: Yes, there are a lot. I've always been a dreamer and there are many characters I want to play. I'd love to play the Psycho Mantis in a **Metal Gear** movie. Someday, I'd love to play The Joker—but who doesn't? I'd like to play a villain in a James Bond movie. As far as monsters and creatures, I've thought about how I'd love to play **Nosferatu** or any type of vampire. I'd love to play a part, no matter how small, in a **Star Wars** movie because I'm a huge fan of those films. But so many of my dreams have already come true, like being a Neomorph in Alien: Covenant. And I'm honored to have filmed a part in the new **Star Trek** series.

DC: Watching your career over that past ten years or so, it's been great seeing you get all these meaty roles. Hopefully, your dreams will continue to come true! What are we going to see you in next?

JB: Besides **IT: Chapter Two** and the new **Star Trek**, I have a small part in **Scary Stories to Tell in the Dark** (produced by Guillermo del Toro). I'm also working on a Spanish drama, but I won't be in any makeup. That's my current schedule.

DC: It sounds like you're keeping busy, and we'll be following your work. Is there anything else you'd like to tell our readers before I let you go?

JB: Every time I get interviewed, I always end by mentioning that I really want to be in a **Star Wars** movie. I just want to keep putting *the word out to whoever will listen until somebody makes it happen. I'm like a little child screaming, "I want to be in **Star Wars**!"*

Myersgate

Reflections: Before I share my interviews with Ryan Turek, I thought it might be helpful to understand some of our complex history. This unpublished editorial is something of a confessional. It's also my attempt to set the record straight. Unless your really into horror journalism, you probably don't recall or even care about this behind-the-scenes drama. But it did, for a hot minute at least, seem like I had put my entire career in jeopardy. This was back when Steve Barton was still the Capitan at Dread Central, and the situation forced him to consider whether or not I had become a liability to the company—a pariah. Thankfully, they agreed that I had been caught up in a crazy situation, and the benefits of keeping me on their team outweighed any potential drawbacks.

Look, it's all in the past. Obviously, I've had a (relatively) long and successful career. At least I stayed on at Dread for years. And I'm not trying to re-stir that pot or drudge up ancient history. I'm all about letting sleeping dogs lie. But, if nothing else, there are some lessons here for ambitious, up-and-coming journalists. Beware anonymous sources!

———

[UNPUBLISHED EDITORIAL]

It's been over a year now since I committed "career suicide".

The call came after midnight. A source I had used during my tenure at **Horror Freak News** had been to an advanced screening of one of 2018's most hotly-anticipated horror releases: **Halloween** 2018. While she/he was only shown a rough cut, they assured me the film was in deep trouble without some major retooling. The ending especially left her/him extremely unsatisfied.

Even though she/he had signed an NDA, they wanted to go rogue. She/he had been given a survey to fill out at the screening's end, but didn't feel the questions addressed the crux of the film's weaknesses. As a huge film fan and a devotee of the **Halloween** franchise, she/he hoped stirring the pot would motivate producers to get their act together.

Of course I was interested in running the story. I had gotten word from this same source that **Unfriended 2** had screened in secret weeks earlier, and that article was immensely popular. What's more, that scoop was picked up by just about every other horror outlet on the net. So simply having confirmation that a screening of **Halloween** had taken place was certain to get reads by itself. My source's gripes with the film would add a salacious slant to the news, but I vowed to maintain journalistic objectivity.

To give my article further validity, my source provided pictures of two pages from the post-screening survey, in addition to the exact time and location of the event. The only catch was, my source wanted to remain anonymous. She/he even took precautions to distance herself/himself from me by unfriending me on Facebook and unfollowing me on Twitter, lest someone at Blumhouse or Universal cross reference my connections with the screening's attendees. I stayed up until past 3 AM composing my piece, titled: "According to One Test Screener, 2018's HALLOWEEN is in Big Trouble". I pressed the "Publish" button and hit the hay.

When I woke up the next morning, all Hell broke loose.

It started with a jolt, but nothing devastating: I received a personal message from *Halloween* producer Ryan Turek. As a formal journalist himself, he totally understood why I published my article, but as an industry insider connected to the film, he was seriously bummed out. He pointed out that my article never mentioned the fact that test-screenings are a common part of post-production on many films, and that reactions are integral to the final product. Essentially, responses to a test screening can't be taken as indicative how the fully assembled product will resonate.

Mostly, Turek was angry at my source, the fact that she/he violated their NDA and smuggled out a copy of the post-screening survey (images of which I had included in my article). Still, he kindly requested that I remove my post. He was professional about it. He didn't make demands or threaten me in any capacity. And since I'd known of Ryan and followed him for years, it hurt me to know that I had hurt him. I'm not sure what kind of response I expected from my article, but I didn't want a dude I respected to have to eat shit on my account. I didn't hesitate to remove my post.

Simultaneously, I had received a Tweet (of all things) from the VP of Development at Universal, Blumhouse's partner on 2018's **Halloween**. He was also extremely polite and professional. He merely pointed out that all of the attendees of the screening had signed NDA's and asked if I would mind removing my article. My response was a single word: "Done". Of course, I had already taken it down after my conversation with Turek, but I would have removed it if the only request I had received was from Universal. As a journalist, I love me a scoop, but I didn't want to end up on a major studio's shit list. It was an easy choice.

You'd think this would be the end of the story, but it wasn't.

Normally, when an article is pulled at a studio's request, people assume that the information was accurate. Otherwise, why would the studio care? If the news was potentially damaging and untrue, they could simply issue an official denial, while holding the writer accountable. But when I pulled my **Halloween** article at the studio's request, for whatever reason, folks took to the internet, insisting that this was proof the screening had actually never happened.

There's a concrete reason the internet crucified me, and a nebulous one.

The same day my article ran and was voluntarily pulled, **Halloween** mastermind and Master of Horror John Carpenter shared a poster for the upcoming film on his Facebook page. When someone inquired about the **Halloween** screening, Carpenter, a man practically worshiped by legions of horror fans, replied: "It never happened." It didn't matter that I had truth on my side.

The word of an up-and-coming blogger carries no weight against a living legend.

A few horror news outlets pounced. They insisted, based on Carpenter's response, that my original article (viewed by over 5K people before it was pulled) was bogus. An online onslaught began that I was simply not prepared for. While many industry insiders would know that Carpenter's response was off the cuff and not necessarily accurate, many younger horror bloggers and "Internet Police" had a field day, reveling in the fact that my integrity had been demolished, my status as a charlatan and a "clickbaiter" confirmed. Soon, news/chatter about the bullshit **Halloween** test screening had gone farther and reached more eyes than my original article ever had.

That's when things took on a life of their own. While I was locked in damage control, fielding calls and DMs from "friends" expressing deep disappointment, meme's popped up, dubbing the controversy "Myersgate". One included the caption: "Spreading Misinformation Since 2018". What's worse, word was going around (propelled by people who had obviously never seen my original article) that my piece had "spoiled" the ending of **Halloween**. One high-ranking member of the horror community even publicly declared it a "hit piece", something designed purely to tank the film. Also stirring the pot was my original source, who had started a new dummy Twitter account in order to provoke many of those crying foul. Though she/he was supporting my claims, it certainly didn't help the situation for me personally. Things might have been different if my source had identified herself/himself, but that wasn't going to happen in a million years.

"The writer who wrote the fake article about the **Halloween** test-screening should be ashamed of himself. It never happened! He has no place in the horror community and any publication that hires him is taking on a liability!"

"I'm ashamed of my profession today," another horror journalist lamented.

"Career Suicide" was a common refrain.

At the time, in addition to producing daily items for **Horror Freak News**, I was a contributor to **Dread Central**, **Scream Magazine**, and even **Fangoria** during its online-only phase.

The irony of all this is that had I invoked my right to freedom of the press, had I left my original article intact, no one would have doubted that the screening took place. The information I provided was indisputable, no matter what John Carpenter had said. And after the shit hit the fan, I had conversations with Turek and Universal proving that the screening had indeed happened. I considered re-posting this proof in order to salvage my reputation. But the conversation with Turek, and guidance I received from some truly sage individuals, kept me from even attempting to combat the tsunami of online abuse I was receiving.

I owe so much to Steve Barton (aka Uncle Creepy) who didn't hesitate to take my call when I rang him up, frantic with panic, my voice trembling. He allowed me to recap what had happened over the last 12 hours, listening with a silent understanding that immediately put me at ease. He advised me to ride it out, to take my lumps and carry on being the best journalist possible, that the Internet has a short memory and this too would pass. He even told me about a personal experience he had (getting skewered over reports of a Rob Zombie *C.H.U.D.* remake). The fact that Steve and other important members of the horror community had my back meant the world to me and gave me the strength to endure the shitstorm that I had, admittedly, brought down on myself.

So, I went back to the grind and got to work, burying my *Halloween* article below dozens and hundreds of new news items. And, as the weeks past, the hoopla did indeed die down. Now, in retrospect, I can evaluate the actual damage Myersgate wrought, and the lessons I've learned.

It's worth noting that, weeks later, when *Bloody Disgusting* confirmed that the *Halloween* test-screening had indeed taken place, I didn't receive a single apology. My most fearsome detractors justified their continued disdain by clinging to the notion that I had printed spoilers, and that I was a "clickbaiter". This is what I meant when I mentioned a nebulous cause for my online pummeling. It was a cocktail of egos, jealousy, and a corrupt spirit of competition among journalists. And there's something seductive about seeing someone else fall from grace, even if it's simply the relief that it didn't happen to you.

The actual extent of damage done to my career can't be quantified. But let it be known that a job offer I had received to be the horror editor for a growing entertainment site before Myersgate was rescinded in the controversy's aftermath. I pleaded with the site's manager, explaining how the situation had been distorted and promising that I would conduct myself with the highest levels of integrity.

"If it was up to me, I wouldn't have a problem with it," I was told. "But some of my other writers have concerns about working with you."

While it was certainly a loss and left a wound, taking that position would likely have prevented me from accepting full time work with Dread Central several months later. Now, as the site's Managing Editor, I've never felt more career satisfaction. I've never been happier about my place of employment. The experiences I've been given over the past year have been incredible—once in a lifetime opportunities that are priceless. I'll never be able to thank Dread Central enough for standing by me, for judging me on the quality of my work and the content of my character; refusing to allow a single mistake to define me or negate the many positive contributions I'd made to the horror community.

I'm not the same journalist or person that I was before Myersgate. Even before I came on board at Dread and committed myself to maintaining the high standards that had been established before my arrival, I turned over a new leaf, steering away from sensationalism and concentrating exclusively on elevating filmmakers and their endeavors. I still struggle with accusations of clickbait. Journalism 101 says a headline should invoke curiosity, get a reader excited about the content within. There was a time when clickbait exclusively referred to those "Miracle Diet" ads and the like, but the internet has hijacked the term, using it to describe anything deemed overly enthusiastic or vague. I don't expect clickbait to be a battle I'll ever win with a certain population, but I think it's important for journalists to refrain from using this term against one another. It's a slippery slope we all have to climb.

As for my Myersgate source, it's impossible to say whether she/he achieved their goal of shaking things up and getting **Halloween** producers' collective attention. The ending that made it into theaters is indeed different than the one that screened. But we'll never know if these changes were motivated by my article or happened organically. Either way, I realize that I was just a pawn in the grand scheme of things. I'm not playing the victim, but I have learned this certainty: If people can't blame the source of bad news, they'll blame the messenger. This is why I'll never use another anonymous source, and I'd advise my peers to make the same commitment. No number of clicks are worth the potential backlash. If a source is sound and the information is legit, there should be no problem going on the record. Those who violate their NDA's are playing with fire and, while I was never personally in danger of litigation, I can't condone or give a platform to those offering embargoed information.

Over a year later, many of us laugh over much ado about nothing. **Halloween** was a hit, so clearly my article didn't scare anyone away from the theater. Turek and I have since met in person where I again apologized. He graciously absolved me and even gave me an exclusive interview a few months later. Still, I'm amazed to discover that many people honestly believe my original article contained spoilers (because that's something I never would have done, even before the maelstrom). And this is really the main reason I decided to put this experience to paper: Not to defend my past mistakes or to elicit sympathy, but to lay bare the truth to anyone who still cares. To kill the urban legends that still swirl about Myersgate.

There's no guidebook for pursuing a career in horror journalist during the internet age (although I'm tempted to write one!). In many ways, the online world still resembles the Wild West of yesteryear. And as soon as we navigate one minefield, we find ourselves smack-dab in the middle of another one. All of us who make a living online and in print need to tread lightly. But if my experiences can benefit one up-and-coming blogger, it will all be worth it.

To those who kicked me while I was down, I don't hold any grudges. My olive branch is right here for any of my peers (or even strangers) who want to turn the page on an ugly chapter. Just reach out and take it!

Ryan Turek

Method: *Phone*

Reflections: Even though I conducted this interview before penning the previously unpublished editorial you just read, understanding the entire situation will give you a more nuanced understanding of the occasion. It was a way for Ryan and I to put the past behind us, to show that there were no hard feelings by engaging in journalistic symbiosis. My words would increase interest for Halloween Kills and the exclusive would bolster my growing reputation as a top-tier reporter.

One interesting note: The anonymous source who sparked Myersgate insisted that the rough cut he viewed contained a connection to the Cult of Thorn, one of the most creative yet divisive elements of the Halloween mythology introduced in 1995's ***Halloween: The Curse of Michael Myers*** . When I asked Ryan about it during Part 2 of this interview, however, he denied it. I'm not taking sides either way, but since Ryan is the only one willing to go on record regarding the issue, we've got to take his word for it.

Ryan Turek set a new model for success, transitioning from horror journalist to horror movie producer. It's a career path many others have been inspired to attempt.

———

ORIGINALLY PUBLISHED: **November 30, 2018**

Those of us who have been obsessed with horror since the early days of the internet have known "Rotten" Ryan Turek for years. He was even influential in the creation of Dread Central, so we consider him family. These days, he's best known as the Director of Development at Blumhouse and a producer of the box-office smash **_Halloween_**, which reunited original Laurie Strode actress (and icon) Jamie Lee Curtis with original Michael Myers actor Nick Castle.

We were lucky enough to catch up with Turek last month for an extensive sit-down that covered a vast spectrum of topics. Of course, we talked about **_Halloween_** at length, but we also discussed his career path from horror blogger to industry insider, including his popular **_Shockwaves_** horror podcast and his documentary **_Still Screaming: The Ultimate Scary Movie Retrospective_**.

Enjoy Part 1 of our exclusive interview below and check back for Part 2 next Friday, when we'll take a deep dive into what it was like being an integral component of one of 2018's hottest horror success story.

Dread Central: Let's talk about your pre-movie producer life, specifically your career as a blogger.

Ryan Turek: Yeah, what would you like to know?

DC: Just give us an overview. Those of us in journalism have known you for years but now there are

all these *Halloween* fans getting to know you for the first time.

*RT: The overview, let's see. I moved out to Los Angeles in 1999. The whole goal was to be a screenwriter. I would say that my two biggest inspirations were Kevin Williamson [**Scream** screenwriter] and Andrew Kevin Walker [**Seven** screenwriter]. And I moved out here and realized real quick that I needed a part-time job just to make some money and cover the incredibly expensive cost of living. Especially since my screenwriting career didn't flourish as quickly as I had hoped. So, I took a part-time job, but I was always very vocal on horror message boards, trading VHS tapes and talking to people about movies. And then I would review movies on message boards or talk about some of the gossip I'd hear in Los Angeles. And basically, my writing career as a horror journalist/horror blogger began with Crea-ture-Corner.com, which no longer exists. I did that for a while. I was writing alongside others like Johnny Butane and going under the name "Rotten Ryan".*

Then we had met Steve Barton, Dread Central's "Uncle Creepy" himself, and we had gone down some paths with him under a company called The Horror Channel (short-lived). But along the way, Dread Central was born out of this partnership. So, Dread Central continued on and we created a name for the website. But, as a blogger or horror journalist, when you're working part-time, you hope to get out of that and make your writing your full-time career. At the time, no one was getting paid at Dread Central, so I left to work for **Fangoria** for a couple years along with doing some stuff for **Rue Morgue Magazine**. Then I heard about a company run by Coming Soon Media and they were going to do an offshoot horror website and they wanted me to be the Editor-in-Chief. They offered me a full-time position with a salary and benefits, and it was music to my ears. I thought, "Now I've made it! I'm my own boss! I can work from home in my underwear and do whatever I want!" Finally, I'd made running a horror website my living. But, boy, have things changed since then!

DC: I was going to ask if your transition from horror journalist to industry insider was something you did intentionally or if it was something that just kind of happened, but it sounds like going into blogging was always an offshoot of your desire to be a screenwriter. Is that correct?

RT: That is correct. When you're a spec screenwriter you're not being paid. Your stuff is just floating around town and you're hoping for that one person who's going to read it and make it. I'm more of an instant gratification kind of guy (or, I was). I really wanted people to read my writing, so this was an opportunity for people to hear my voice and hear what I had to say about the horror genre. So, it was an extension of it, and I think over the 14 years I did it, there was a desire to explore getting into the industry. Being more creative and producing.

But there was a shift in focus, and that was from being a screenwriter to being a producer instead. That was mostly because of the contacts I had built since moving to Los Angeles. When you live in Los Angeles, you become part of the horror community and, let's just say my Rolodex got a lot larger. I knew that I could apply those contacts and the talent I was meeting into film.

DC: While your main gig is with Blumhouse as Director of Development, you're also one of the co-hosts of the hugely successful *Shockwaves* podcast. Can you give us a brief overview of *Shockwaves*, how it started, and where you guys are headed in the future?

RT: **Shockwaves** began when I was running ShockTillY-ouDrop.com and it was myself and Lawrence Raffel over at

FearNet. Podcasting still wasn't necessarily a big thing and we just recorded it in my dining room. We did that for a little bit and it was a fun experience. I was also doing **The BloodCast** with Clarke Wolfe while the **Killer POV** team (Rob Galluzzo, Rebekah McKendry, and Elric Kane) were doing their thing. So, when I started here at Blumhouse, I kind of barraged [Jason] Blum and the company with all of these ideas: "We should do this, we should do a book, we should do that…"

I had all these ideas and podcasting was one of them. They were, like, "Oh, it's low-cost? Sure, play around with it and do what you want. See what you can come up with." I said, "I know a trio of people who might be willing to jump over here." So, I asked Rebekah, Elric, and Rob to do a then-untitled podcast. As we talked about ideas for a name we came back to **Shockwaves** *and adopted that. Now, it's just one of those things that's an extension of the Blumhouse brand and we hope to see it grow. It's a very fan-oriented podcast but our television department is working on unscripted podcasts and exploring true crime stuff—even a political podcast.*

DC: Before we transition into your participation in the new *Halloween* I wanted to discuss how you were also deeply entrenched in the *Scream* franchise. Tell us about the documentary you produced.

RT: I'd say around 2009 and 2010 we were seeing the likes of the **Friday the 13th** *and* **Nightmare on Elm Street** *documentaries [**Crystal Lake Memories** and **Never Sleep Again**] that were being made, being made well, and actually offering insights into these beloved franchises. I was thinking about doing one myself and somewhere along the way I teamed up with Anthony Masi and we made a Scream Trilogy documentary [called **Still Screaming: The Ultimate Scary Movie Retrospective**].*

Scream *was always near and dear to my heart, obviously, because I was so inspired by Kevin Williamson while I was in film school. And* *Scream* *always just made a mark on me when I saw it opening night in 1996. And with* *Scream 4* *coming out, it felt like the right time to do a documentary, something that would get everyone up to speed on the franchise and how it was created. I wrote and directed* *Still Screaming* *and it was a labor of love that came from our own pockets. We sold the digital rights to FearNet and then we shared it with Miramax and they included it in their Blu-ray box set.*

It was a lot of fun, but I look back on it now and see all of the production warts of it all. It's a little rough! But what people connected to was the ambition and the obvious love I have for the *Scream* *franchise. We did all sorts of kooky stuff. We had little animations and an opening sequence where someone is actually commenting on horror documentaries. It was fun, and I played Ghostface, so now I look back and just think, "How goofy was that?" But it was fun.*

DC: Awesome! Now, let's talk about *Halloween*...

Check back next week for Part 2 of our exclusive interview with Ryan Turek where we discuss his role in the production, what it was like working with John Carpenter and Jamie Lee Curtis, and even addresses those "Cult of Thorn" subplot rumors.

If you missed **Halloween** when it was in theaters, you'll be able to own it on Blu-ray/DVD on January 15th, 2019. In the meantime, you can check out the synopsis and trailer below.

Synopsis: *It's been 40 years since Laurie Strode survived a vicious attack from crazed killer Michael Myers on Halloween night. Locked up in an institution, Myers manages to escape when his bus transfer goes horribly wrong. Laurie now faces a terrifying showdown when the* *masked madman returns to Haddonfield, Ill. — but this time, she's ready for him.*

Ryan Turek

Method: *Phone*

Originally Published: December 7, 2018

Today, it's all about ***Halloween***! Below, find out how Turek's efforts took the new ***Halloween*** movie from an idea to the top-grossing slasher film in history!

Dread Central: I saw *Halloween* at Fantastic Fest in September. In the Q&A that followed, Jason Blum gave you this incredible shout out, stating that you were integral to the film's success. Can you tell us about your role in making *Halloween*? Being a producer doesn't necessarily mean you're hands-on in the day-to-day mechanics of filmmaking, but in this case, you certainly were.

*Ryan Turek: It was very kind of Jason to say and it's always unexpected when people do that. **Halloween** was always one of those movies that was very close to my heart for various reasons. But basically, the story is: I had heard Dimension Films was going to do a third **Halloween** and it was in production, according to certain* *websites. So, I did a bit of digging and I found out it was not shooting. I continued to dig and found out Dimension no longer had the rights. I reached out to Jason and I said, "Jason, if there's any franchise we should get involved in,* **Halloween** *should be it. Do your thing. Do what you do, talk to the rights holders, get involved, and I think this would be a great investment for the company."*

Cut to many months later and we're working with all parties and— yeah, the whole thing was a labor of love. From finding the right director and screenwriter to developing it and being on set. I flew out to South Carolina and I lived in Charleston for two months, away from my family. But being there every day was an incredible experience. I was there for the wardrobe fittings and saw James Jude Courtney wearing the jumpsuit for the first time. I saw Jamie Lee Curtis coming out as Laurie Strode for the first time. I was there for everything! I was there every day, whether people wanted me or not, just to help out or lend guidance or offer input or whatever.

But honestly, this movie wouldn't have been a success if it wasn't for David Gordon Green and Danny McBride and Jeff Bradley. These guys knew exactly what the franchise needed and what the movie needed. The fact that we got Jamie back was just the cherry on top. And her enthusiasm and dedication—her energy brought life to the set every day. It was just an incredible experience.

DC: It sounds like you assembled a dream team.

RT: Yeah, we absolutely did. You talk about those movies that are just perfect fits all around… everybody on set from our props master to our makeup effects guy to wardrobe, everybody was just so into bringing Haddonfield and these characters to life. There was this arthouse theater in Charleston and, just before principal photography began, we rented it out to show the original **Halloween**. Everyone came out and got really pumped up. We knew we were making history!

DC: Is it true that there was a Cult of Thorn subplot that was edited out in the final cut?

RT: No [laughs]. No, no. Look, the first draft of the script was different than the final incarnation, but that's always the case. Characters will shift, their motivations will shift. But it was always something that took place 40 years later.

DC: Before it even went before the cameras, John Carpenter stated that this would be the last *Halloween* movie ever. But now that the film is enjoying record-breaking success, a sequel seems like a foregone conclusion. Are you hoping to convince Carpenter to return again?

RT: Never say never about anything! And it's way too early to talk about it now. But we all know how things work. If everything falls into place just right, etc., etc. We'll see. Never say never.

DC: As a blogger, you were able to celebrate horror movies as finished products without dealing with the nuts and bolts and nightmares of filmmaking. Now that you're in the thick of it, has it changed the way you look at and appreciate horror movies? Has going behind the curtain diminished your pure love of experiencing cinema?

RT: Well look, I'm 42-years-old and many things that have challenged my love for horror, especially when you live here and you're looking behind the curtain. You're meeting all your heroes, you're meeting all these people who are making the cinematic magic happen. There was a period when I had moved out of Los Angeles just to distance myself from it. And during that time, I really reflected on what I wanted to do with my life. I was like, "Well, do I want to continue blogging or pursue my creative career?" You don't want to do anything that robs you of the love for the genre, that love we grew up on.

So, I took a couple years to kind of recalibrate and then I realized, "No, I have to be in the thick of it. I need to work and I want to find an opportunity to get in the industry again and be part of it." I came back to L.A. just after Dread Central got started and I had made some sacrifices. I put a lot on my credit card and I even ended a relationship. I put everything into moving back to Los Angeles to do exactly what I want to do.

*So, as an older horror fan, of course, my perception of the genre is going to change, but that love never goes away. It's just about how… how can I put this… Being on set [for **Halloween**] and being part of the production only amplified my love of the genre. I think what I look for in horror now is much different than what I looked for when I was 13. I think when you're in your teens you don't have a whole lot of life experience. You're getting that experience through horror movies and you're seeing the world in a certain way.*

I'm constantly dissecting my love for the genre and analyzing it. Right now, I wake up every day super pumped about it whereas, when I was a blogger, I would wake up and go, "Ok, what are the horror movies that are getting me excited and how do I evoke that in my writing?" It was draining because it became less about that enthusiasm I had in my early days of journalism and more about numbers and traffic. It bummed me out because I would look at my past articles and be like, "Wow, look at how pumped I was back then!" But I've been at Blumhouse now for four years, on this side of the business, and that feeling hasn't disappeared at all. I still wake up every morning going, "What fucking horror movies can we make, what projects can I help push along, and which directors will I get to work with next?" It's a lot of fun.

I've run into a lot of people who aren't focused and don't know what they want to do with their life. I think I realized about halfway through my journalism career that I'm a really good producer. I have an eye for movies that I'd like to see that will also do really well. Once you put out that energy and position yourself in the right way, people will look at you different. Some people were, like, "No, you're going to The Dark Side!" But I was, like, "No, I'm going to be creative!" Then of course, when you get to this side, you meet with executives and agents and they're, like, "Oh, we pulled you over from The Dark Side." So which side is The Dark Side? Being a producer or being a journalist?

DC: What are you working on next?

RT: **Fantasy Island** and a couple of other new projects. Besides than that, I'm just tinkering away: Looking at new scripts, looking for new properties, looking for new stuff and playing around with that.

DC: Is there anything else you'd like to tell our readers before I let you go?

RT: We're living in turbulent times but a really cool time for the genre. As a journalist, there are a lot of cool things to write about right now. I'm actually on my way to see **Suspiria**.

If you missed Halloween when it was in theaters, you'll be able to own it on Blu-ray/DVD on January 15th, 2019. In the meantime, you can check out the synopsis below.

Synopsis: It's been 40 years since Laurie Strode survived a vicious attack from crazed killer Michael Myers on Halloween night. Locked up in an institution, Myers manages to escape when his bus transfer goes horribly wrong. Laurie now faces a terrifying showdown when the masked madman returns to Haddonfield, Ill. — but this time, she's ready for him.

Christopher Nelson

HALLOWEEN 2018 MAKEUP/FX DESIGNER TELLS US WHAT HE'S MOST PROUD OF

Method: *Phone*

Originally Published: January 14, 2019

Despite those who claimed it simply couldn't be done, Blumhouse and Universal made 1980s horror icon Michael Myers relevant again—and scary enough to thrill 21st Century genre fans. Sure, you can't please all the people all the time, but ***Halloween*** 2018 was a record-breaking success becoming the most lucrative slasher film of all time.

There were many components that made ***Halloween*** 2018 a hit, like brilliant directing by David Gordon Green, a throbbing soundtrack from original ***Halloween*** mastermind John Carpenter, and the return of the OG Scream Queen, Jamie Lee Curtis reprising the role of Laurie Strode. Still, all of these hot ingredients were bolstered by incredible makeup and special effects work, and for that we can thank designer Christopher Nelson.

You might not know his name, but you know his work. He's contributed to some of today's most celebrated genre films and TV shows, but he's also successful in other genres. In fact, Nelson's skills seem to have no bounds. Still, his first love and main squeeze when it comes to his job remains horror. If you missed **Halloween** when it was in theaters, you'll be able to pick it up on Blu-ray/DVD tomorrow.

Dread Central was lucky enough to sit down with Nelson where we hit on a variety of topics, paying special attention to **Halloween**. Find out what aspect of the film he's most proud of in the interview below.

Synopsis: *It's been 40 years since Laurie Strode survived a vicious attack from crazed killer Michael Myers on Halloween night. Locked up in an institution, Myers manages to escape when his bus transfer goes horribly wrong. Laurie now faces a terrifying showdown when the masked madman returns to Haddonfield, Ill. — but this time, she's ready for him.*

Dread Central: How did you get your start in makeup and special effects?

Christopher Nelson: That's a really long story that will bore the hell out of you. [Laughs] I just started doing it when I was a little kid at about six or seven-years-old, watching horror and sci-fi movies and being a huge fan of Lon Chaney and Dick Smith as all makeup effects guys are. I started messing with household stuff, you know, playing tricks on people. From there I graduated to grease-paint and doing KISS makeups and London After Midnight makeups. I graduated from that to doing professional stuff and just constantly being obsessed with it and being a complete nerd in my bedroom listening to heavy metal music. I moved to Los Angeles from Pittsburg when I was 15 or 16 and just started knocking on people's doors, meeting effects makeup guys, and getting odd jobs in the industry. I spent my time paying attention and learning, asking for what I want and—here I am! I can't believe it!

DC: You already mentioned Lon Chaney and Dick Smith. Who are some other effects artists, films, or actors who inspired you and nurtured your love of horror?

CN: Yeah, Rick Baker…I mean the list goes on and on. There are just so many films and people who have inspired and influenced me. As far as actors go, Gary Oldman really inspires me because he loves makeup.

DC: Your IMDB filmography is impressive, making it clear that you're an artist with extremely versatile talents. You've worked in ever genre, on major films and independent films. So, how does horror compare to other genres?

CN: All film is storytelling and that's the way I look at any genre. It's all storytelling aimed at eliciting different feelings and certain responses. Of course, I lean towards horror because it's such an extreme way of storytelling and it makes me feel at home. It's just something I love even though I love all films across the board. Horror gets a bad rap and is considered lowbrow, but over the years we've been able to pull it out of the basement, so to speak, and give it the respect it deserves. I think I've always approached horror in this way: It's a viable method of story-telling and I love it. As far as comparing all genres, I've never been one to do that. It's all just different methods of storytelling. I love horror and I'm always thrilled to work on horror movies because I always feel like I'm at home. It's like comfort food.

DC: You haven't just worked on a few horror movies, you've hit on just about every related subgenre! Some of my favorites are Return of the Living Dead 3, Ghost Ship, Identity, The Walking

Dead, Halloween, Constantine, and Hostel. So, I guess my question is: Do you have a favorite subgenre of horror? Like, would you rather work on a slasher movie or a ghost movie or a zombie movie?

*CN: Again, I can't pinpoint one. I do get excited about slasher movies, I really do. I love ghost stories, and I really love films like **Jacob's Ladder**, which I don't think we get enough of. Psychological horror. As a fan, that's what I enjoy watching most. So, I'd love to do something like **Jacob's Ladder** or **Hereditary**. Psychology fascinates me. If I wasn't an effects guy, I'd probably be a psychologist. The human condition and the way people think fascinates me and always has. But I do love a good slasher film, I really do. I'm just now getting started on a project that's kind of a combo ghost-slasher. I can't tell you what it is, but I'm super excited.*

DC: We need more supernatural slasher movies, so definitely keep us in the loop!

*CN: Yeah, hell yeah. I also love monster stuff and sci-fi. I wish I could have worked on John Carpenter's **The Thing** or **An American Werewolf in London**. They just don't make movies like that anymore, but I wish they did, because I'd be all in!*

DC: *Halloween* had a smaller budget than many of the films you've worked on. Did you feel constrained by the resources available to you? Was there anything you would have liked to have done but couldn't?

CN: Yeah, I mean, you always have grand ideas when you're thinking outside the box and trying to do things a little different. Those things take time and money and both of those were limited for this production. But no, I never felt restrained. I went in there, first and foremost, with *passion and excitement as a huge **Halloween** fan. We were ready to make stuff happen, no matter how much money we had. We were going to make it work! The excitement was too palpable to get concerned about money. Also, we knew the way we were approaching it was going to create a better film. In order to make it work everyone, collaboratively across the board, had to approach it with passion and figure it out. That always makes it better. That's the beauty of working with smaller budget film. You're always approaching it from a place of love. So I didn't feel restrained at all.*

DC: Loved the decapitated head carved into a jack o lantern. What aspect of your work on *Halloween* are you most proud of?

CN: The Michael Myers mask, absolutely. I was really happy with it. I know fans went back and forth about it. I got a lot of hate mail about it, but I also got a lot of love mail about it. But the fact that it elicited such a strong response really says something. I was super proud. Were there things I would have done differently? For sure. I love the jack o head too, and that was David Gordon Green's idea. I had an amazing crew and we all had a great time with that. And now, it's turned into something people love so much that it's an accessory in the action figure. That's always the coolest for me: To make something that the rest of the world can enjoy at home. Whether it's a Myers mask or a prop or accessory or a toy, that's the best feeling because you know you're making a ton of people happy every day.

DC: You're definitely making a ton of people happy. Anything else you'd like to tell our readers about Halloween before I let you go?

*CN: I just hope people enjoy **Halloween** and take it for what it is. Sit back, have some popcorn, and approach it as another chapter in a story that people love so much. Maybe, you know, be happy its back and that it is what it is and, hopefully, we'll do more. It's all about* *being a fan, being passionate, and making people happy. And I hope that my little contributions do something to bring people happiness.*

DC: I'll only correct you on one small detail: Your contributions were not little. Your contributions are amazing!

Tony Todd

SETS THE RECORD STRAIGHT ON UNMADE CANDYMAN VS LEPRECHAUN CROSSOVER

Method: *Phone*

Reflections: First and foremost, getting to interview Tony Todd was an honor. The actor's contributions to the horror genre cannot be understated. Also, I do believe this is the first time the scrapped ***Candyman vs. Leprechaun*** crossover was discussed on any major horror outlet.

In this interview, we refer to the recent ***Candyman*** remake as "Jordan Peele's ***Candyman***", a fact that may cause consternation. Hollywood had always made a habit of billing films with the most famous name attached. Like Tim Burton's ***A Nightmare Before Christmas***, for example. Most people reading this book probably name the guy who actually directed that film. Still, referring to the most recent ***Candyman*** as "Jordan Peele's ***Candyman***" will upset those who believe it undermines the contributions of director Nia DaCosta. In this case, nothing could be farther from the truth.

When this article was penned, a director had yet to be announced for the film Jordan Peele was producing via his Monkeypaw Productions. Much respect to Nia DaCosta for her brilliant work.

Historically, it's worth noting that we were just a year away from the onset of the COVID-19 pandemic. It's interesting to reflect on what people thought they would be doing (and the films they thought they would be releasing) in 2020. What a year that turned out to be! And no, Nia DaCosta's ***Candyman*** was not released that year.

―――――

ORIGINALLY PUBLISHED: **January 21, 2019**

When it comes to horror icon Tony Todd, all conversations start and end with ***Candyman***—and for good reason. ***Candyman*** was and is important, both cinematically and culturally (as we'll discuss later in this article). Also, we recently received a new, definitive re-release of 1992's ***Candyman*** via Arrow Video. Then there's the fact that Oscar winner Jordan Peele is rebooting ***Candyman*** with a set release date in June of 2020.

But Todd was in another excellent film recently. ***Hell Fest*** was a surprise horror hit in 2018 and the movie is now available to own on Digital HD and Blu-ray/DVD. Though the actor's role was small, he made an incredible impression. ***Hell Fest*** represents the actor's most impressive work since the ***Hatchet*** and ***Final Destination*** franchises.

Dread Central had the honor of sitting down with Todd recently. Of course, we spent considerable time talking about the enduring legacy of ***Candyman*** (even addressing those **Candyman vs. Leprechaun** crossover rumors), but we also discussed representations of minorities in media and ended our conversation with **Hell Fest**.

We even got an update on the Nazi zombie/flying sharks movie **Sky Sharks**, which was scheduled for a 2017 release before pretty much dropping off the face of the Earth. Will we ever get to see the irreverent mayhem? Read on to find out!

Hell Fest Synopsis:

On Halloween night, three young women and their respective boyfriends head to Hell Fest — a ghoulish traveling carnival that features a labyrinth of rides, games, and mazes. They soon face a bloody night of terror when a masked serial killer turns the horror theme park into his own personal playground.

Dread Central: *Candyman* is enjoying a return to the limelight following a new, definitive release from Arrow video plus news that Jordan Peele is producing a remake slated for 2020. How do you feel about the fact that the character you made iconic has endured for over two and a half decades and is still relevant and scary in the 21st century?

Tony Todd: It's a fantastic occurrence for me that I never could have imagined. Most films have a shelf life of maybe one or two years. But I think that with horror films in particular, once they click with fans, they never let them go. So, I'm honored that, A: Someone would want to bring **Candyman** *back and, B: That someone of Jordan Peele's caliber wants to produce it. That's extraordinary and I think it's going to be a great boon for horror fans and for* **Candyman** *fans worldwide.*

DC: Fantastic! Will you be involved in the reboot?

TT: No one has reached out to us yet, but I can't imagine that I won't be a part of it.

DC: I don't think fans can imagine it without you participating in some capacity as well. You really deserve to be a part of this.

*TT: What will be will be. Even if I'm not involved in it (God forbid), it will draw attention back to the original **Candyman** so it's really a win-win situation no matter what happens. I love the character and I know it's in good hands and I just want it to continue the legacy of the original.*

DC: Back in 2016, Bernard Rose was on an episode of *The Movie Crypt* podcast where he claimed that, following the success of *Freddy vs. Jason*, someone pitched a *Candyman vs Leprechaun* movie since the same studios owned the rights to both franchises. Rose claims they were seriously considering it until you personally shot the deal down. The story has become something of an urban legend, which is ironic since *Candyman* is about urban legends. Can you tell us what you recall about the situation?

*TT: Absolutely! This was right around the time of **Freddy vs. Jason** and [**Candyman vs Leprechaun**] did come across my desk. I saw it and I said, "I will never be involved in something like that." I respect the character. Once a horror character becomes something of an icon [like Candyman], reluctantly or not, you have to treat that with respect that. I remember watching **Abbott and Costello vs. Frankenstein** continuously as a kid and being amazed that my horror legends were making a comedy. So, I guess there are some ways to make something like that work, but I wasn't interested in doing that with **Candyman**.*

DC: We also heard there was going to be a *Candyman 4* at one point with a plot that centered on an all-girls school in New England and a professor who doesn't know she's related to Daniel Robatille [aka Candyman]. What happened there?

*TT: That was actually an idea I had pitched. One reason it never came together is because there were three owners of the **Candyman** franchise at that time, and for some reason, they couldn't all get on the same page. So now, I guess the smoke has cleared and people see a way to make money so people are signing off on it. Plus, I think Jordan Peele's track record also helps. But I'm glad that they've announced a specific release date (June 21st, 2020), which happens to be the birthday of my aunt who raised me, so it all feels really good.*

DC: That definitely sounds cosmic—like an extremely good omen.

*TT: I believe in that path. I've learned how to let things go. I've lost roles I really wanted. I've lost roles because I was involved in other projects, and I'm pretty loyal. You mentioned [before the interview] that you saw **Candyman** when you were back in college. I've been at this for almost three decades now. And it hasn't dried up. Every year, things become more concrete. So, I'm in a good place. 2018 was a terrific year for horror. We had the **Halloween** remake which was a hit both creatively and critically, and that was good. Then there was **A Quite Place** and **Hereditary**—a lot of good work this year. And I think 2019 is going to be even better.*

DC: And hopefully that trend will continue into 2020 with the Candyman reboot!

TT: Absolutely.

DC: I wanted to get kind of serious for a minute: *Candyman* is important for many reasons, but, at

least as far as I can recall, the character was the first African American horror villain (who wasn't a parody, like Blackula). Not only that, he was scary but also seductive and sexy. While African Americans have often been cast as criminals and thugs, even today, Candyman remains the only truly iconic Black horror villain. Why is it so easy for Hollywood to cast African Americans as criminals but not slashers?

TT: I don't know, maybe it's part of a deep-rooted fear of seeing something that could really happen on a national level. But I think now is a good time to examine these issues. With all the things that are going on politically in our country, the division. If Candyman is a product of division, and a product of not being not being accepted by a specific group of people, the timing is better than ever.

*When [**Candyman** director and screenwriter] Bernard Rose did his adaptation from Clive Barker's short story, **The Forbidden**, he hit a stroke of genius by setting it in Chicago. It's not only one of our most iconic American cities, but there's a long history of criminality, from bootlegging to underground black markets. And it's still going on. Chicago's homicide rates are outrageous. And I think they're going to keep the reboot in Chicago, so I think they might explore the whole gentrification angle because Cabrini–Green is no longer there. It only exists beneath the surface. So, that's what I'm hoping for. I can't wait to take a look at the script!*

DC: As far as racial equality and accurate representations of African Americans in the media goes, do you see things improving?

*TT: It's certainly gotten better over time. My first film was **Platoon**, released in 1986, so I really hit the ground running. Everybody in that film was placed on a certain list. But I remember being the only*

African American, or even person of color, on set, and we're talking over 100 people. The first decade for me acting, I would show up and it was like being alone. Like I was working in a cultural echo chamber. But lately, in the last couple years, I've shot five projects in Atlanta, and the Atlanta workforce is a more accurate reflection of America's cultural diversity. You've got people of all colors and nationalities on both sides of the camera, which is fantastic. This is a Dream Factory that we work in and everyone should be allowed to at least taste the dream.

DC: *Hell Fest* surprised a lot of folks in 2018, not just because it came out of nowhere, but because it was really damn good!

TT: I was great! I had a ball working on it. It had a great young cast who weren't just cookie-cutter teenagers. We really get to know them and their unique, individual situations. And my character was kind of like a mash-up of iconic, rock and roll performers.

DC: Anything else you want to tell our readers before I let you go?

*TT: I'm a big fam Dread Central! You guys have always been so good to me. We do have a new film coming out this year called **The Final Wish** and another one called **Immortal** which is one of those films that posits the question: What happens in a relationship if one person can never die? So, we've got those two films and a couple pilots I've signed on to. I'm really excited for this year.*

DC: You just reminded me: What ever happened to *Sky Sharks*? The trailers for that film are just nuts and we were looking forward to seeing you as Major General Frost. Will we ever see it?

TT: I got pulled into that at a German horror convention where they were just grabbing everyone who showed up and putting them in these scenes. This was during the **Sharknado** *craze, so we'll see what happens there.*

DC: Well now, *Overlord* just made Nazi zombies cool, so mash them up into a *Sharknado* and I say, "Bring it on!"

TT: I get to say, "Let's slay this motherfucking catfish!"

"Munky" Business

TALKING MIND OVER MATTER, MUSIC & HORROR
WITH THE GUITARIST OF KORN

Method: *Phone*

Reflections: "Do you know you look like Jonathan Davis from KORN?"

Actually, I've been compared to three core members of KORN, Jonathan, Head, and Munky, depending on what I'm wearing. That's what happens when you're a white dude with dreadlocks (even though, these days, I'm compared to Rob Zombie much more than any of these guys).

Dread Central, during the Steve Barton all the way through the Josh Millican eras, was friendly when it came to exploring the fringes of the horror genre. In other words, it wasn't uncommon for the site to report on the happenings of spooky and heavy bands like Ghost, Mushroomhead, Slipknot, and yes, KORN.

I bought KORN's second album, ***Life is Peachy***, on CD from Tower Records in Marina Del Ray, back when it still existed. I wasn't a huge fan, but I liked their vibe and style (obviously) and love watching their rendition of "Freak on a Leash" from the infamous Woodstock '99 music festival. Epic.

So maybe it's because I'm a white guy with dreadlocks, or maybe that had nothing to do with it, but Jonathan Barkan asked if I'd be interested in interviewing Munky from KORN about an upcoming heavy metal documentary? Seemed like something Dread Central would do, and so I was happy to do it. More recently, Dread Central has narrowed its focus when it comes to coverage. There are fewer articles about bands. This interview might not have happened in the post-COVID era, so I'm glad to have it documented here.

Munky was fun to talk to, and I honestly think he was smoking a joint (we were on the phone). At one point, he had to stop in order to ask me, "What was your question again?"

———

ORIGINALLY PUBLISHED: **February 25, 2019**

Since there's a huge area of Venn space that incorporates both metal-heads and horror hounds, we recently reported on the inspirational documentary **Mind Over Matter***. It tells the story of KORN fan Brandon Mendenhall who self-rehabilitated parts of his body (para-lyzed by cerebral palsy) in order to form his own hard rock outfit: The Mendenhall Experiment.*

It's more than just a compelling and engrossing film for anyone following their dreams (no matter the odds). **Mind Over Matter** serves as a sort of guide book for those with

rock and roll aspirations in the 21st Century. Along his journey, Mendenhall got to meet and work with many of his
idols, including guitarist Munky (born James Shaffer) from
KORN, who he felt a special bond with (more on that later).

What's so awesome about **Mind Over Matter** is that it
tells the story of Mendenhall's life up until now, but it also
sets the stage for his next chapter. He needs complicated
surgery on his foot to prevent the need for amputation, but
with The Mendenhall Experiment taking off and hitting
stages across the country, the band's founder isn't willing to
derail his potential juggernaut. It's sort of like a "borrowed
time" situation that adds urgency to the film while serving
as a reminder to never put off until tomorrow what must be
accomplished today.

Dread Central was lucky enough to sit down with Munky
from KORN, who appears prominently in **Mind Over
Matter**. He inspired Mendenhall who learned the ax man
had once suffered a near-debilitating hand injury in his
youth, and used music (specifically, learning how to play
guitar) as a method of rehabilitation.

"Losing the end of my left index finger [in a motorcycle
accident] actually launched my career," the simian-
monikered hard rocker explains. "When I went to the
doctor, he asked if I had ever wanted to play a musical
instrument. I said, 'How about the guitar?' and he said,
'That's perfect because it will rehab your finger'. So, my
dad bought me a guitar and the rest is history."

Today, the two musicians are close friends and Munky is
elated at Mendenhall's well-earned recognition. Check out
the rest of our exclusive interview below where we discuss
The Mendenhall Experiment, KORN's upcoming album,
and the connection between dark, heavy music and horror.

Mind Over Matter is now streaming on multiple VOD platforms.

Synopsis:

Brandon was born with cerebral palsy, a neurological condition that affects movement, coordination and balance. More than one doctor told him he would never play an instrument, but Brandon had other plans. The film documents Brandon's unbelievable journey to rehabilitate his then-paralyzed left hand in order to play guitar, while also overcoming bullies and stereotypes. Along the way he found friendship and mentors with members of the Grammy-award winning band KORN.

Dread Central: How does it feel to know that your band, and you specifically, had such an inspiring and emotional impact on one of your fans [Brandon Mendenhall] that it literally set a course for his entire life and living out what he had been told were impossible dreams?

Munky: When KORN first started out, we had our own passionate desire to change music and forge our own path when it came to creating and being original. It's really just hitting us now, that we've inspired people in these incredible ways. We're so grateful that the music became more than just songs. It became something that resonated with so many people, a way to ease their day-to-day suffering and pain by giving them hope for a moment. I didn't expect that out of a music career, and that's only been uncovered for me in recent years. It fulfills us as people, forming these bonds and connecting with people in ways we never imagined. That's a level of success you can't buy. And it's priceless.

DC: KORN just celebrated their 25th Anniversary. How does it feel knowing that you've been a nu-metal pioneer for a quarter century now? How does it feel to look back at this amazing ride you've been on?

M: It hurts. I'm in pain. I've got heavy metal neck! But seriously, out of a billion bands, only one gets the chance to live their dream to this extent. [Co-guitarist] Brian ["Head" Welch] has been back for six or seven years, and it feels like everyone has a renewed sense of creativity and passion. We're starting to see the generation gap between our fans start to merge. We have original fans who are bringing their kids to our shows. It's beyond anything we've ever dreamed. A wild roller coaster, man!

DC: In addition to being an incredibly inspirational film, *Mind Over Matter* is kind of like: "How to Make it in Rock and Roll 101". What would you say are the biggest obstacles for today's up-and-coming bands?

*M: Yeah, Brandon kind of lays it out like a checklist [in **Mind Over Matter**]. When you move to a city with a huge music scene, you have thousands of bands all competing for the same resources. Professional recording studios, promotion, marketing... You do all of this to try and break a band and your chances are still very slim. When he breaks that down in the film, it's kind of a shocking revelation.*

DC: It really is.

M: Then, on top of all that, you still have to have that drive and passion to succeed no matter what, because it's your destiny.

DC: You have to do it for the love first and foremost.

M: Yeah, you have to. And everything else follows.

DC: New KORN Album in 2019: Yes or no?

M: New KORN album in 2019... It's definitely coming.

DC: Nice! Can you tell me anything else or are you keeping those cards close to your chest?

*M: I can't say too much... but we put a whole year into this record. That's something we hadn't done since **Untouchables** in 2002. So, we really sat with these songs, lived with them, had time to reflect on them, and then went back and worked on them some more. We didn't rush it through just to put something out in order to get back on tour. I know a lot of bands do that. We've done it in the past too—I'm guilty. But this time we wanted to spend time with our families and take our time to make some great music. So, we spaced things out and really enjoyed being in the moment.*

DC: Most KORN fans know that vocalist Jonathan Davis has had a really tough year, losing his wife in 2018, and we genuinely worry about him. Can you tell us how he's holding up?

M: I can tell you that he's doing great. He's a real champion of courage and someone to be looked up to on so many levels. Being a father and having so many things thrown at him, and him handling it like a man. Holding his chin up and knowing that everything is going to be okay when everything looks so dark. Given the circumstances that he's been dealt, he's been such a courageous role model.

DC: That's fantastic and really touching. Be sure to wish him the best from all of us here at Dread Central when you get a chance. Now to switch gears a bit: Since Dread Central is all about horror, I've got to ask: Do you like the horror movie?

M: I loved horror movies when I was younger, but now I'm old and frail. I'm not strong enough now to block the demons and they get into my dreams [joking].

DC: What were your favorites growing up?

M: The classics like, **Friday the 13th**—*anything with Jason or Freddy. The first horror movie I saw growing up that had a really profound effect, and definitely has something to do with why I write dark music, isn't necessarily a horror film but at the end gets really scary: It was* **Apocalypse Now**. *My dad took me to see that movie when I was six-years-old and my mom freaked out on him when we got home. I remember she really yelled at him and let him have it. Then I saw* **The Exorcist** *around the same time, and the first* **Omen** *movie.*

Listen, this is a scary detail: That Damien kid, he was born on June 6th and my birthday is on June 6th. I was, like, 'Whoa!' My dad was like, 'You're a devil baby!' and then I'd stare at him and try and freak him out. I really thought I had special powers when I was around seven, eight-years-old.

DC: So, I guess it's not a leap to say KORN owes some of its sound and style to horror movies.

M: For sure! There are real misconceptions about scary movies. For people who love them, they're such an outlet for creating an alternate world where anything can happen. We can express those scary, fearful moments so we don't have to experience them in real life. We can exercise those demons in a playful way that's artistic. I don't think people really understand that, and it's the same for metal music when it comes to people on the outside looking in. 'They're Satanists, they're fucking crazy. They must worship the devil' and that sort of thing. I want to break those stereotypes.

DC: You definitely hit on the fact that there's a huge crossover between horror fans and metal fans. It's a family spirt, it's an outcast spirit. Despite the way we look on the outside, we're (for the most part) good people on the inside.

M: Exactly. And when something crazy actually does happen, it's usually some guy-next-door type who kills his whole family even though he seemed so nice, not a horror fan or a metal fan. The outcast kid on his skateboard who you're afraid of, he's going to be okay, because he's self-sufficient. Those kids usually turn out pretty good.

Riding the Inferno with Preston Fassel

HOW WORK AS AN EXTRA ON A HORROR FLICK LED
AUTHOR PRESTON FASSEL TO A BOOK DEAL, MOVIE
DEAL AND DREAM JOB

Method: *Phone*

Reflections: Book reviews have never been a significant element of Dread Central or most horror outlets that focus primarily on movie news. It's a shame, especially since I recently found myself transitioning from horror journalist to horror author. Still, we gave ***Our Lady of the Inferno*** coverage for one main reason: Preston Fassel is a hell of a good spokesperson, for himself and for the fledgling literary imprint Fangoria launch in 2019.

Of course, it wouldn't be long before Preston's dream job with Fango turned into a royal nightmare when the fabled magazine's corporate owners, Cinestate, crumbled amid accusation of covering up sexual assaults. I did write about the whole situation in a piece called "Fandom Fractured: 72 Hours That Split the Horror Landscape," published on June 11th, 2019. But since this is a celebration of my career highlights, not an expose of horror's low-points, I see no reason to re-hash those details here.

Of course Preston had nothing to do with it, but it lead to the staff at Fangoria resigning in mass in an effort to separate themselves from the tainted company.

It should be made clear, however, that the situation I'm hinting at unfolded under past Fangoria ownership and does not reflect the magazine's current owners.

In 2022, Preston and I reunited as imprint-mates. Encyclopocalypse Publications had re-issued *Our Lady of the Inferno* and released my debut horror novel, *Deeper Than Hell*, in June of 2022. In the months and weeks leading up to my books release, Preston was a valuable mentor. He remains one of my trusted advisors to this day.

ORIGINALLY PUBLISHED APRIL 3, **2019**

It's been over half a year since we announced that *Our Lady of the Inferno* by Preston Fassel would be the first novel published by the newly launched Fangoria Presents imprint. Now, *Our Lady of the Inferno* is about to sell out for the 4th time on Amazon. Plus, Fassel has a movie deal and a dream job with *Fangoria*. While the writer put in years of hard work, it was a job as an extra in a horror movie that may have sparked his rise to literary stardom. It's a story that also serves as a reminder to never pass up an opportunity to make a connection. You never know where it might lead.

"A couple of years ago, I was working at Cinedump.com and Jessie Hobson told me they were filming Puppet Master: The Littlest Reich," Fassel explains. "He thought I should go and maybe write an article about the experience.

So, I spent a week running around a hotel, getting killed and, of course, I met a ton of people." While Fassel never wrote about the experience for Cinedump, it was a life-changing experience—although he didn't realize it at the time.

"Later that year, I was attending Texas Frightmare, and I was hanging out in the lobby. This guy comes down the stairs and says, 'Hey, Preston!'" It turned out to be Cinestate CEO Dallas Sonnier. Fassel mentioned that he had written a horror novel and wanted to give Sonnier a copy for consideration as a possible movie. "I didn't hear anything for a couple months—and then I got an email!"

Sonnier told the author that he loved the book, ***Our Lady of the Inferno***, and wanted to acquire the film rights. It was a dream come true for Fassel, and he didn't plan on wasting this opportunity. "I explained to them that the publisher who released ***Our Lady of the Inferno*** had gone out of business. I said, 'If you want the movie rights, why don't you buy the publishing rights as well and we can re-release it." Sonnier was definitely open to the prospect.

Then Fassel asked for a job.

This was before Cinestate had announced their plans to purchase and relaunch ***Fangoria Magazine***.

Fassel got the movie deal, he got the book deal, and he now works as a story editor and a staff writer at ***Fangoria***. But career success isn't the only thing he's enjoyed since finding support with Cinestate and ***Fangoria***. He's effecting people's lives with ***Our Lady of the Inferno***, specifically, the book's positive, human portrayal of sex workers in Times Square during the 1980s.

Our Lady of the Inferno was published last September; for an overview, check out the synopsis below:

"Spring, 1983. Sally Ride is about to go into space. Flashdance is a cultural phenomenon. And in Times Square, two very deadly women are on a collision course with destiny— and each other.

"At twenty-one, Ginny Kurva is already legendary on 42nd Street. To the pimp for whom she works, she's the perfect weapon— a martial artist capable of taking down men twice her size. To the girls in her stable, she's mother, teacher, and protector. To the little sister she cares for, she's a hero. Yet Ginny's bravado and icy confidence hide a mind at the breaking point, her sanity slowly slipping away as both her addictions and the sins of her past catch up with her…

"At thirty-seven, Nicolette Aster is the most respected woman at the Staten Island Landfill. Quiet and competent, she's admired by the secretaries and trusted by her supervisors. Yet those around her have no idea how Nicolette spends her nights— when the hateful madness she keeps repressed by day finally emerges, and she turns the dump into a hunting ground to engage in a nightmarish blood sport…

"In the Spring of 1983, neither Ginny nor Nicolette knows the other exists. By the time Summer rolls around, one of them will be dead."

"I was at a book signing in Dallas last October," Fassel tells me, "and this young woman approached me and said 'I'm a sex worker and I just wanted to thank you.' She wasn't used to seeing positive representations of sex workers in the media. She thanked me for portraying these women as multidimensional and human without sugarcoating the realities of that life."

We aren't the only ones singing the praises of ***Our Lady of the Inferno***. The book made ***Bloody Disgusting***'s list of the best horror books of 2018. The movie deal followed in February. Not only are we extremely excited to see how the film comes together (there's no cast or director attached at this time), we can't wait to see what Fassel produces next. His story should serve as inspiration for all horror writers and filmmakers hoping that, with patience and perseverance, their dreams will come true.

How Sweet to Walk on Sour Ground!

PET SEMETARY SET VISIT, PART 1: THE DIRECTORS SPEAK

Method: *Set Visit*

Reflections: Nobody pursues a career in horror journalism to make big bucks. It's pure love for the genre that motivates most of us to get through the grueling hours, seeking out our next scoop, transcribing notes, or doing research. But there are some perks that come with writing for a respected genre outlet that are priceless. I'm talking about set visits. My first one was incredible.

It was also my first experience with NDAs and information embargos, which was exciting and frustrating. Imagine walking through a recreation of Stephen King's titular Pet Cemetery and not being able to talk about it for five months!

I was flown out to Montreal! I was put up in a fancy hotel! I ate poutine!

These are experiences I'll never forget. I was part of a small group of journalists including Meagan Navarro from ***Bloody Disgusting***, Michael Gingold of ***Rue Morgue*** and *Fangoria* fame, and Chris Evangelista from *Slash Films*. These guys are all legends in the industry and I was humbled to be in their company.

In some ways, I'll admit, the experience was overwhelming. And maybe I wasn't as focused as I should have been. As Gingold made verbal notes on a tape-recorder and Navarro and Evangelista scribbled notes furiously, I spent most of the visit with my jaw on the ground! I remember soaking in the immensity of it all. And mosquitos—big as mosquitos that could bite you through your hoodie!

Seeing a movie from creation through fruition is wild, and I saw 2019's *Pet Sematary* at an advanced screening at The Egyptian Theater in Hollywood. As a member of the press, I didn't even have to wait in line. In fact, I was seated comfortably for a good 20 minutes before they officially opened the doors. And when it was over, I drove my ass nonstop back to Oakland, because I still didn't live in Los Angeles yet.

————

ORIGINALLY PUBLISHED: **February 7, 2019**

2018 was a landmark year for me, both personally and professionally. It was the year I solidified my position as the Managing Editor here at Dread Central and, as such, became eligible for some of the job's most coveted perks: Set visits! I think being on the set of a major film is some-thing all horror fans dream of, and my first time set the bar extremely high. Last fall, the good folks at Paramount flew me and a few other journalists out to Montreal to interview the directors, actors, and producers of the upcoming *Pet Sematary* remake (based on the best-selling novel by Stephen King), arriving in US theaters April 5th.

I'm a huge Stephen King fan, so I was extremely excited from the get-go. And, as a child of the 1980s, I still have vivid memories of being absolutely terrified by Mary Lambert's adaptation—especially the hideously twisted Zelda! So how, I wondered, would **Starry Eyes** directors Kevin Kölsch and Dennis Widmyer revamp this horror classic for the 21st Century? All my questions (and more) were answered over the course of my eight-hour set visit, which also included a tour of the titular "Pet Sematary".

That's right, I stood inside the somber and infinitely creepy site—and felt as though I had walked straight into the novel. The makeshift headstones of hundreds of pets spiraled out from a center point. The attention to detail was impeccable, as each "grave" included appropriate trinkets: Dog and cat collars, empty bird cages, and even a cloudy, cracked fishbowl. And there, at the far end of the "Sematary" was a hill-sized mound of brambles and branches. Though we didn't venture over, those familiar with **Pet Sematary** know exactly what lies yonder: An ancient Native American burial site, where the ground has gone sour.

Of course, photographs weren't allowed. In fact, the information embargo I signed means I've only recently been able to share these experiences with anyone besides the event's participants. Needless to say, my mind soaked up the imagery like a sponge. I need only close my eyes to find myself right back at the center of the "Sematary", complete with the smell of rural Montreal wafting into my nostrils. Okay, I admit it: I pocketed a few pebbles from the forest floor, little gray rocks indistinguishable from ordinary, jagged stones. But these are special, even if only I know it. Magic stones from sour ground!

Since the second trailer for **Pet Sematary** just hit the internet this morning it's the perfect occasion to unfurl Part 1 of my set visit recap. Today, I'll be relaying portions of our conversation with Kölsch and Widmyer where we discussed Stephen King fandom and persistently attempted to get the duo to give up more details than they were willing to. While they remained tight-lipped on some key questions (spoilers) they nonetheless spoke volumes, making clear their goals and aspirations for the project. Read on...

Synopsis:

Dr. Louis Creed and his wife, Rachel, relocate from Boston to rural Maine with their two young children. The couple soon discover a mysterious burial ground hidden deep in the woods near their new home. When tragedy strikes, Louis turns to his neighbor Jud Crandall, setting off a perilous chain reaction that unleashes an unspeakable evil with horrific consequences.

When Kölsch and Widmyer emerged from the set for our interview (an actual house in rural Montreal that had been converted into Jud Crandall's residence) they looked exhausted. In truth, I was kind of worried about the pair. The duo rose to indie prominence following the release of **Starry Eyes** in 2014, a completely unnerving supernatural and psychological horror that becomes a metaphor for the pursuit of fame. But **Starry Eyes** was an indie film and now, they're helming a major motion picture for a major studio. Expectations are high. There are literally millions of Stephen King fans ready to dissect the final product, so the pressure must be immense. Are they worried, I wondered, about losing their indie "street cred" by transitioning into the big leagues? More importantly, would executive interference dull the duo's razor-sharp creative edge? After a lengthy conversation, I'm pleased to report that the answers are "No" and "No"!

Sure, the pressure is real, and Kölsch and Widmyer are feeling it. But the most important thing to them is staying true to the source material. "We're fans of Stephen King and the book and the original movie, so we want it to be respectful to that," Kölsch explains. "When we came in, obviously this was a project that, unlike everything else we've done before, we didn't write ourselves. There's a script in place. We worked with the writer [Jeff Buhler] to actually try and get closer to the book than what the original script was. There are a lot of things in the book that we were always big fans of, or things that didn't even make it into the original movie that we always wanted to do in the movie, and we worked hard to get those into the script. So, that has been our approach: To kind of be faithful to the book, but knowing the best remakes are the ones that stay faithful to the essence, not necessarily every single thing that happens."

As for losing the insidious edge that made **Starry Eyes** so exceptional, Widmyer assured us they're pulling no punches for Pet Sematary:

"It's a dark fucking movie. It's **Pet Sematary**! A lot of Stephen King's work is sentimental. The good guys win. Even at the end of **The Shining**, Wendy marries Dick Halloran. People forget that, [because] that's not in the movie, but Stephen King has a heart. And a lot of his work has a heart. [**Pet Sematary**] is one that [King] put in a drawer for, like, a year and he felt really disturbed by what he had written. So, you have to make that story. It's definitely very **Starry Eyes** as far as it's very emotional, very psychological. It's very grounded in its horror, and it goes pretty far. It's really not a studio film."

Indie "street cred" remains intact! The pair also discussed balancing the source material and fan expectations with the desire to make *Pet Sematary* a 21st Century adaptation. "We're making some changes or doing some decisions based on things that we think would be really cool, but it's all sort of within the spirit of the original source material," Kolsch explains.

Widmyer elaborates: "Here's what I'll say: We've refreshed some things, in the essence of the novel, but I would actually say that there might be more things from the novel that weren't in the first movie that are going to be in ours. Things that everyone loves, fans love, that's all in the movie. I'm shocked that they let us get away with some of i]!'"

It sounds like fans can expect a bloody romp so, of course, the question of CGI vs practical effects was floated. "It's as practical as we could get it," Widmyer assured us. "That was one of our first pitches. We had to go fully practical, you know?" Best of all: "No CGI cats! We're working with a trainer who has, like, six different cats. And there are some days, we wake up and we're like, 'What the hell were we thinking?' You know, it's hard to get a cat to act! But a CGI cat would look like crap." Agreed!

Of course, I couldn't let the duo go before grilling them on Zelda, the character played by Andrew Hubatsek in Lambert's *Pet Sematary*, who basically stole the show in terms of producing palpable, pulse-pounding terror. It's since been revealed to the public that Zelda does appear in the upcoming Pet Sematary (and will be played by Alyssa Brooke Levine), but she'll be a far cry from Hubatsek's version. "[In the novel, Zelda is] an 11 or 10-year-old girl with a debilitating disease in bed," Widmyer explains. "So, if you look at the psychology of the Zelda situation, it's a family that was dealing with a horrible situation that had a daughter that they couldn't fix, wasting away up in their bedroom. And they had a younger daughter [Rachel] who was in charge of basically, like, going in and taking care of her and being there as she disintegrated. That in itself is pretty horrific."

There was a moment when the pair considered cutting Zelda from the script altogether, but eventually came back around to the idea. I'm pretty sure a huge percentage of 1989's **Pet Sematary** fans would have called for the film-makers' heads on sticks had they excluded her!

"We just sort of accepted the challenge and said, 'We gotta try to do something on our own and do something that honors the book but is our own thing,' which is just as scary if not scarier than they did in the first one."

The two are also keenly aware that they are part of a Stephen King resurgence that was ignited by the mega success of Andy Muschietti's **IT**, released in 2017. "We're lucky that **IT** did as well as it did, because now we're in another Stephen King renaissance and we shouldn't blow it," Widmyer says. "We should be making great movies out of this material, because the material warrants it. [**Pet Sematary**] is a very seminal book. It's very different from [King's] other books. Our approach to the material is very mature, very grounded, and we really understood the material."

And that's the ultimate message: **Pet Sematary** is true to the spirit and intention of King's novel, and Kölsch and Widmyer are treating the project with legitimate reverence. "This is literary horror. This isn't just concept and shlock,"

Widmyer insists. "This could be something more. I think we're excited to try to tell an elevated, really smart, mature version of [*Pet Sematary*]."

In the weeks leading up to *Pet Sematary*'s release this April, we'll bring you more from my set visit.

Look, I don't think anyone goes into journalism to get rich. The majority of us who cover entertainment do it for the love of cinema. But visiting the set of *Pet Sematary* was a once in a lifetime experience that literally millions of horror fans would have died to experience—and that makes it priceless. These memories are now vaulted where I can treasure them for the rest of my life!

Is Jud Crandall Actually a Villain in Pet Sematary 2019?

SET VISIT PART 2: READING BETWEEN THE LINES

Method: *Set Visit*

Reflections: Jason Clarke is either a method actor or else he's a jerk. That's why I didn't include anything from his interview in my set coverage of **Pet Sematary**. He wouldn't make eye contact with anyone. He spent 15 minutes looking annoyed at us, picking at his fingernails (which were very dirty from the scene he had just filmed). His responses were terse, bland, and delivered in a tone that clearly sought to end the interaction, refusing to elaborate on anything.

If he was stuck in the mindset of a family man enduring a personal apocalypse, then I forgive him.

John Lithgow, on the other hand: I love that guy! I'd actually seen **The Twilight Zone Movie** in a drive-in movie theater, and it left an indelible impression. It might even be partially to blame for my childhood fear of flying!

As far as this installment of my **Pet Sematary** set-visit recap goes, I used it as an opportunity to float my own personal fan theory. I was wrong, but it was still a fun prospect to ruminate on.

––––––

ORIGINALLY PUBLISHED: **March 15, 2019**

Spoiler Warning: Though I haven't seen the film and can only make postulations, this article includes spoilers for both the novel *Pet Sematary* and the 1989 film adaptation directed by Mary Lambert. If you plan on seeing *Pet Sematary* 2019 knowing as little as possible, bookmark this page and come back in a few weeks.

One of the most fascinating aspects of *Pet Sematary*, the novel by Stephen King and Mary Lambert's 1989 film adaptation, is that it's a story without a central villain. Sure, the book and movie are full of scary characters – Pascow, Zelda, Gage, and that goddam cat for example – but there isn't a single antagonist for us to blame the story's atrocities on. No one is blatantly evil, but several good characters do questionable things.

Regular readers of Dread Central know that I was lucky enough to participate in a set visit for the upcoming remake of *Pet Sematary*. Directed by Kevin Kölsch and Dennis Widmyer (*Starry Eyes*), the hotly-anticipated horror movie will enjoy its world premiere on the closing night of SXSW (this Saturday, March 16th) before hitting US theaters nationwide on April 5th.

Today, I'm continuing my *Pet Sematary* set visit report with an analytical eye on a specific character: Jud Crandall, played by John Lithgow in the upcoming iteration. By examining statements Lithgow made when journalists grilled him during a roundtable interview, along with information provided by **Pet Sematary** producer Lorenzo di Bonaventura, I'll be presenting a somewhat controversial postulation: What if Jud Crandall is the overarching villain the novel and previous film never had?

It's almost sacrilegious to imagine, as Jud Crandall in Lambert's **Pet Sematary** was good as gold. Played by Fred Gwynne in a performance that became iconic, the character's thick Maine accent, soulful eyes, and affinity towards children immediately endeared him to both the Creed family and readers/audiences alike. So how could Jud possibly be a bad guy?

First, it's important to remember that there will be many significant differences between Lambert's **Pet Sematary** and **Pet Sematary** 2019. Trailers have already revealed that it's Ellie (played by Jeté Laurence), not Gage, who gets hit by a truck and reanimated. We've also seen hints of a Wendigo, a creature from Native American folklore that featured prominently in King's novel, but was absent from **Pet Sematary** 1989. So, it's prudent to assume that Lithgow's Jud Crandall will be different in many respects from Gwynne's portrayal of the same character. And as someone who was able to interview Lithgow on set, I can confirm the differences are indeed profound.

For starters, Jud Crandall 2019 won't have the signature Maine accent that made Jud Crandall 1989 something of a tender counterbalance to the scenes of intense terror.

"We all talked about [the accent]," Lithgow told us, "and we even tried it different ways. I did a whole reading with a Maine accent. I personally felt that even people who are from Maine, even actors who get it absolutely right – an accent like that kind of takes you out of the story. I myself think that, especially how they have reimagined this script, which is changed from the book and the first film, it has evolved and Jud has become a more serious character, in a sense. He is a character in the pull of a kind of deep, deep regret, deep guilt, great longing, great feelings of loss, love. And because of that, I just felt he had to be a very genuine person. Listen, I have Boston roots. My father was born there, all my uncles and aunts were from there, I went to Harvard and I know Boston well. I can do an accent. But as soon as I start, that's all you're listening to."

Indeed, Lithgow's Crandall doesn't evoke the warm fuzzies of his predecessor, Gwynne (whose turn as Herman Munster may also have added to his "gentle giant" vibe, if only on a subconscious level). Lithgow's Crandall is gruff, prickly, tobacco stained—and, frankly, intimidating! You might not realize it unless you're in the same room (or in my case, trailer) with him, but Lithgow is a big, tall man. In costume, and in character, he's a far cry from Gwynne's portrayal of the exact same character.

This isn't an accident. In an earlier interview, producer Lorenzo di Bonaventura explained how the Jud character was given intense attention during the **Pet Sematary**'s development stage.

"The one thing that I always struggled with in the book and in the movie was Jud's reasoning behind telling Louis about the burial ground, or taking him to the burial ground," di Bonaventura told us. "It was an interesting process to go through the development of it because we kept trying to find a rational reason – this is why Jud would do it," di Bonaventura continues. "But what we ended up on, which I think is an incredibly satisfying result – which is an evolution, I'll say from the book – is that Jud is this lonely man who suddenly has a family that moves in who touches his heart. So, it's an emotional decision he makes, not a rational decision."

It's not hard to read between the lines. In Lambert's **Pet Sematary**, Jud's motivations for telling Louis about the cursed burial grounds beyond the branches and brambles is never explicitly discussed, but he seems to have come from a place of genuine caring (and, later on, he seems to genuinely regret his decision). So, we accepted it when Gwynne's Crandall sums it up succinctly, explaining he was only thinking of Ellie and how sad she'd be over the death of her cat, Church.

This makes di Bonaventura's statements incredibly intriguing. We can at least begin to suspect that Jud Crandall 2019 has an agenda, unlike Crandall 1989. But what could it be? If Crandall knows about the burial ground's "sour" properties, why would he get the Creed family entangled in its curse? "It's an emotional decision he makes, not a rational decision," remember. And what could possibly stir more emotions in a man than his wife of forty-some odd years.

Yes, Jud Crandall has a wife. Mrs. Crandall never appeared in Lambert's film adaptation, but she was present in Stephen King's novel, though often in the background. In the early stages of their friendship, Jud tells Louis about her chronic arthritis and the terrible suffering she endures on a daily basis. We don't know for certain if Mrs. Crandall will appear in 2019's **Pet Sematary**, but I did notice an old woman in the film's first trailer, someone I hypothesized could be Jud's wife.

Whoever this woman is, she's in a chair that might have wheels, and she's definitely wringing her hands, as though her fingers are in pain.

So, here's my theory: Jud Crandall has been emotionally wrecked watching his beloved wife deteriorate. He's heard legends of the burial ground's ability to reanimate the dead, as well as the warnings that those who come back aren't the same. Still, he fantasizes about ending his wife's suffering (killing her) and resurrecting her (hopefully) without the pain that made living unbearable. When the Creed family endures an unthinkable tragedy, he sees an opportunity to use them as guinea pigs, essentially.

He manipulates Louis (played by Jason Clarke in 2019) into burying Ellie to see what might happen if he did the same for his wife. "It's an emotional decision he makes, not a rational decision," after all. Of course, there's always the possibility that he's under the control of the Wendigo, and that the creature is the true villain of *Pet Sematary*, pulling all the strings by exerting supernatural influences.

Those attending SXSW will learn the truth behind Jud's motivations before the rest of us, and my hypothesis may actually be disproven. Still, it's something the majority of us can think about as we continue our march towards April 5th. I'll be posting my final set visit recap in the day's leading up to *Pet Sematary*'s theatrical release date. In the meantime, there's plenty to ponder.

Synopsis:

Dr. Louis Creed and his wife, Rachel, relocate from Boston to rural Maine with their two young children. The couple soon discover a mysterious burial ground hidden deep in the woods near their new home. When tragedy strikes, Louis turns to his neighbor Jud Crandall, setting off a perilous chain reaction that unleashes an unspeakable evil with horrific consequences.

"Dark F***ing Movie!"

PET SEMETARY SET VISIT PART 3: CONCLUSION

Method: *Set Visit*

Reflections: This "conclusion" to my *Pet Sematary* set-visit is really more of a recap. But it illustrates the process of ongoing promotion.

———

ORIGINALLY PUBLISHED: **March 15, 2019**

Regular readers of Dread Central know that I was lucky enough to visit the set of *Pet Sematary* when it was filming outside of Montreal last Summer. What struck me profoundly at every turn was just how seriously everyone involved was taking the project. While it would have been easy to play up the most salacious elements of the novel by Stephen King for this adaptation, those behind the scenes and in front of the cameras were always striving to make something deeper and more universal than moviegoers might be expecting.

Producer Lorenzo di Bonaventura, for example, told us "I thought [*Pet Sematary*] was a great idea because it is. I don't know if it's my favorite Stephen King book, but it's close if it's not that. Because it deals with something that's utterly timeless, which is death, and our relationship to it. And as a father, that really interests me."

But if you're worried producers sacrificed scares for drama, don't be. **Pet Sematary** co-director Dennis Widmyer promises: "It's a dark fucking movie."

"It's **Pet Sematary**," Widmyer continues. "A lot of Stephen King's work is… sentimental. The good guys win. Even at the end of **The Shining**, Wendy marries Dick Halloran. People forget that, but Stephen King has a heart. And a lot of his work has a heart. This one, he put in a drawer for a like a year and he felt really disturbed by what he had written. So, you have to make that story. I think it's very emotional, very psychological; it's very grounded in its horror, and it goes pretty far. It's really not a studio film."

Kevin Kölsch, Pet Sematary's other co-director, explained the duo's approach to adapting the novel: "We're fans of Stephen King and the book and the original movie, so we want it to be respectful to that. When we came in, obviously this was a project that, unlike everything else we've done before, we didn't write this one ourselves. We worked with co-writer [Jeff Buhler] to actually try and get closer to the book than what the original script was. There was a lot in the book that we were always big fans of, or things that didn't even make it into the original movie, that we always wanted to do, and we worked hard to get those into the script. So, that has been our approach: To be faithful to the book. But the best remakes stay faithful to the essence [of the source material], not necessarily every single thing that happens."

Producer Mark Vahradian had an approach similar to the directors. "It's actually a family drama," Vahradian says of the *Pet Sematary*. "There are a lot of interesting thematics. There's this notion of nature and the power of nature and a family that moves from the city closer to nature, into the woods. They're unfamiliar with that kind of savage power and don't really know the dangers of being outside of civilization. It's technically a horror movie, and it has scary stuff, but that's generally at the back end of the story, and it's really about dealing with all these other issues, human choices, and behaviors. So, I think this is much deeper than most of the horror that's out there, and I think even most of the horror literature that's out there. And that was what was always so exciting for us."

The actors were especially aware of the emotional intensity that would be needed to plumb the depth of *Pet Sematary*. "You know, when you make a horror film," John Lithgow, who plays Jud Crandall, explained, "the emotions have to be so authentic and everything that happens in the story has to really come out in various deep emotional needs from the characters. And that's built in to the way [Widmyer and Kölsch] have reimagined this story. You believe these feelings and you identify strongly with these characters and their needs, their longings, their feelings of love and anger... and regret."

Pet Sematary finally lands in US theaters nationwide tomorrow, Friday April 5th (tonight in many markets). Give the film's synopsis and trailer a look-see below.

Synopsis:

Dr. Louis Creed and his wife, Rachel, relocate from Boston to rural Maine with their two young children. The couple soon discover a mysterious burial ground hidden deep in the woods near their new home. When tragedy strikes, Louis turns to his neighbor Jud Crandall, setting off a perilous chain reaction that unleashes an unspeakable evil with horrific consequences.

Tom Holland

"I BECAME A DIRECTOR IN SELF-DEFENSE"

Method: *Phone*

Reflections: Nothing but love and respect for horror icon Tom Holland. Much of my history with the man who helmed ***Child's Play*** and ***Fright Night*** is outlined in the preface of this interview, so I won't repeat it here. Still, it was wonderful to have ended up on the same publishing imprint as Tom years later (I'm talking about Encyclopocalypse Publications, of course).

Wikipedia might not realize it yet, but this interview smashes the long-standing rumor that Chucky was inspired by Robert the Doll.

There's something Tom said in this interview that I reflect on a lot a potential warning about the future of horror, even as the genre is enjoying unprecedented popularity: *"There's a growing critical acceptance to the genre. It might even have come too far, actually. When it becomes didactic, that's usually the first sign of dying or atrophy."*

———

ORIGINALLY PUBLISHED: **April 6, 2019**

With films like **Psycho II**, **Fright Night**, and **Child's Play** under his belt, writer/director Tom Holland was one of the most creative and impactful horror practitioners of the 1980s. That's why he'll be featured prominently in the upcoming documentary **In Search of Darkness**, a project that aims to be the definitive retrospective of the genre in that decade. But those of us who truly love and live horror know that Holland has remained a constant since first rising to prominence.

Tom Holland's Terror Time, for example, is a must-visit internet destination for horror fans. It's part genre news site and part merchandise store where aficionados can procure autographed copies of Holland's movies along with other rare memorabilia. And when he's not at work on **Terror Time**, he's writing novels. **The Notch** will be published by Cemetery Dance and is eying a late-Summer release. Then, there's the novelized sequel to Fright Night he's got in the works (more on that later).

When I was first getting my start in horror journalism, Holland and his son Josh (who co-manages **Terror Time**) brought me on board for daily news and occasional reviews. It was this gig that launched me into a full-time career (eventually landing me here at **Dread Central**), so I've always felt a special bond with the Hollands. That's why, when offered the opportunity to interview Holland in connection with **In Search of Darkness**, I jumped at the opportunity.

In addition to thanking him profusely for the start he gave me in horror journalism, Holland and I discussed 1980s horror in general, paying specific attention to his filmography. Read on to hear the filmmaker's thoughts on horror's Golden Age, the pride he feels regarding his work on **Psycho II**, and how he feels about the upcoming **Child's Play** reboot at Orion (arriving in US theaters this June). But before we begin, check out the synopsis for **In Search of Darkness**.

Synopsis:

*Featuring compelling critical takes and insider tales of the Hollywood filmmaking experience throughout the 1980s, **In Search of Darkness** will provide fans with a unique perspective on the decade that gave rise to some of the horror genre's greatest icons, performers, directors, and franchises that forever changed the landscape of modern cinema. Tracking major theatrical releases, obscure titles and straight-to-video gems, the incredible array of interviewees that have been assembled for **ISOD** will weigh in on a multitude of topics: from creative and budgetary challenges creatives faced throughout the decade to the creature suits and practical effects that reinvigorated the makeup effects industry during the era to the eye-popping stunts that made a generation of fans believe in the impossible. **In Search of Darkness** will also celebrate many of the atmospheric soundtracks released during that time, the resurgence of 3-D filmmaking, the cable TV revolution and the powerful marketing in video store aisles, the socio-political allegories infused throughout many notable films, and so much more.*

Dread Central: As someone who was a major player in horror for several decades, what would you say made the 1980s so special?

Tom Holland: I don't know. At the time, none of us [in horror] knew that the 1980s were going to be so noteworthy. At the time everybody was too busy working and trying to get their next job. I don't think anyone I knew had any semblance that we'd be talking about it 30-40 years later. It's pretty amazing, Josh. I see it everywhere now, people referring to the 1980s as the decade where horror came out of the subbasement and went on its way towards being a vibrant and profitable genre. At the time it was considered "slumming" to work in horror.

DC: You're well-known for helming *Fright Night* and *Child's Play*, but you're also as much of a writer as you are a director. In addition to the films I just mentioned, you wrote *Psycho II* and *The Beast Within* in the 1980s. Which hat do you like wearing best: Writer or director?

*TH: Don't forget **Cloak and Dagger**!*

DC: Never!

*TH: I like all of it, but I started directing in self-defense. I had a movie called **Scream for Help** [directed by Michael Winner and released in 1984] that didn't turn out so well. I was so in love with the script for **Fright Night**, it was the most joyous writing experience I ever had. So, after the experience I had with **Scream for Help** I didn't trust it in anybody's hands except my own.*

DC: A couple of years ago, we heard that the rights to *Fright Night* are about to revert back to you. What does the future hold for that franchise?

TH: I'm writing… well, I'm trying to write a sequel as a novel.

DC: Fantastic! Please keep us posted on that. Now, Stephen King was popular in the 1980s and we're in the midst of a Stephen King renaissance in the 2010s. Can you talk about your experiences working on *The Langoliers* or Thinner and postulate why the 1980s and Stephen King specifically are so popular again?

*TH: When I did the adaptation of **The Langoliers** he had some notes for me on that. We became friendly when I shot in Bangor and he was actually in it. What Stephen did was he took horror literature out of the basement, out of the ghetto, and brought it up to the middle class. Up until then, horror was something you'd see in comics and probably hide from your parents. But Stephen made it safe for the middle class. He transformed horror literature, made it respectable. And all these things came together to make horror the vibrant, money producing genre it is today. It was something you were likely ashamed of but now when we're getting the films of Jordan Peele's for example. it's like Pauline Kael is writing horror movies now because of all the socio-economic subtexts. There's a growing critical acceptance to the genre. It might even have come too far, actually. When it becomes didactic, that's usually the first sign of dying or atrophy. But horror's now taught in college classes! Who would have ever thought that? But everything that's being done now is still working off of 1980s horror primarily. That's what Jordan Peele did. **Get Out** is really **The Stepford Wives**.*

*John Carpenter's **Halloween** was a big one in terms of influencing the genre. It was the commercialization of slashers. You could lay out a timeline and watch the growing acceptability and intellectual heft that's been growing for all these decades. And 1980 is when it really opened up. I don't know why.*

DC: *Psycho II* is becoming something of a cult phenomenon with folks saying it's one of the best horror sequels ever made. How do you feel about *Psycho II* and the fact that it's taken decades for that film to get the accolades it deserves?

*TH: That probably makes me more grateful than anything else. That was my breakout film and it was the last gathering of the people who had worked with Mr. Hitchcock on **Psycho**. Vera Miles came back. Our producer Hilton Green was Hitchcock's first AD. The script* *supervisor was the same guy who worked on* **Psycho***. They're all gone now. But that was the thrill of my life and I worked harder on that script than I have any other. And this is interesting: I think it was actually the top movie for the Summer of 1982. It was a huge hit and no one expected it—certainly not the folks at Universal. It started as a cable movie. It's a terrific movie and that's what spawned the whole* **Psycho** *legacy. Off of my film's success they did two or three more sequels and a couple of TV series. They've never stopped making money off of* **Psycho** *since* **Psycho II***.*

And you're right that it was somehow forgotten. But I went to a dinner four or five years ago and every big horror director there. I had **American Psycho** *author Bret Easton Ellis sitting next to me, and* **Psycho II** *was voted the best horror sequel ever made. That was the first time I realized it was gaining its own critical cache. That's something I feel grateful for and I want to support that movie in every way.*

DC: I think our readers would probably kill me if we didn't talk about a little film called *Child's Play*! Let's talk about that long-standing urban legend that Chucky is based on Robert the Doll. True or false?

TH: False.

DC: How did that rumor get started?

TH: No idea.

DC: What's your opinion on the upcoming *Child's Play* reboot in the works at Orion?

TH: I think it's terrific. I hope they can make the doll scary again!

DC: Do you and Don Mancini keep in touch?

TH: I've never met him. He wrote the original script, but I'm the one who made it into a slasher. I'm the one who brought suspense in. The reason I did the film was because of **Trilogy of Terror**, *the 1968 TV movie. Remember? In "Amelia", which is based on Richard Matheson's short story "Prey", there was this Zuni doll. That was the first time I knew I wanted to do that. When they did "Amelia" they didn't have steady cams. Then steady cams exploded with* **The Shining**. *I wanted to take the steady cam and put that into a killer doll movie.* **Child's Play** *is built on visual set pieces. In other words, there are cuts in that movie that move things forward with visuals and the minimal amount of dialog. That's Hitchcock: Very carefully crafted. The opening scene is a hook. You know the doll is evil because you see Charles Lee Ray put his soul into it. Then you give that evil doll to an innocent single mother and seven-year-old boy. The audience knows something the characters in the movie don't and that's a ticking timebomb. And that is Hitchcock's definition of suspense. I learned that by doing* **Psycho II**, *because what I did there was I ran every Hitchcock movie, even the silent ones, and I studied the visual set pieces he did. I think I put five of them in* **Psycho II**. *I was learning all the time if that makes any sense.*

DC: Give Josh [your son] my regards the next time you see him. He told me stories about being on sets with you when he was growing up.

TH: You know what, he thought **Child's Play** *was the stupidest idea he ever heard! He told me "No one's going to buy this!" But here we are 30 years later and we're still talking about it.*

DC: Yes, we certainly are!

Lauren Ashley Carter

BLACK SITE STAR WALKS THE WOMAN, JUG FACE, IMITATION GIRL & FILMING IN A HAUNTED BUNKER

Method: *Phone*

Originally Published: April 22, 2019

Most horror aficionados first became familiar with the name Lauren Ashley Carter when the actress burst onto the scene as Peggy Cleek in Lucky McKee's ultraviolent, uber-controversial flick *The Woman* in 2011. Since then, she's become a powerhouse in indie horror, featuring prominently in *Jug Face*, *Darling*, *The Mind's Eye*, and *Imitation Girl* with other creepers coming down the pike. In my opinion, she's just one role away from breaking through into mainstream superstardom.

Her most recent release is Dread's *Black Site*, a genre mashup of futuristic sci-fi and old-school, Lovecraftian cosmic terror. The film is currently available on Epic's online store.

Dread Central was lucky enough to sit down with Carter recently for a conversation that covered her past, present, and future. In addition to talking about some of her most impactful roles, she shared some of her personal, real-life horrors. Specifically, unexpected challenges that come as a byproduct of fame and notoriety.

Synopsis: *Members of an elite military unit encounter supernatural entities known as the Elder Gods, forcing them into a battle against an army from another world.*

Black Site *is written and directed by Tom Paton. In addition to Carter, the film stars Sophia Del Pizzo, Henry Douthwaite, and Angela Dixon.*

Dread Central: You graduated from the University of Cincinnati's College-Conservatory of Music with a Bachelor of Fine Arts degree in Dramatic Performance in 2008. How did you get from Ohio to Hollywood? And I'm using Hollywood in the figurative sense, meaning moviemaking in general.

Lauren Ashley Carter: We had showcases where we go to New York and L.A. to perform in front of casting directors and agents in the hopes that someone will want to meet with you. I was pretty sure I wanted to go to Los Angeles because I was interested in filmmaking and being in film more so than theater at that time. But I went to New York and there were a lot of people who wanted to meet with me. I had a really good time there. I'd been to New York a lot just because of the proximity. I'd been there a lot with friends and family many times but I never really felt like I wanted to live there. But after I left university, I thought, "Well I could actually see myself working and living here." Then, when I went out to L.A., I was certain I wanted to move there, but once I got there, I didn't feel the same way.

DC: Very understandable.

LAC: Yeah, I didn't realize how spread out it was and the insane amount of driving involved. I guess I just didn't feel it. What really put the nail in the coffin was that the writers' strike was going on that year in 2008, and I think it had just lifted the day we got there. So, because there had been such a lull when it was lifted everyone was rushing to get back to work and no one showed up to our showcase. I thought, "Well it doesn't make sense for me to move out here when no one wants to see me, but I have lots of meetings in New York." And plus, I felt I really wanted to be there. So, I made the big leap to New York and I signed with one of the agents that I had an interview with.

I started auditioning right away and I think for my first role, I had I ended up going to Europe for a few months. It was for a motion capture animated film in France. Unfortunately, the translation wasn't that great so the film didn't do too well. But the next one I did was an independent film, **Rising Stars** *that Andrew van den Houten was producing. When we were shooting that together, he was talking about how he made horror movies. He had heard me talking about* **Martyrs** *at the lunch table, and he was like "No way, Carter, you like horror movies?" and I was like, "Yeah," and he was like "No way! We've got to get you in one!" And so later Lucky [McKee] was making* **The Woman** *and we got in touch again and—things just kept going from there. So, I moved to New York for about ten years. I did these indie films and was also performing in theater, off-Broadway in states all over America.*

DC: There isn't a lot of information about you online. Is this on purpose? Are you a private person when you aren't acting?

LAC: Yeah, I am. I 've just always been that way. But what really did it for me is that I had a stalker.

DC: Oh no, I'm really sorry to hear that.

LAC: It was really terrifying.

DC: I bet!

LAC: Yeah, and she was able to find out so much about me online—even, like, pictures of my family and things, because it was all there. I think I had Facebook links to my family and you could see who my mother was and who my sister was at the time. And I got really paranoid that she was going to find my friends and family and start harassing them—or do something. So, I immediately got off Facebook and kind of severed my ties with a lot of people. It was kind of a good thing because as soon as I did, I felt so much better. Not only because of her not having access to me and my friends and family, but also just that pressure of being online in general—and it was such a great excuse to let that go. Since that happened, I've just been super paranoid, and I've had some other… odd encounters. I actually set up a block for myself, so I can't go on Instagram or Twitter. I won't delete my accounts so if I have to tell people something I can still get back on. I'm happy to talk about anything people want to ask me, I just don't want my information readily available for everyone.

DC: That's a good idea in this day and age—and it makes you more mysterious.

LAC: There's something to that in the sense that you always want people to watch you as a character and not so much as your actual personality. I just remember, growing up with my father, he had so many judgments about famous people who were open in the media. He's like, "You're an actor! Just keep your mouth shut!"

DC: I like the way you explained how it really keeps the focus on your characters as opposed to you as a person. Now, I've heard you're a life-long fan of horror and sci-fi. When did you first discover your love of these genres and what are some of the first movies that hooked you?

LAC: It was because of my father and I can't remember what really happened—I don't remember if we were watching TV or if it happened when we went to the video store first. But I do know that I

217

always wanted to go to the horror section. And I've heard a lot of people say that, that when they were kids, they liked the scary covers and titles, and they were just drawn to that dark VHS box art. And I think that was a huge thing for me, for sure, because when I was five and six, I would just point at covers of things and my dad would let me take them. I think it was just an unspoken rule that we wouldn't tell my mother. But the first movie that we rented that I remember watching over and over was **Sleepaway Camp***. The original kept getting stolen from the store so we usually rented* **Part 2** *and* **Part 3***.* **Part 2** *was my favorite. Then there was the first* **Hellraiser***. I did see the other ones,* **Hellbound** *and* **Hell on Earth***, but the original was always the one I always wanted to rent.* **Puppet Master** *and all the* **Puppet Master** *movies.* **Halloween***, all the* **Halloween** *moves. I wasn't a big Jason fan, and Freddy—I got pretty tired of him early on and stopped being scared of him. I remember telling my dad I wanted to watch scarier movies. At some point, he rented* **Faces of Death** *and I screamed and cried. I think we had to put on Rocky and Bullwinkle after that!*

DC: You already mentioned *The Woman*, which was super intense. What was that experience like for you and do you think the themes explored in *The Woman* are more relevant now that when the film was released?

LAC: Well, hmm… **The Woman** *was a little taboo when it came out. There was a lot of controversy about possibly exploitive imagery. People thought it was just torture porn, but we obviously never thought it was. We all knew the movie we were making. But it was a really challenging film for everyone involved.*

There's so much pressure when your shooting independent films in general. You're not always working under the greatest conditions. I always say, "It's either way too hot or way too cold!" The food sucks and people are really stressed out and overtired. We were sleeping on rubber mattresses… The rooms had no locks on the doors and people were always coming in and out. There was a frog living in one of the showers. But we really loved working together. We were such a family and such a team and I ended up staying friends with a lot of the people involved afterward. But we came to work every day to work on this really heavy material. And working with Sean Bridgers and Angela Bettis and Pollyanna McIntosh was so helpful for me and that movie taught me a lot. It was the film that made me 100% certain that I wanted to move forward with my acting career. Before that, I wasn't quite sure and I wasn't taking everything as seriously. But working alongside all those other actors gave me that figurative slap in the face I needed—in a good way. And Polly I remember she came on set and, initially, she didn't intend on speaking to any of us. She wanted to keep herself isolated. But she said that when she saw how much fun the rest of us were having, she said, "Ah, forget it!" I think that's a good way to be when you're doing independent movies because of the factors I spoke about earlier. You don't really have the luxury of just staying in character and retreating to your trailer. I think that in some cases it's to your benefit that you talk to people and hang around them so you know that you can trust them. Feeling taken care of, when you're in the middle of nowhere with no cell phone reception, you need to feel safe, and that created a very nurturing environment—and that leads to better performances. You can take care of one another.

I'd be interested to hear what people think after watching **The Woman** for the first time now and compare that to what people thought when it first came out. Because of the rape scene that's in it and the incest/molestation that's happening. I think it's important to show these things in a real light. But there is a line though. I'm one of those people who thinks that the rape scene in **Irreversible** was absolutely unnecessarily long. People will argue with me about that, and that's fine. But people will say to me "Well, how can you be OK with the rape scene in **The Woman**?" For me, they're *completely different. I think it's important to show abuse and also to show the men who do it getting their hearts ripped out through their stomachs!*

DC: I'm a huge fan of *Jug Face*, from the animated opening credits to the way the story immediately pulls you in. At the same time, there's something almost oppressively bleak about it. It's like, no matter how hard you try, you can't escape your destiny. Do you agree that the film is completely dark, or is there something more positive going on that I'm missing? What's the takeaway?

LAC: No, you hit the nail on the head I'm afraid! When I'm doing a film, I always try to find at least one scene where my character has joy and the whole time, I was really searching for something. I remember looking at director Chad Crawford Kinkle, and he was just smiling like, "What's it going to be? Where's your joy?" And I told him, "I don't think there's anything—she has zero joy. There's absolutely nothing for her!" One of his writing teachers had told him to just put your protagonist through hell—scene after scene after scene. And that's what he did.

DC: True that. Your character really goes through the wringer in *Jug Face*!

LAC: The only positive takeaway from Jug Face is my character's relationship with Dwight.

DC: Yeah, that was sweet.

LAC: She did find some kindness in all of it, even though she was doomed.

DC: *Imitation Girl* is a difficult film to describe. It explores what it means to be American by focusing on a very unique family. How would you describe

Imitation Girl and what messages do you feel that movie conveys?

*LAC: I think that was beautiful what you said. That was always writer/director Natasha Kermani's goal: To feature this immigrant Iranian-American family, because she's Iranian, and it's such a beautiful underrepresented culture in film. It's about belonging and it's about identity and we have a huge issue with that in America at the moment. Because I think that so many of the battles we're fighting, offline and online, and with the president at the moment, it's all about who belongs and who doesn't. And what does that mean? And also, I think that even this idea of "the other" being good or bad. There's an identity crisis at the moment. There are a lot of white people feeling stressed about their guilt and their duties and responsibilities. And I think a lot of anger and hate comes from white males who are uncertain about their identity and where they belong now. They start lashing out. You hear the argument, "I didn't come up with money… I didn't have privilege… I grew up with nothing…" and not really understanding that yes, you have more because you are white. That's what Julianna's struggle is: She has no identity and she isn't embracing anything. And she's this middle ground average chick, and that's not enough. But that's the point of the immigrant experience in the film: Immigrants have to work so hard just to be considered average and to have what everybody else has while people who were born average all want to be superstars or special or important. It's that struggle to be somebody, and putting these experiences side by side is kind of ridiculous in a way. I always think that Julianna is such a pathetic character, but she's also she's got hope. And, compared to **Jug Face**, Ava never had any hope, she was a hopeless character. Julianna, on the other hand, kind of represents the Ava who got out, who escaped her destiny. It's a difficult subject.*

DC: I love how you tied that back to _Jug Face_. Let's talk a bit about _Black Site_ before I let you go. _Black Site_ deals with cosmic horror, which can be more difficult to convey than fear of the supernatural or

fear of an attacker. What was it like working on that film compared to some of the other films you've worked on?

LAC: It was really cool because, first of all, it's in England. The sets are a lot different and the energy is a lot different. It was very laid back but everyone was really professional even through it was a low budget film. They crossed all their t's and dotted their i's. The coolest part was that everyone rehearsed for a really long time before filming. That's something we usually don't get enough of—there's just no time in indie films to rehearse anything. We were in this huge bunker and it was really creepy and I guess they do ghost tours there all the time. So, every day we were trying to beat the ghost tour before they would bring their people in. They would spend the night in there. It was really weird. They put handprints on the walls to make it look like people had been trying to escape. It was a lot of fun. The place was so huge I didn't even get to see all the sets. And it was dark, so we needed a chaperone to lead us around just so we wouldn't get lost. And, of course, it was absolutely freezing!

DC: What are you working on next?

LAC: I've got two films coming up that I'll have much bigger roles in. **Gags the Clown** *is one that will be On Demand soon (I hope) and* **Artik**. **Gags** *was so much fun for me, shooting in Wisconsin, and* **Artik** *was shot in Mexico and I play a more sinister character.*

DC: Anything else you want to tell our readers before I let you go?

LAC: I'll keep making movies if you guys keep watching them.

DC: It's a deal!

Chris Roe

Method: *Phone*

Originally Published: April 24, 2019

I recently had the pleasure of screening *A Tale of Two Sisters*, the first in a planned universe of *Cemetery Tales* created by Chris Roe. I know critics and journalists use the "time machine" metaphor liberally, but it truly was like being transported into a different era of cinema, one where horror was more about existential terrors and personal hells.

Synopsis (via *Deadline*): *Roe's film is set in 1949 and stars Traci Lords as an aging Hollywood star who is mourning her beloved sister on the first anniversary of her death. When the truth about her murder is revealed, a visitor adds new layers to the dark mystery.* ***Cemetery Tales: A Tale of Two Sisters*** *is a Tea Time*

Production; the film also stars Bruce Davison, Ros Gentle, Michael Broderick, and Monte Markham.

I knew that **A Tale of Two Sisters** had screened at the Sitges Festival in 2018, so I was anxious to sit down with Roe to discuss the film's journey and what's next in the realm of **Cemetery Tales**. To find out about the film's connection to horror royalty George A. Romero and what it took to roll back the decades, read on!

Dread Central: How was *A Tale of Two Sisters* received at Sitges?

Chris Roe: I thought the film was very well received. It was a real dream to have its premiere at Sitges, and be in competition! It's the greatest genre film festival in the world, and well over 50 years running. For a filmmaker to make a genre movie, and to have it screen there is a dream come true. All the great directors and actors love that festival. It was George Romero's favorite, Clive Barker's and Malcolm McDowell's too! European audiences get film better. They really understand cinema differently. It's always a joy to watch a movie with a European audience.

DC: The ending says "Dedicated to George Romero". How, specifically, does *A Tale of Two Sisters* pay tribute to the iconic filmmaker?

CR: It was important for me to dedicate the film to George because we were very close. I loved him dearly. I was his manager for over 15 years until he passed in July of 2017.

DC: Oh wow, I didn't realize you have such a profound, personal connection with him.

*CR: Absolutely. He taught me a lot in those 15 years. I had talked to George about **Cemetery Tales** back in 2010 and 2011. He loved the concept. He loved those half-hour shows **like The Twilight***

Zone and *Night Gallery*. *Of course,* *Creepshow* *was very similar too! He thought it would make a great series or anthology film. Shortly after George passed, I was going through papers and files and found all these notes and outlines I had written for* *Cemetery Tales* *back in 2010 through 2012. I remembered George always saying that if you started something, to finish it if you could. So, I decided to do just that and began getting* *A Tale of Two Sisters* *ready to go.*

DC: We're glad you did! I was lucky enough to get a screener, but where can everyone else see *A Tales of Two Sisters*?

CR: Currently, *A Tale of Two Sisters* *can only be seen on the festival circuit. It's been successful. We have been accepted into six I believe. It won Best Short Thriller at the 19th Hollywood Reel Independent Film Festival in Los Angeles a few months ago. It always feels good to win at home. We had most of our cast and crew present, and a nice party after the screening. Audiences have really enjoyed it. I wasn't sure how they would at first. Since it's a period film, shot in black and white, that can cut away some of your viewers. Especially, with the younger generation. They often don't care for black and white. But I'm very pleased with all the support and response to it.*

DC: So, obviously, you're planning on making more Cemetery Tales, am I right?

CR: My hope is to definitely do more. Right now, I would like to do five more and have a limited series to pitch. I have the outlines and scripts for the next five ready. If the series doesn't work, then we can take those six shorts and make a great anthology movie out of them. So, I have several platforms I can work with this. I also have a lot of other great talents in mind for some of these.

DC: Fantastic! We can't wait to see what you come up with next. Now, I've been a huge fan of Traci

Lords since her knockout performance in *Excision*. What was it like working with her and the rest of the cast?

CR: Working with Traci was fantastic! Hard at times actually. She's a perfectionist and a complete professional. She really got to play a part that you don't always see her do. It shows her diversity and range as an actor. She's so glamorous. Watching her on set, and seeing her on the screen, she really looks like she walked out of the '30s, '40s, and '50s. She fits right into that lineup of actresses like Joan Crawford, Marlene Dietrich, Gloria Swanson, Lana Turner, and Joan Fontaine.

DC: Agreed!

CR: Bruce Davison was a dream! First of all, he's a first-class actor and professional. Totally collaborative and just fun to be with. Bruce is very underused in Hollywood and that's a shame.

Monte Markham, I grew up watching on TV. In the '70's he was on everything. Again, a total professional and old school. He's been a star of stage, TV, and the big screen. And his voice you want to use in everything!

Ros Gentle and Michael Broderick are both fine actors with great talent and work ethics. Each person was cast specifically for their character. Each person's character was fully written with them in mind. So, I got exactly what I wanted out of my cast.

DC: Fantastic! Were you just as pleased with your crew?

CR: I had a pretty good crew. My director of photography, Alex Wysocki, was amazing. We literally worked out every single scene before filming started. He knew exactly what I wanted, and he delivered. My editor, Michael Bruining, was the real savior. I think that's when making a movie really begins. He took all the pieces and made it work. He had great ideas and was completely collaborative. And

Jonathan Hartman did my music. He understood musically what I was going for. I could have paid for some boring synth score, and it would have not elevated the film at all. Jonathan's music is brilliant. The musicians were all total pros. I wanted something in the style of Bernard Herrmann, and I got just that.

Working on a film set with all that talent, ego, and ideas make it a priority to have your chemistry really solid. Most of my crew I will always work with again and again. A few, I would never work with again. On a film, you really get to know people. Especially, those who just are users and out for their own gain. I had one of those, all sets do. If a friendship can survive the making of a film and still be there when it's all over, you probably have a good friendship!

Tim Meunier

Method: *Email*

Reflection: I have deep roots in Southern California and Los Angeles specifically. Three generations! And when you grow up in Los Angeles, you think the entire world is like L.A. Not only is it all you see in your day-to-day-life, but it's all you see on television and in movies as well.

But I went to college at UC Santa Cruz in the 1990s, and immediately noticed that Northern California has its own vibe. I liked it a lot, and so after I graduated, I decided to stick around for a couple of years or 20. I eventually settled just east of Oakland in the San Francisco Bay Area.

Now, you might think that a city known for its artistic free-thinkers and countercultural tendencies would be a hot-bed for horror fans. But you'd be wrong. While San Francisco is infamous for its Halloween festivities, including the annual Edwardian Ball and fantastic theater experiences, it seems void of horror happenings the rest of the year. In all my years covering horror, I've never heard of a convention or genre film festival taking place in San Francisco.

No, if you want to find the bleeding heart of horror fandom in Northern California, you have to go someplace you might consider unlikely: Sacramento. Despite being that state's capital, Sacramento feels like a small town (especially when compared to gargantuan Los Angeles). But the horror community there is vibrant, diverse, and thriving—and that has everything to do with Tim Meunier.

I met Tim a full ten years ago when I covered the Sacramento Horror Film Festival for a small, now defunct site. In addition to this annual festival, Tim organizes an annual short-film festival at the historic Colonial Theater—and so much more. In 2015, Tim (along with his consummate right-hand-man Brian Jones) founded Sinister Creature Con. Though small, it's one of my absolute favorite horror weekends on the planet. As a member of the press, Tim has always treated me incredibly well. And I can honestly say, I've never met anyone who works harder than this guy. Sometimes it drives him crazy, but his love for horror and his community can never be understated.

Tim also organizes shows with a horror burlesque company ("gorelesque") called The Scream Queens, and it was at one of these events that I met my beautiful wife. So, yeah, I love the hell out of Tim Meunier and practically consider him family.

———

ORIGINALLY PUBLISHED: **June 3, 2019**

Since its launch in 2015, Sinister Creature Con in Sacramento has become one of California's most lauded bi-annual horror events. What it lacks in size and scope it more than compensates for with incredible special guests, engrossing panels, educational workshops, and raging after-parties. Sinister Creature Con happens every Spring and Fall and we're just under two weeks away from the next one (June 15th-16th).

About Sinister Creature Con: *Quakes ripple around the known universe as a new convention beast breaches through the Earth's surface. The Sinister Creature Con announces its presence from the primal depths of our humanity with volcanic might and jubilant fanfare. Located in Northern California, Sinister Creature Con's expansive tentacles ensnare a massive array of horror genre craftsmen and craftswomen that give monsters and the genre its tangible essence, such as painters, filmmakers, sculptors, tattoo artists, comic book artists, graphic designers, practical FX companies, actors, writers, haunted attraction engineers, and much more. So come one and come all to the belly of this new convention beast and learn how your fears are imagined so you may celebrate in the conquering of them.*

Sinister Creature Con is a horror convention unlike any other. We celebrate both the past and present. From the nostalgic to the contemporary we celebrate it all and have something for every horror artist and fan alike. Above all, we strive to serve and promote the art and artists. Come, be inspired, create, and scare us. We invite you to Northern California's Horror Convention, Sinister Creature Con.

Special Guests confirmed for this month's convention include David Howard Thornton (Art the Clown in ***Terrifier***), Kane Hodder, Doug Bradley, Ashley Laurence, Sherilyn Fenn, Felissa Rose, Joe Bob Briggs, and many others.

This year, Dread Central is thrilled to offer our readers a 50% discount code to attend Sinister Creature Con. Just enter "DREAD" at checkout.

As a member of Team Dread Central, I'm lucky enough to attend many of the biggest and most prestigious horror conventions across the country. That said, Sinister Creature Con is an event I look forward to more than any other. I've been to every one since its founding and don't plan on stopping. In fact, I'll be working at Dread Central's table, so come by and say "Hello"—and pick up some of our incredible DVDs/Blu-rays.

We recently sat down with Sinister Creature Con founder Tim Meunier to find out what it takes to establish one of today's best horror events from the ground up. Check out our conversation below.

Dread Central: How did you go from being a horror fan to a horror promoter?

Tim Meunier: This began in 2006 when I saw under representation of independent horror shorts and features and the many multi-genre independent film festivals in my home town of Sacramento. With my background as a filmmaker and experience as a promoter I elected to dive head first into the field of film festivals, screenings, and exhibitions. I wanted to give horror a home where fans like myself could benefit from such events.

DC: What motivated you to launch Sinister Creature Con? Were you inspired by any other conventions or was your goal to create something unique?

TM: I honestly wasn't into conventions until I was offered a challenge by my former business partner to produce the first successful horror con the city of Sacramento has seen. Having a built-in horror following from all my horror film festivals, shadow cast screenings, one off events, etc., I felt I had enough of an audience to take the dive. With the focus being on the art of creation, SFX, nostalgia/appreciation, I was given the reigns to produce an event I myself would pay to go to. I admired haunt-focused conventions where things were interactive and you could roam the halls as a voyeur and spy on folk's creations as they were being assembled. Currently I don't have the venue space for such an event so I decided to blend the elements of conventions I did enjoy to fit the space we have effectively. I think what attaches many horror fans to the genre is its tangibility. So, the craft of monster building and FX creation is something I feel is of interest to all, even just the casual viewer.

DC: You've always had great guests, but you've got some serious heavyweights coming to the con this June. Does this reflect Sinister Creature Con's reputation?

TM: We have some fantastic team members that help give each of our featured guests, artists, and celebs the red-carpet treatment as much as possible. These amazing staffers have afforded us a great reputation in regards to guest treatment. When you treat a guest right and they do well financially they spread the word amongst other horror celebrities and artists in their network. Many times, it is not us who seeks out the guest but the guest who seeks us out to experience Sinister Creature Con and our fans. That's a beautiful thing and lets us know we are doing something right.

DC: What advice would you give to up-and-comers looking to launch horror conventions in their own cities?

TM: Don't blow your wad. Be smart. Realize your first event will probably be a loss if you don't have a fanbase already built. I had nearly eight years of producing horror film events across Northern California before I launched Sinister Creature Con. I had a built-in fanbase to entice to our newest project. If you are starting fresh, I advise to keep it simple. Don't book any celebrity guests. Curate your vendors so you have a fantastic assortment of items for your patrons to browse. Horror fans are loyal. Shine that bright blood smear in the sky like the bat signal and they'll eat up what you provide. Don't buy into the celebrity guest trap too soon or it could mean the end of your convention if you blow your budget getting them in the building and you don't have the attendance to make up your investment.

DC: What's been your biggest success so far? What are you most proud of?

TM: I couldn't do this alone. My team supports this show and gave it legs. I'm proud that through the thick and thin my team has been able to help me produce a quality show in a city, Sacramento, I was told would never support horror events. The fact that I began in 2007 with one film festival and in 2019 I stand with six film festivals, two conventions a year, and an assortment of other one off, semiannual events that all revolve around horror makes me incredibly proud.

DC: Where would you like to see Sinister Creature Con go in the future?

TM: Eventually nostalgia will change with the aging generations. Legends will become too old or will die and booking marquee guests will become more of a challenge. At Sinister Creature Con, we wish to stay ahead of this shift. Eventually, we will reduce the number of media guests and be more artist-focused and place a focus on outside-of-the-box type bookings. I want to include more LGBTQ representation, horror drag queens and drag kings. Podcasters. Twitch broadcasters. Youtubers. Of course, until that shift happens we are proud to bring the best guests we can for fans who aren't able to afford to attend the bigger veteran horror cons. We stay in our wheelhouse and focused on our market. We hope to launch a 3rd convention in the February or March months in Central California once we find a suitable venue. Of course, I'd love to see attendance grow to justify moving into a much bigger venue where we can have so much more flexibility in creating a horror paradise for fans for a weekend.

DC: Can I get you to tell me a bit about the horror scene in Sacramento?

TM: Horror fanatics in Sacramento are loyal, intelligent, passionate, LOUD, and so sweet to engage in discussions with. Other horror promoters in the city all play nice together and we have a great relationship with them all. Local media is usually wide-eyed and awkward when they cover our events or other events but we appreciate their enthusiasm and willingness to give the weird and esoteric some exposure. Like many cities, Halloween season is 2nd to Christmas in terms of how much entertainment there is to be had. Sacramento is no different. Night clubs, haunted houses, playhouse performances, bar crawls, film festivals, you name it, get in the spirit of the season. It creates so much competition but that's great for fans as they have so much to select from.

Gary Dauberman

ANNABELLE WILL BE A "MAESTRO OF MAYHEM" IN ANNABELLE COMES HOME

Method: *Junket*

Reflections: This interview took place on the Warner Bros. Studios' lot, in an editing bay. Gary Dauberman was working with an editor on assembling the film's final cut. It was a great way to show clips and a behind-the-scenes look at filmmaking I'd never experienced before.

———

ORIGINALLY PUBLISHED: **June 4, 2019**

Dread Central was lucky enough to sit down with ***Annabelle Comes Home*** writer/director Gary Dauberman while the film was still being pieced together. Now that it's slated to be released in a matter of weeks, we're finally able to share excerpts of our extended conversation with a filmmaker who's already left quite an imprint on ***The Conjuring*** Universe launched by James Wan in 2013.

When **Annabelle Comes Home** on June 26th, it'll be the diminutive devil doll's third feature film—but this won't be the conclusion of a trilogy. Dauberman assured us:

"When I think of trilogies it's like, I don't think [**Annabelle:**] **Creation** was necessarily the **Empire** [**Strikes Back**], you know what I mean? The doll connects the stories and I think the mythology connects the stories. But I don't think this puts closure to the Annabelle story in any way."

So what can we expect from the evil vessel on her third outing? For starters: Madness and mayhem!

"I looked at her as sort of that the maestro of the madness or the mayhem. Kind of a master of ceremonies is a great way to put it. And how she sort of charges up the other artifacts that are in the room. What's that interaction like? That's something I dive into."

While **Annabelle Comes Home** is the third spinoff for the doll (and the seventh **Conjuring** Universe film), this upcoming release will definitely have its own identity. One of the things that will really set **Annabelle Comes Home** apart from her peers is that the majority of this installment takes place in a single evening.

"I wanted a little sense of playfulness because it is teenagers," Dauberman explained. "It's teenage girls in a house. I wanted to have that sort of vibe to it, like seventies style horror movies. I think there's a couple of more moments of levity in this movie just because I like that. I like a little bit of laughter because if you get them laughing and then you get them scared, it's a sharper contrast. [**Annabelle Comes Home**] takes place over the course of just one night. We haven't done that before, for the most part. It's usually a couple of days or a week or whatever."

Synopsis: *Determined to keep Annabelle from wreaking more havoc, paranormal investigators Ed and Lorraine Warren lock the possessed doll in the artifacts room in their house. But when the doll awakens the room's evil spirits, it soon becomes an unholy night of terror for the couple's 10-year-old daughter, her friends, and their young baby sitter.*

Annabelle Comes Home stars Vera Farmiga, Mckenna Grace, and Patrick Wilson.

Chloë Sevigny

TALKS THE DEAD DONT DIE, AMERICAN HORROR STORY & AMERICAN PSYCHO

Method: *Phone*

Reflections: Chloë Sevigny was an absolute delight to speak with, and I love how she turns the tables on me several times throughout my interview—putting me on the hot seat!

———

ORIGINALLY PUBLISHED: **June 12, 2019**

After breaking onto the indie film scene following an arresting performance in ***Kids***, Chloë Sevigny became one of the 1990s most prominent "It" girls. It's a title she's had an evolving relationship with as she's developed as an actor and a woman. She's no longer a kid! In the decades since her emergence, Sevigny has participated in films of every genre. But she's still got an independent streak, choosing to gravitate towards projects that speak to her artistic sensibilities.

Sevigny plays Officer Mindy Morrison in Jim Jarmusch's upcoming zombie comedy **The Dead Don't Die**, arriving in theaters nationwide this Friday (June 14th). Dread Central was lucky enough to sit down with the actress recently for an exclusive interview. In addition to **The Dead Don't Die**, we discussed **American Horror Story**, **American Psycho**, and the films of Jarmusch in general. Give it a read after the synopsis for **The Dead Don't Die**.

Synopsis: *In the sleepy small town of Centerville, something is not quite right. The moon hangs large and low in the sky, the hours of daylight are becoming unpredictable, and animals are beginning to exhibit unusual behaviors. News reports are scary, and scientists are concerned, but no one foresees the strangest and most dangerous repercussion that will soon start plaguing Centerville: the dead rise from their graves and feast on the living, and the citizens must battle to survive.*

In addition to Sevigny, **The Dead Don't Die** stars Bill Murray, Adam Driver, and Tilda Swinton.

Dread Central: I was reading your bio on IMDB and it sounds like you had something of an aversion to Hollywood and mainstream moviemaking early on in your career. Is this still the case?

Chloë Sevigny: No, it's not the case [laughs]. I think maybe the movies of the mainstream then just weren't speaking to me because of the things that I was seeing. I had an aversion to that. It wasn't the path I wanted to take and I was pretty vocal about it. I was also pigeonholed by the media and everything. I became the indie ingenue, actress, starlet, whatever. Now, looking back on it, not that I regret any of my choices, but I regret that I was stuck in that. In people's minds, I was just that. It's hard to break out of.

DC: Your filmography is all over the place in terms of genres. You've done horror movies like *Lizzie*, *Antibirth*, and *American Psycho* but you've also done drama and comedy. What do you enjoy about horror movies and how do they compare to other projects you've worked on?

CS: I don't really know how to compare it because every project is so different. I also did American Horror Story which was my most outwardly scary project, you know? It would be project by project.

DC: I'm glad you mentioned *American Horror Story* because *Asylum* is still my absolute favorite season and your character was definitely a highlight…

*CS: You didn't think the first season [**Murder House**] was the best?*

DC: Not personally. But I'm curious if we'll be seeing you on that series again?

CS: I don't know. If they'll have me, I'd love to come back.

DC: *American Psycho* will be turning 20 years old in April and it's still considered one of the best horror movies of the 21st Century…

CS: You really think it's a horror movie?

DC: Yeah, absolutely! It's got ax murders and dismemberments and chainsaws and sexual sadism! What do you think about *American Psycho*'s legacy when you look back?

*CS: With so much being discussed right now about toxic masculinity, I think **American Psycho** was ahead of its time. I think it would be interesting to go back and watch it now. It was early in Christian*

Bale's career after he was previously known as a child actor. The performances are so strong and the commentaries on excess are very topical now. It always has been, but it's coming around again. That's why it's remained so relevant.

DC: Let's talk about *The Dead Don't Die*. What attracted you to the script?

*CS: Well, just wanting to work with Jim [Jarmusch] again. I've done two other films with him. I was in **Broken Flowers** and we did a short film together a few years before that. Also, knowing the cast that he was going to pull together. I loved his vampire picture, **Only Lovers Left Alive**, and I was excited that he wanted to jump into another genre like that, to see how he would make [zombies] fresh and new. I loved reading the script and the meta aspects of the film. I'd never seen zombies speak before, but you'd probably know better than I. Have zombies ever spoken before?*

DC: It's rare, but they spoke in *Return of the Living Dead*. That's where the moaning "Brains!" refrain comes from.

CS: Oh, right. I just thought it was so original the way they were speaking about their addictions.

DC: I just caught a screening of The Dead Don't Die last night and found it hilarious. At the same time, I feel like there's a socio-political message in the subtext, beyond the obvious environmental allegory with fracking. How would you describe the message of the movie?

CS: It's about the desire to consume and consumerism in general, our relationships to material goods and our addictions. And it's about how we treat other people. It's a reminder to be more conscious about how we interact with other people and the Earth.

DC: As a journalist, I really see the marketing for *The Dead Don't Die* pulling in younger moviegoers. At the same time, Jarmusch is so unique, I feel like people need a primer in his work so they'll know what they're getting into. How would you describe the work of Jim Jarmusch to someone who's never seen one of his movies before?

CS: I would say the tone is very specific. There's a droll, deadpan delivery to his movies, wherein lies the humor. You have to just give in to that and go along for the ride. Things are very measured and it gives things specific weight.

DC: Anything else you'd like to tell our readers before I let you go?

*CS: There's a short film I directed called **The Echo** that's going to be playing at festivals. It's about a bunch of girls upstate playing with a Ouiji. One girl has "the gift" and it's about how she convinces other people of that and how they react to it.*

DC: We can't wait to see it.

CS: Thank you!

Culture Shock Aims to Wake You the F*** Up

SET VISIT RECAP

Method: *Set Visit*

Reflections: Gigi Saul Guerrero is the future of horror, a director with uncanny prowess and uncompromising vision. She's also one of the nicest people I've ever met in my life.

I first met Gigi all the way back in 2015 in Little Rock, Arkansas of all places. I was there for the 1st Annual Fantastic Cinema and Craft Beer Festival as a brand ambassador for a fledgling Crypt TV. Gigi was there with her Luchagore Productions team, Raynor Shimabukuro and Luke Bramley, screening a few of shorts and serving as festival jurors. It was a blast, and I'll never forget laughing as we consumed a platter full of "mud bugs"!

Over the years, it's been an absolute pleasure seeing Gigi's star rise high. My set visit for **Culture Shock** gave me an opportunity to see her in action and let me just say: She's a powerhouse. Today, Gigi and I are still in touch and I'm honored to call her a friend.

While this was another set-visit, it was just a one-day affair. The film was shot in Southern California and the other attending journalists were all local. So it was a shorter experience than I had with **Pet Sematary** and **Doctor Sleep**, but it was impactful nonetheless.

———

ORIGINALLY PUBLISHED: **July 2, 2019**

Culture shock is an experience a person may have when one moves to a cultural environment which is different from one's own. It is also the personal disorientation a person may feel when experiencing an unfamiliar way of life due to immigration or a visit to a new country, a move between social environments, or simply transition to another type of life. One of the most common causes of culture shock involves individuals in a foreign environment. Culture shock can be described as consisting of at least one of four distinct phases: honeymoon, negotiation, adjustment, and adaptation.

Culture Shock is also the 10th installment of Hulu & Blumhouse's **Into the Dark**, a monthly series of feature films, each with a holiday theme. **Culture Shock** hits the streaming powerhouse this Thursday, July 4th and, obviously, the theme is Independence Day.

So it might seem strange, at first, to learn that **Culture Shock** is directed by Mexican-born, Canadian filmmaker

Gigi Saul Guerrero. Then again, someone who truly understands life on both of America's major borders is perhaps uniquely qualified to offer an objective, artistic examination of our current socio-political climate—especially in the South.

In 2010, during the height of the "Minute Men" movement (when a group of self-proclaimed vigilantes took it upon themselves to patrol remote corners of America's border with Mexico), the film ***Undocumented*** presented a horrifying look at this disturbing and misguided mindset. Now, as migrants are coming to the U.S. in record number, illegally, resulting in overcrowded detention centers, ***Culture Shock*** aims to wake us all the fuck up!

As politicians and their constituencies pontificate about what should or shouldn't be done, Guerrero's film is both a warning and an ugly mirror. It's never been timelier, which is why everyone I spoke to during my set visit (Guerrero and actors Martha Higareda, Richard Cabral, and Shawn Ashmore) all used the word "important" (repeatedly) when discussing ***Culture Shock***.

There are two different worlds on display in ***Culture Shock***: Harsh reality and the American Dream incarnate. The sets I visited were part of the darker world. It was a place of claustrophobic corridors and grimy, make-shift medical banks that one might expect to see on an active battlefield—or the bowels of Hell.

The clapboard snaps and someone yells "Action", but there is no quiet on this set. As Higareda performs an emotionally grueling scene with minimal dialog, Guerrero is literally screaming: "Come on Martha! Dig deep! Remember how hurt you are, how much you hate him! Now's your moment for revenge, Martha! Do it! Do it! Do it!"

At least that's what I imagine Guerrero is saying. Her passionate and equally urgent directions are delivered in Spanish.

"I told Blumhouse that I was going to give them a true, authentic piece of Mexican culture–that this was really important to me," Guerrero explains and, obviously, this isn't lip-service. The majority of the actors and crew are Mexican-American, hence Spanish being the language of choice on set. Now I was experiencing mild culture shock; I've been on a number of sets, but never one where business was being done in a foreign tongue.

When I asked Ashmore, a white man, how it felt to be a minority on the set of a feature film in Hollywood, he paused before responding, "I hadn't really noticed"–and bless his fucking heart. This could be proof of permanent change, when a young actor sees a culturally diverse production as completely normal. Hopefully, his entire generation will be as color-blind and artistically devoted when it comes to quality filmmaking. Because while it's worth noting that Guerrero is a woman and an immigrant in an industry dominated by white men, the goal is to create a world where diversity is commonplace.

Responses to festival screenings of ***Culture Shock*** have been tremendous, meaning Guerrero is well on her way to super-stardom. As someone who's followed her and her production company, Luchagore, for years, I know there's plenty more glorious gore and socially relevant horror in the tank. She's smart as a whip with a wicked mind for arresting and engrossing cinema.

Check out the synopsis ***Culture Shock*** below.

Synopsis: *This thriller follows a young Mexican woman in pursuit of the American Dream, who crosses illegally into the United States, only to find herself in an American nightmare.*

Guerrero directs **Culture Shock** from a screenplay she developed with James Benson and Efrén Hernández.

Does the Dog Survive?

ALEXANDRE AJA DISCUSSES THE FATE OF "SUGAR" IN
CRAWL

Method: *Phone*

Reflections: My first interview with Dread Central was hardly my first interview as a horror journalist. I'd already scored a bunch of exclusives, including with heavy hitters like Dee Wallace, Elvira Mistress of the Dark (aka Cassandra Peterson), and Linda Blair.

What you are about to read is my second interview with Alexandre Aja and, I have to admit, the one I did for **Horror Freak News** was just as interesting (and probably more historically relevant). That one is probably lost to the ages; it might still be up on the latest incarnation of **Horror Freak News**, or a draft might exist on my last laptop's hard drive.

But I remember that my first interview with Aja focused on New French Extremity, a powerful but ultimately short-lived subgenre that peaked in the mid-2000s. It was a world I discovered thanks to Netflix, and I was floored by movies like Inside, **Martyrs**, **Irreversible**, and **Frontier(s)**. Aja wrote and directed **High Tension** (aka **Haute Tension**), released in 2003. It's a film that is widely regarded as a crown jewel of New French Extremity.

Aja lamented that French horror practitioners didn't get much love in their home country and that, objectively, New French Extremity had died in the early 2010s. Still, the influence of this nihilistic and uncompromising brand of horror can still be seen in the works of filmmakers like Julia Ducournau, the maverick behind 2018's **Raw** and 2021's **Titane**, which took home the top prize at the Cannes Film Festival that year.

Aja's continued success as a filmmaker comes from his efforts on American movies. 2006's **The Hills Have Eyes**, for example, is one of those rare remakes that actually improves on the original (Wes Craven's **The Hills Have Eyes** was released in 1977). The interview below was in support of **Crawl**, released in 2019.

———

ORIGINALLY PUBLISHED: **July 12, 2019**

Whenever I see a dog in a horror movie, my heart sinks. Nine times out of ten, when you see a pet in a horror movie, it's going to get killed, delivering an emotional gut punch. If the movie is rated R—forget about it! So, when I realized that one of the main characters in **Crawl** (now playing in theaters nationwide) is Sugar, a shaggy terrier mutt mix, I decided not to get too attached to her.

Crawl is directed by Alexandre Aja, one of the pioneers of New French Extremity, who savagely slaughtered two dogs in his remake of Wes Craven's **The Hills Have Eyes**. "Sugar doesn't stand a chance," I lamented.

So, when I had a chance to discuss *Crawl* with Aja this morning, I couldn't help but discuss sweet Sugar's surprising fate.

Spoiler Warning: To find out what happens to Sugar—and what could have happened, continue reading. If you've yet to see *Crawl* for yourself, bookmark this page and come back later.

Sugar lives, but was that always the plan? Not necessarily. Aja explains:

"We went back and forth a lot [about what to do with Sugar]. We had different versions of the script, including a contingency plan for if the dog turned out to be a nightmare on set. There was even a really dark idea about the characters sacrificing Sugar to save themselves. It's funny because we discussed things like Sugar living in peace and Sugar jumping into the water to save her humans. In the end, I think having the audience wondering what's going to happen to the dog is a good suspense builder."

That's when the conversation took a really wacky turn.

"We even talked about doing a sequel entirely from Sugar's perspective."

Now who wouldn't want to see that?

You can check out the synopsis for *Crawl* below.

Synopsis: *When a massive hurricane hits her Florida town, young Haley ignores the evacuation orders to search for her missing father, Dave. After finding him gravely injured in their family home, the two of them become trapped by the rapidly encroaching floodwaters. With* *the storm strengthening, Haley and Dave discover an even greater threat than the rising water level — a relentless attack from a pack of gigantic alligators.*

Crawl stars Kaya Scodelario, Barry Pepper, and Morfydd Clark. Sugar was played by a dog named Cso-Cso!

Richard Elfman

TALKS ALIENS, CLOWNS & GEEKS

Method: *Email*

Reflections: I first met Richard Elfman when a contingency from Dread Central had assembled in Los Angeles to cover the E3 Convention in 2018. Richard had become an associate of then-Editor-in-Chief, Jonathan Barkan, having recently submitted an editorial. Richard threw one of his famous roof-top parties in our honor—and it was mind-blowing. We were served blood-colored cocktails over dry-ice, creating a smoky mini-cauldron of imbibement. Richard had also invited a handful of well-known horror directors to the event, making it a truly once-in-a-lifetime experience.

Sure, I'll name drop. There was Darren Lynn Bousman (***Saw*** franchise), Jackson Stewart (***Beyond the Gates***), Brian Yuzna (***Return of the Living Dead III***), and Don Mancini (***Child's Play*** franchise). Oh man, Don told me the most hysterical story about Jennifer Tilly and Leonard Maltin. I'd love to re-tell it here, but I'd probably get in trouble. After all, I was attending the party as a guest, not a journalist. Still, maybe I'll recount the tale on a podcast interview or something.

I'm still not exactly sure how it happened, but Richard and I struck up a genuine relationship that was both professional and personal. In the months that followed, I'd find myself attending several more of Richard's famous rooftop soirees. I even scored a coveted spot at one of Richard's artistic salons, "The Barbecue Bacchanals." I'll never forget Anastasia performing a blistering, visceral act with live electronica spun behind her. Amazing! I couldn't wait to attend the next event.

And then, the pandemic happened. But even though the world went on lockdown, our friendship persisted. And when it was safe to emerge, Richard and I reunited with a vengeance! As many of my followers know, he and I are now working together on his authorized biography. There's also a chance I'll be penning a novelization of **Forbidden Zone**. I also adore Anastasia and the entire Elfman clan and hope our lives will be intertwined indefinitely.

_____

ORIGINALLY PUBLISHED: **August 20, 2019**

Richard and Anastasia Elfman are like the real-life Gomez and Morticia Addams: A spooky-ooky-kooky couple who hold elaborate dinner parties on the upper level of their home in the Hollywood Hills. (They're also sickeningly in love!) Recently, I was lucky enough to attend one of their legendary shin-digs, where I was treated to a rough-cut of Richard's upcoming feature film, *Aliens, Clowns & Geeks*.

For the uninitiated, Richard Elfman is the founder of Mystic Knights of the Oingo Boingo and writer/director of the cult hit *Forbidden Zone* (released in 1980). Anastasia Elfman is a burlesque dancer and Scream Queen who recently starred in the short film *Karma's a Bitch* which screened at Etheria 2019.

Aliens, Clowns & Geeks is an absolute hoot, a madcap and irreverent romp that will put a huge grin on your face and a serious stitch in your side. It has all the makings of the next great cult classic. Look out *Rocky Horror Picture Show*! *Aliens, Clowns & Geeks* is arriving soon to give you a run for your money! At the same time, there's almost a spiritual link between *RHPS* and *AC&G*, as both are populated by mad scientists and aliens participating in bizarre (and hilarious) couplings.

Eyeing a Fall release, *Aliens, Clowns & Geeks* is a crowd-pleaser as likely to tickle horror fans as scaredy cats. It's a near-hallucinatory kaleidoscope of colorful characters and comic lunacy. If you're a connoisseur of upper-echelon B-movies like *Killer Klowns from Outer Space*, *Critters*, *Troll 2*, and the like, you won't want to miss *AC&G*!

After the Hollywood festivities, I was able to sit down with Richard for a one-on-one where ***Aliens, Clowns & Geeks*** was the main topic. Give our convo a read below.

Synopsis: *An out-of-work actor stumbles upon the key to the universe and is drawn into an intergalactic war between clowns and aliens.*

Dread Central: It's been quite some time since your 1980 cult hit, *Forbidden Zone*. What have you been up to in the interim and what got you back into directing?

*Richard Elfman: I'd been a hired gun after **Forbidden Zone**. I directed some Matthew Bright dark horror-comedy scripts (**Shrunken Heads** and **Modern Vampires**) and did some dance documentaries. Plus, I write and direct for the stage and play in bands. For five years I ran a small media company, wrote articles, produced 300 red carpet events, made music and celebrity videos—but was spending way too much time behind a desk. I wanted to get back to directing, especially to make **Forbidden Zone 2**. **Aliens, Clowns & Geeks** somehow came up first. You might say as a warm-up—although we were blessed with a dream cast, dream crew and I am quite pleased with the way **Aliens, Clowns & Geeks** came out.*

DC: *Aliens, Clowns & Geeks* was Verne Troyer's final film. [The actor, perhaps best known for playing "Mini-Me" in the Austin Powers movies, passed away in 2018.] What was it like working with him?

RE: I had initial reservations over Verne's health. He actually wanted to do an additional second role. We kept it to the megalomaniac Clown Emperor. But Verne was a prince to direct. Total pro, worked his ass off. He even did some great comic improv we all loved. He hung out with the cast and crew, literally charming everyone. A huge talent in a little package.

DC: *Aliens, Clowns & Geeks* is kind of a family affair: Your son Bodhi Elfman is the main protagonist and your wife Anastasia Elfman plays a number of roles. Was it weird directing them?

*RE: Ha! Everything about this film is weird! Bodhi may not be as famous as his wife Jenna Elfman (**Fear of the Walking Dead**), but he's got like a hundred IMDB credits. Mostly bad guys in serious dramas. For this film, his comic instincts really knocked it out of the park. An out-of-work actor wakes up with the key to the universe stuck up his ass. Yes, that took years of dramatic training, but Bodhi thoroughly nailed the nuances of the role.*

And my lovely wife Anastasia played five roles—everything from a nun to a carny slut. She also did second unit wardrobe, make-up, even some stunt driving—plus choreographed the cabaret numbers. AND had to come home to me each night…what a trooper!

DC: Your brother, Danny Elfman, scored Aliens, Clowns & Geeks, correct?

*RE: Yeah—and on a modestly budgeted film it really helps when your little brother is Danny Elfman. **Aliens, Clowns & Geeks** is a 90-minute film with a mammoth 75-minute soundtrack. And Danny laughed and howled at his nephews' comedy every damned minute. Also, my buddy Ego Plum (Guerrero) did the music with Danny. He and Danny work with the same people, like arranger (Oingo Boingo lead guitar) Steve Bartek. Ego is Hollywood's TV cartoon genius, presently scoring and music editing all the Sponge Bobs plus other top shows. We have a band together—Mambo Diabolico. it's on the soundtrack. In a few weeks we'll go to Belgium to mix in state-of-the-art Auro 3D surround. Although I prefer seeing **Aliens, Clowns***

& Geeks in a theater, our game boys and girls will get mind-blowing 9.1 surround in their headphones.

DC: *Aliens, Clowns & Geeks* is constantly skewering Hollywood culture. It's almost like you have a love/hate relationship with the entertainment industry, true?

RE: Not at all. When I threw that studio head into a pool at a black-tie party, he really deserved it. Rudely insulting my wonderful Afro-Brazilian musicians!! (Afro-Latin percussion being my other true love, btw.)

DC: What was the most challenging aspect of making *Aliens, Clowns & Geeks*, and what did you find most rewarding?

RE: Well, lack of money is always a challenge—it stretched things out with our huge musical score and tons of special effects. The rewarding part was watching it all come together, from scribbling the script in my rooftop garret to finally editing the chingadera. We've done a few rough-cut previews and watching an audience laugh, yell and scream is the ultimate reward though. Aside from whatever "art statements" and surrealistic dream sequences we play around with—my greatest joy is simply to entertain—and I think the film does that well.

DC: We've heard that after *Aliens, Clowns & Geeks* is released, you'll be diving into a sequel to *Forbidden Zone*, something Oingo Boingo fans and lovers of cult films have been craving for decades. True?

*RE: Damn straight! **Forbidden Zone 2** IS my "bucket list" film. Danny's already written some great music (Ego's onboard as well). **Forbidden Zone 2** will make people laugh, cry, and piss in their pants!*

DC: You and your wife Anastasia have quite the reputation for throwing wild, elaborate dinner parties and entertainment at your place under the Hollywood sign. How does that fit into everything?

RE: You might say, how does writing and directing fit into our party schedule? Whether it be the written page, the stage, screen, or at my table—my greatest joy is to entertain. I seriously grill and cook for cast and crews at the end of each shooting week. Anastasia and I currently host an underground food and performance salon, the Barbecue Bacchanals! Too much damned FUN!!

Aliens, Clowns & Geeks

IN A WORLD OF ABSOLUTE ABSURDITY, EVEN
NIGHTMARES CAN BE FUN! [UNPUBLISHED
EDITORIAL]

Reflections: The original distributor for ***Aliens, Clowns & Geeks*** went belly-up. Then Covid happened. So when the movie was finally gearing up for its Blu-ray/DVD release in late 2021 via MVD Visual, Richard Elfman asked me to pen the inner booklet, a request I felt honored to oblige.

Ultimately, however, MVD released a more stripped-down physical copy than what had been expected. No inner booklet, no essay by Joshua Millican.

While it's not an interview, I think my introduction to the ***Aliens, Clowns & Geeks*** makes a great companion to my conversation with Richard. And I'm pleased to rescue this piece from the dust-bin of history!

———

PREVIOUSLY UNPUBLISHED EDITORIAL

For over a decade now, I've managed to turn my obsession for horror movies into a full-time career. I use the analytical skills developed as a writing and literature double-major to dissect themes and subtexts buried in slasher flicks, supernatural horrors, torture porn affairs—everything across the spectrum from mainstream genre offerings all the way into the outer fringes. My appetite was voracious, and it wasn't long before I had consumed the majority of horror cinema from the 1970s through the present. Since then, I've made it my goal to see as many new horror movies as possible, earning my title as a self-proclaimed Horror Expert.

I've always considered journalism to be a noble profession. Journalists are on the front line of history and, ten years ago, horror entertainment was still fighting to prove its legitimacy. It's my duty, therefore, to celebrate the achievements of the immensely creative individuals dedicating their lives to giving us nightmares. While the big studios are never lacking when it comes to marketing budgets, independent artists and producers often depend on intrepid journalists and critics to get the word out. Nothing brings me more joy than introducing readers to a new shocker or an up-and-coming writer/director/actor/producer who may be worthy of our attention. Additionally, I've made it my mission to expand the very definition of horror, elevating it from an aisle in a video store (or a section of a streaming service) into something akin to an emotion—a pervasive feeling of impending dread... something we experience and process much more often than we realize.

I often ask both my readers and myself, "How do we commemorate films that don't fit into traditional genre parameters?" More importantly, how do we assure that films considered "horror-adjacent" get the recognition they deserve before potentially falling through the cracks? How do we convince those trapped in a feedback loop of mainstream entertainment to dip their toes into unfamiliar waters? With so many films at our fingertips in the era of digital entertainment, wonderful creepers can get lost in the mix. As brave as horror fans can be for facing down their fears, some can be surprisingly meek when it comes to experiencing something truly unique. This is why I feel compelled to champion films that may not otherwise get the recognition they deserve—cinematically unique misfits like *Aliens, Clowns & Geeks*.

I first met Richard Elfman at his home in the Hollywood Hills back in 2018. He and his wife, actor, dancer and burlesque star Anastasia Elfman, were holding a shin-dig for the staff of *Dread Central* with more than just a few famous horror directors in attendance. I've often called Richard and Anastasia "The real-life Gomez and Morticia Addams" because they're delightfully kooky and spooky—but mostly because they are passionately, unabashedly in love. In the years since that first meeting, Richard and I have maintained a professional and personal relationship that's blossomed beautifully. Though "drug-free" for 50 years (he prefers cigars and whiskey), I was even able to convince Richard and Anastasia to try a little cannabis with me one night. When I launched my TV Series, *Chronic Horror*, back in 2019, they were two of my very first guests! The show's premise is having horror stars join me for some intoxicating smokables, genre-themed munchies, and, of course, a frightening flick!

As the Editor-in-Chief of *Dread Central* and a friend of the Elfmen, I was one of the first critics to see *Aliens, Clown & Geeks*. I've seen an early cut that ran under a different title and the final cut on several occasions. I've seen the film in Richard's home, at my own home, and at a drive-in screening as part of a double-bill with **Forbidden Zone**. With each viewing, I became slightly more enamored by the film, which reveals its subtexts and subtleties to the truly attentive. Obviously, I absolutely adore **Aliens, Clowns & Geeks**—even if I've always struggled with how to describe it. Yes, it's a comedy, but not slapstick; rather it's an experience of immersive absurdity. No, it's not a horror movie, but we're told a tale of intergalactic, grease-painted freaks on a mission to destroy our planet—an objectively terrifying scenario. At any given moment, **Aliens, Clowns & Geeks** can feel simultaneously uproarious and unnerving.

There're aren't any jump-scares in **Aliens, Clowns & Geeks**; no excessive gore or unrelenting fright. Although the overall arc is a classic three-act story structure, the film unfolds almost as a series of vignettes, a presentation reminiscent of **Forbidden Zone** (also a singular story broken-out into nearly self-contained segments). And like **Forbidden Zone**, **Aliens, Clowns & Geeks** abides by a nightmare logic, unbound by the constraints of linear reality. The textures and tonal shifts have a psychedelic quality, perhaps owing to Richard's unwitting recruitment into Ken Kesey's "Electric Kool-Aid Acid Test" as a youth (an experience that obliterated both his fears of death and authority). In addition to the titular aliens, clowns, and geeks, this film includes a kaleidoscopic ensemble of colorful characters: Carnies, hipsters, churchies, scientists, nymphomaniacs, addicts, and dregs.

Aliens, Clowns & Geeks follows Eddy Pine (played by Richard's son, Bodhi Elfman), an out of work actor and lothario Casanova who finds himself in a very uncomfortable situation (he wakes up one morning with an obelisk up his ass). Suddenly at the center of interstellar mayhem, Eddy crosses paths with mad scientist Professor von

Scheisenberg played by French Stewart, priestly Father Mahoney played by George Wendt, and amorous Swedes Helga and Inga Svenson played by Rebecca Forsythe and Angeline-Rose Troy respectively. Angeline-Rose is also hysterical as Eddy's junkie mother. Hulking Steve Agee and diminutive Nic Novicki slay as terrestrial clowns Lenny and Fritz, foils to the film's legions of extraterrestrial clowns! The colorful alien horde is commanded by Emperor Beezel-Chugg played by the tiny but talented Verne Troyer in his final film role. Plus, *Aliens, Clowns & Geeks* sees Richard and Anastasia in multiple cameos.

Your ears will be tickled by *Aliens, Clowns & Geeks*' wall-to-wall dynamic score by Danny Elfman and Ego Plum. Circus flare collides with sci-fi sounds to create an eccentric auditory experience that's festive but also creepy and foreboding. The soundtrack includes tracks from Oingo Boingo and Richard's current band, Mambo Diabolico— bona fide fire!

Aliens, Clowns & Geeks is equal parts irreverent satire, raunchy comedy, and surreal fever-dream; a nonstop thrill-ride that will have you clutching your stomach with laughter. It's great entertainment and perfect for chasing away the COVID-19 Blues. Simultaneously a love letter to Hollywood and a self-deprecating send-up of the entertainment industry, the film is a 90-minute party you'll be glad you attended!

Aliens, Clowns & Geeks isn't for everyone—but horror fans aren't known for being easily offended. This is one of those films that can't be compared to anything else—a particularly bizarre experience with the ability to enrage, enthrall, but most certainly entertain!

So, what exactly is ***Aliens, Clowns & Geeks***? It's a one-of-a-kind experience you won't want to miss. It's exactly what we'd hope for from the founder of The Mystic Knights of the Oingo Boingo and the unhinged mind that created ***The Forbidden Zone***. It's a film certain to herald the next exciting chapter of Richard Elfman's artistic existence. ***Aliens, Clowns & Geeks*** is proof that in a world of absurdity, even nightmares can be fun!

Devon Sawa

ON THE FANATIC & THE NATIONAL TRAGEDY THAT TANKED POTENTIAL IDLE HANDS FRANCHISE

Method: *Phone*

Reflections: Devon Sawa: I love this guy. Recently, he's been in a string of truly amazing indie horrors. Specifically, **Hunter Hunter** deserves to be lauded as one of the best, most nihilistic, most soul-crushing experiences since **Hereditary**. It'd been great to see him most recently in a prominent role in the **Chucky** TV series. But I've had a bro-crush on Sawa since way back in the day.

In the late 1990s, my horror lust was still on the back burner, playing second fiddle to my hybrid punk/metal/electronica band, which was peaking in popularity. In the Back then, I was a frequent ritualistic and recreational user of cannabis, as I remain today. But things were so much different back then. There was a time, living in Los Angeles at the turn of the Millennium, where it was easier for me to score cocaine than cannabis. No lie. Medical Marijuana was still in its infancy and reserved, for the most part, to AIDS and cancer patients in Northern California. Legalization still seemed like an impossible dream.

But I remember watching *Idle Hands* on VHS, sitting on my friend's sofa, consuming copious bong rips, and really feelings seen. Seen and appreciated. Sure, the comedy angle didn't reinvent the wheel *Cheech & Chong* perfected in the 1970s, but the hybridization with horror was brilliant. I've probably watched *Idle Hands* 20 times over the years. Not only is Sawa brilliant as Anton, Elden Henson and Seth Green killed it (pun intended) as zombies with munchies. Jessica Alba was perfect as Molly and Vivica A. Fox slayed (okay, I'll quit the puns) as Debi LeCure. Over the years, I'd sometimes wonder why *Idle Hands* never got a sequel. Well, I'd get my answer.

I interviewed Sawa when he was making the rounds in support of *The Fanatic*, a film that had been produced under the working title *Moose*. The film was written and directed by Fred Durst. Yes, that Fred Durst, the frontman for the rap-rock outfit Limp Bizkit. I admit it, when news of *Moose/The Fantastic* began to come to light, I was intrigued—but not necessarily in a good way. I kind of expected it to be a disaster. I mean, what on Earth made Fred Durst, the guy who does it all for the nookie, think he had the skills to make a genre flick?

I've always had a chip on my shoulder about Fred Durst and Limp Bizkit. My own band was seeking fame when they broke. Not only did I abhor comparisons between my band and LB, I resented the fact that they had scored major fame while we struggled. Really petty shit, I acknowledge. A bit of a superiority complex, for sure

Before the film was released, I saw a clip of John Travolta on an entertainment new program where he said that Durst was the best director he'd ever worked with. Remember, Travolta has worked with Quentin Tarantino (*Pulp*

Fiction), Brian De Palma (*Carrie*), and John Woo (*Face/Off*) among many others throughout his illustrious career. Naming Durst as the best director he's ever worked with is no small compliment. Could it be true?

As you'll be able to tell from the interview that follows, I did eventually see *The Fantastic*, and I was genuinely impressed. I felt bad for throwing shade, for assuming that Durst's wacky, on-stage personae was proof that he was an inferior artist; for being a dick. And, ironically, I'd meet Durst in person at the Shockfest Film Festival in Las Vegas towards the end of 2019.

He looks so much different these days than he did in the 1990s. I had always predicted that Fred Durst would get fatter with age, but he's in great shape. He was also sporting a huge gray beard that gave him an almost professorial aura. I introduced myself as Josh from Dread Central and told him how much I had thoroughly enjoyed his film.

He, in turn, told me that he had read my interview with Sawa, and that he appreciated the fact that I was one of the few critics of *The Fanatic* to actually "get it". He also confided that he was unhappy with the final cut of his film, but had no recourse against the film's producers and distributor. It was a brief interaction, but one that completely changed my attitude towards Fred. I owe him an apology—and mad props.

———

ORIGINALLY PUBLISHED: **August 26, 2019**

When I first heard that Limp Bizkit frontman Fred Durst had written and directed a horror movie, I confess my knee-jerk reaction was less than objective. "Is he doing it all for the nookie?" I asked myself? Having just seen **The Fanatic**, however, I'm reminded of the adage advising against judging books by their covers. **The Fanatic** is fantastic!

Is Durst the next James Wan or Mike Flanagan? Probably not. Still, the rap-rocker delivered a riveting indie with genuine suspense, a film that benefits immensely from top-notch performances by its leads, John Travolta and Devon Sawa. Named Moose and Hunter respectively, Durst is obviously setting up a stalker/prey relationship—but it's deceptively straight-forward. In fact, this exploration of the dark side of fandom is anything but predictable.

I was lucky enough to sit down with Sawa last week to discuss **The Fanatic**, a film based on actual events. Give our exclusive convo a read below the film's synopsis.

Synopsis: *A rabid film fan stalks his favorite action hero and destroys the star's life.*

Dread Central: I know that I should be asking Fred Durst this question (and hopefully, I'll get the opportunity), but what do you know about the actual events that inspired *The Fanatic*?

*Devon Sawa: I met the guy the [Moose] is based on and he was actually on set while we were filming. So, if he was really as crazy as he was in the film, obviously he wouldn't have been there. But I think this guy, back in the Limp Bizkit days, just crossed a couple of lines, and Fred just thought, "What if he went all the way with this [obsessive fandom]?" And that's how **The Fanatic** started.*

DC: John Travolta is amazing, and I don't think I'm exaggerating when I say his portrayal of Moose was *Rain Man* caliber. What was it like working with him?

DS: I'm lucky because this was my second film working with John Travolta. But he was amazing and completely immersed himself in the role. Everyone on set, from craft services on up had to call him Moose. When he and Fred talked off set, he would still be Moose. He was completely dedicated and it shows. We all enjoyed watching that ride, man. It was great.

DC: This is more of an observation than a question, but I'd love to hear your thoughts. I loved how *The Fanatic* completely upends the concepts of villains and heroes. You have a bad guy antagonist in, Moose, who's so sympathetic he's almost lovable. And Hunter (your character) is a protagonist who you can relate to, but he's such an asshole you practically hate him. It's like the terms "antagonist" and "protagonist" don't even apply!

DS: That's exactly what we were trying to achieve and I'm so happy you picked up on that. When you're watching the climactic scene at the end of the movie, Moose is obviously doing things that he shouldn't be doing. At the same time, we don't like Hunter because it's like, does this guy have the right to be a dick just because of all this shit going on in his life? It's confusing, like, who should you be rooting for in this situation, and that's kind of what we were going for. Fame can be stressful and some people just handle it better than others.

DC: How have you handled the dark side of fame? Like the character Hunter, you actually are a horror movie star with a large following. So, what's the creepiest, real-life fanatic experience you've had and how did you deal with it?

*DS: I'm lucky because, for the most part, I've stayed under the radar. I don't go to premieres or big parties or whatnot, so I've been pretty blessed not to have these kinds of negative experiences. Back in my childhood when I was on **Teen Beat** and all that stuff, I'd get some* *crazy fan letters and boxes with girls sending me their braziers and locks of their hair and stuff like that. But other than that, unlike Fred Durst, I haven't had a psycho yet!*

DC: Let's switch gears: *Idle Hands* turned 20 years old in April. How do you feel looking back on that film?

*DS: I just did one of my first horror conventions ever because it's the 20th Anniversary of **Idle Hands**. It was nice to hear the love people have for that film. It's crazy because it didn't do that well at the box office, and it came out at the same time as Columbine, but people loved that film. It's still to this day one of the best times I ever had on a set.*

DC: That's interesting because I didn't connect the dates up until you just mentioned it. Do you think that the timing with the Columbine massacre in Colorado had a negative impact on the film's box office draw?

*DS: I do. We were supposed to have a premiere for **Idle Hands**, but that got cancelled after Columbine happened. The film was completely removed from a lot of theaters, especially in Colorado. **Idle Hands** came out right around the same time as **Scream** and **I Know What You Did Last Summer**, and that big teen horror film craze. So, while we were making it, **Idle Hands** seemed like a shoe-in to be the next successful franchise. But then Columbine happened and—it is what it is. But I did **Final Destination** a couple years later, so it was definitely an important stepping stone for me and something I'm extremely proud of.*

DC: You should be! *Final Destination* was definitely your big breakout moment, but those of us who enjoy horror and cannabis in equal measure

have always had a soft spot in our hearts for *Idle Hands*!

DS: I've got to give it a watch again soon to see if it stands the test of time.

DC: Is there anything else you want to tell us about *The Fanatic* before I let you go?

DS: It's one of those indie films that all of us just put our heart and soul into. John Travolta put his entire life into this film, and it really shows, so I hope people check it out!

The Fanatic arrives in select theaters this Friday, August 30th and on digital and On Demand beginning September 6th, 2019.

Return to The Overlook Hotel

TALKING TO MIKE FLANAGAN ABOUT DOCTOR SLEEP

Method: *Set Visit*

Reflections: Stephen King enjoyed quite a Renaissance in the late 2010s, one that continued into the 2020s (though with arguably less fervor). And I was lucky enough to enjoy two set visits for productions based on the lauded author's works. The first, as you already know, was ***Pet Sematary***. And while my coverage of ***Doctor Sleep*** was objectively thin, I'm glad to have an opportunity to expand upon my experience here.

Doctor Sleep was shot on a soundstage in Atlanta. So while, on paper, it might seem a less exotic destination than, say, Montreal, it was nonetheless an epic expedition for this horror fan. I was part of a larger group than my previous set visit; whereas there were only four of us on the set of ***Pet Sematary***, there were about a dozen genre reporters in attendance this time. Still, the experience felt intimate and intense.

It was the first time I had the opportunity to meet Michael Sprague in person. Mike, as I call him, had been a staff writer at Dread Central since before I was brought into the fold. In this instance, he was covering **Doctor Sleep** for JoBlo, another entertainment website where he also featured prominently. I've always had a ton of respect for Mike. Like me, he's a journalist who is inspired by love of cinema as opposed to monetary gain or elevated status. And he loved being on set—like a kid in a candy shop. We all were.

After the interview, Mike Flanagan personally gave us a tour of the exact replica of the Overlook Hotel. Keep in mind, this was before anyone knew that the location would feature at all in **Doctor Sleep** (it was destroyed in the novel, but not in Stanley Kubrick's adaptation). They went to great measures to recreate the iconic multi-leveled main lobby, down to the smallest detail. Then aged everything by about 40 years as though it had been abandoned all this time. There were even blood stains at the bottom of the stairwell from when Wendy Torrance (Shelley Duvall) clocked Jack Torrance (Jack Nicholson) with a baseball bat. And did you know that we never actually see an entrance or exit in The Overlook? The only time we ever see someone leaving is when Wendy and Danny (Danny Lloyd) escape out the window.

Best of all, a treat every adult horror fan would treasure: There was an oversized Big Wheel that we were all invited to ride along the upper level of hotel rooms. It was a giddy blast and, even though it was all fun and games, I half expected to encounter The Grady Twins (Lisa and Louise Burns) around every corner. What a fantastic experience.

So why, given how much I enjoyed the experience, was my ultimate coverage of **Doctor Sleep** so slim? All I can say is, those were crazy days at Dread Central. Between my daily responsibilities and the amount of traveling I had been doing (back and forth from Oakland to Los Angeles on the reg, plus trips to big conventions and prominent film festivals) I was spread thin. I remember feeling like I barely had time to stop and breathe sometimes.

But I've said it before and I'll say it again: When you love what you do, you never work a day in your life. I was living the dream, fully immersed in the world of horror, and I wouldn't trade it for the world. Things were changing at Dread Central, and I had plenty of opportunities to prove my worth.

Mike Flannagan is an absolutely wonderful human being. His successes are well-earned. I'd treasure another opportunity to hang out, professionally or otherwise, should the opportunity present itself.

———

ORIGINALLY PUBLISHED: **September 5, 2019**

I'm sitting in Room 237 of the Overlook Hotel, talking with director Mike Flanagan about his sequel to **The Shining**, **Doctor Sleep**. For a life-long horror fan, it's an experience both exhilarating and surreal. In spite of the missing walls and ceilings, in spite of the cameras, equipment and crew running in all directions, it feels like I'm inside a genre classic, a piece of horror history—and a future masterpiece. The attention to detail is profound, and Flanagan exudes an infectious passion for this project.

The mechanics of producing a sequel to **The Shining** are complex and surprisingly political. Stephen King was infamously dissatisfied with Stanley Kubrick's 1980 adaptation of his novel, which deviated immensely from the source material. Still, when most people hear "**The Shining**," they think of the film, not the novel. So how will **Doctor Sleep** stay true to both the novel it's based on and fans' expectations? It's a tightrope walk to be certain.

"The thinking behind that was, you know, trying to straddle that line between honoring the source material of the novel and the importance of Kubrick's film," Flanagan explains. "For us and, I think for a lot of the readers, when I first read [**Doctor Sleep**], I loved what he did with Dan and I loved kind of revisiting that universe. But I just had this real ache to go back to The Overlook and I was really, you know, kind of bummed when the book didn't do that. And so, for us it was a question of how do we try to combine those two worlds in a way that's going to make Stephen feel really satisfied with what we did and also honor the legacy of the Kubrick film and what it means to cinephiles. It's one of the most influential, if not the most influential horror movie of all time. So, that was a tough call, and we needed to get Stephen on board, but when we explained how we wanted to do it he was actually really enthusiastic about it, which was quite a pleasant surprise."

Synopsis: *Struggling with alcoholism, Dan Torrance remains traumatized by the sinister events that occurred at the Overlook Hotel when he was a child. His hope for a peaceful existence soon becomes shattered when he meets Abra, a teen who shares his extrasensory gift of the "shine." Together, they form an unlikely alliance to battle the True Knot, a cult whose members try to feed off the shine of innocents to become immortal.*

Richard Brake

TALKS JOINING THE FIREFLY CLAN IN 3 FROM HELL
& DOOM HEAD SPINOFF

Method: *Phone*

Originally Published: September 9, 2019

Theatergoers checking out Rob Zombie's *3 From Hell* during its three-day run next week will meet the newest member of the murderous Firefly clan: Winslow Foxworth Coltrane (aka "Foxy") played by Welsh actor Richard Brake. Fans of Zombie's catalog will remember the actor from his arresting portrayal of Doom-Head in *31*. he also played Gary Scott in *2009's Halloween II*. But even though this isn't Zombie and Brake's first collaboration, it is the actor's first appearance in *The Devil's Rejects* franchise.

We were lucky enough to sit down with Brake to discuss what it was like being a newcomer in the already-established Firefly clan, while also addressing those persistent rumors about a Doom-Head feature film. Check out our conversation below.

Dread Central: Between playing Doom-Head in *31* and the mad chemist (and tiger owner) in *Mandy*,

it seems like your horror pedigree has really risen. How does it feel to be a burgeoning icon?

Richard Brake: Oh I love it, mostly because I love the roles I've gotten to play. I'm really lucky. First Rob asked me to do Doom-Head [in **31**] *and then Panos [Cosmatos] asked me to play that crazy, drug-manufacturing madman in* **Mandy**. *It's been great and it's been really lovely to meet fans of these films. It's a real treat.*

DC: Years ago, we heard rumors of a potential Doom-Head spinoff movie. What's the scoop?

RB: You know, Rob has so many irons in the fire all the time. He's such a creative force. If the idea comes to him and he gets the creative urge, then it'll happen. And it'll happen like it always does: I'll get a phone call [impersonates Rob Zombie] "Hey man, what are you doing in July or… next week?" And that'll be it. We'll be out making it. But you never know. With Rob, it may happen or it may never happen. It all depends on Rob's creative urges, and that's what I love about him.

And that's what I love about this film. I think it's been 13 or 14 years since **The Devil's Rejects**. *And everybody was wanting some kind of sequel or trilogy. But as much pressure as he was getting, Rob didn't make* **3 From Hell** *until he really felt he was ready and it was something he wanted to do. As an artist, you've got to respect that. So hopefully, for the lovely character Doom-Head the day will come!*

DC: Well, I can tell you for certain there are a ton of fans who would love to see a Doom-Head movie. Now, *3 From Hell* **is your 3rd Rob Zombie movie, but your first in the** *Rejects* **saga/trilogy. How did it feel to enter this established franchise with such a major role?**

RB: Well first of all, when Rob asked me, I was totally over the Moon. I was beyond excited when I first heard. Then I sat down and thought about the character. I did the same work I would on any job. And whenever I work with Rob, I always get this creative inspiration. I'm sure everyone does. There's a feeling of "I never want to let him down," and, "I want to do my best to help achieve what he's going for". So, when I go in with that attitude it never goes wrong.

I came on set about four days late because I was working on another film in Spain. I literally flew home to London, changed my clothes, and flew out to LA to work on **3 From Hell***. And the first scene was with Otis, myself, and Baby. Otis [Bill Moseley] and I were in the room and Sheri [Moon Zombie] walks in in full Baby-Mode. And the camera's on me but I'm watching her just absolutely going for it. Crazy and just brilliant. And I'm sitting there as Richard thinking, "Man she's incredible, she so good!" And then I thought, "Oh shit, the camera's on me!" And then I realized that's probably what Foxy's thinking. And so, what I love is that it was written in a way that felt like I really belonged in the family and we really gelled. One of the things I loved about the whole experience and becoming part of the Firefly world was the chemistry between the three of us. And I hope that's reflected in the film, because it was definitely there while we were shooting.*

DC: It does, and the *3 From Hell* feels almost like a celebration of that bond. How did the vibe on set compare to the vibe while shooting *Halloween II* and *31*?

RB: There's always a celebratory vibe on the set of Rob's films. Everyone's creative juices are on full flow. That's one of the things I love about Rob and why he's, without a doubt, my favorite director. All the directors I've worked with have been fantastic, but if someone put a gun to my head and said I could only pick one, it would be Rob. He inspires me and everyone on set to be the best. There's a real feeling of family. Celebratory is a good word. Even though you're making a film about slaughtering people and committing all kinds of mayhem and madness, you're having a blast doing it.

DC: *The Devil's Rejects* felt like an ending, but *3 From Hell* feels like a new beginning. Did Zombie talk at all about making another Firefly movie?

RB: Once again, it's totally up to Rob and his creative urges. He won't do it until he's ready—if he ever does it at all. But if he does do another one, it's going to be fucking brilliant, that's for sure.

3 From Hell will reunite the Firefly clan (Bill Moseley, Sheri Moon Zombie, and Sid Haig); the film will also feature Richard Brake, Emilio Rivera, Danny Trejo, Kevin Jackson, Wade Williams, Jeff Daniel Phillips, Pancho Moler, Daniel Roebuck, David Ury, Sean Whalen, Austin Stoker, Dee Wallace, Bill Oberst Jr., Dot-Marie Jones, and Tom Papa.

Rob Zombie

EXPLAINS HOW 3 FROM HELL COULD HAVE BEEN MUCH DIFFERENT

Method: *Phone*

Reflections: "Hey, you remind me of Rob Zombie," say half the people I meet walking down the street. We're not twins or anything, but there just aren't that many heavily-tattooed middle-aged white dudes walking around Los Angeles these days.

People I meet over social media sometimes tell me they're initially intimidated by me, again siting the Rob Zombie resemblance. Of course, anyone alarmed by my appearance is usually immediately disarmed when I open my mouth. Yes, I may look like Rob Zombie, but I sound like Jeff Spicoli.

Love him or hate him, the films of Rob Zombie simply can't be ignored or pigeonholed. And while I never really followed him as a musician, I've watched his career behind the camera with morbid glee. Of course I was excited to talk to the man, the legend, when the opportunity presented itself.

This was published just days before the release of *3 From Hell* and, therefore, mere days before Sid Haig would pass from this world. It makes Zombie's reflections regarding the iconic actor even more poignant.

I remember this interview took place at 8 AM, and I was surprised that the rockstar maverick would even be awake at such an ungodly hour. But that's the thing about Rob Zombie, isn't it? He refuses to be stereotyped and constantly defies expectations.

———

ORIGINALLY PUBLISHED: **September 16, 2019**

Global content leader Lionsgate and Saban Films are unleashing horror icon and heavy metal mastermind Rob Zombie's *3 From Hell*, the follow-up to **House of 1,000 Corpses** and *The Devil's Rejects*, as the next chapter in the blood-soaked crime saga. The film will be released in nearly 900 select movie theaters on September 16, 17 and 18, 2019 through Fathom's Digital Broadcast Network. Fathom Events will broadcast the unrated version to theaters with each night featuring unique bonus content.

No one really expected a sequel to *The Devil's Rejects* for one specific reason: The central Firefly Clan was killed 15 years ago! Even Rob Zombie considered *Rejects* the end of the story. It was only after a decade + of seeing how much these characters meant to fans that the shock-rocker-turned-filmmaker considered revisiting the saga first launched in 2003 with *House of 1,000 Corpses*. The potential return of the Firefly Family was a common topic of conversation during horror convention panels.

When the urge finally hit him, Zombie knew time was of the essence: "Everyone's getting older and you never know how much time you have left," he tells us. "It was now or never." While it's difficult to acknowledge (and hard to even write about) the health of Captain Spaulding actor Sid Haig was a major concern and had a profound effect on the direction of *3 From Hell*. Read our exclusive interview below to find out how.

Dread Central: How hard was it for you to come up with a way to essentially bring the Firefly Family back to from the dead?

*Rob Zombie: I used a lot of Terry Reid songs in **The Devil's Rejects** off his album **Seed of Memory**. And there was one song "Faith to Arise" which I used for the end titles. And that song would always make me think of a way to start the next movie. I'd go, "Oh well, whatever, I'm never going to do it," and I would put it out of my mind, but it would just never go away. That track, always sounded like a missing track off **The Devil's Rejects** and that's what inspired me to get the next one going.*

DC: Even though Captain Spaulding only has a small part in 3 From Hell, his presence is felt throughout the film. Can you talk a bit about how his absence is as important as his presence?

RZ: Well, his absence is just something that was unavoidable. Because the "3" from Hell are Captain Spaulding, Otis, and Baby, and that's the script I wrote. That was the movie I was getting ready to make. And then, about three weeks out from the first day of shooting, I remember it so clearly: I was driving to the set, you know, the sound-stage to oversee the building of the sets and I thought to myself, "This is the most prepared I've been for a movie—ever! What could possibly go wrong?" And my phone rings and its Sid calling, saying, "I've been in the hospital for a while. I'm out of the hospital but now I'm in a physical rehabilitation facility." And I thought, "Oh my God, what is going on!" So, we talked for a while and he told me what was wrong (which I'm not going to say). I went and visited him and when I went, he looked like he had lost about 80 pounds. And I thought, "Well, I've got to do something because he isn't physically capable of playing the part as I wrote it. Not possible." So, I kept rewriting the movie, lessening Captain Spaulding little by little, thinking "Okay, he can do this much. In a week he'll be better and he'll be out of there and feeling good." But it just never really worked out that way.

With him being almost 80-years-old, he had to get cleared by a doctor and an insurance company before Lionsgate would let him work. He couldn't pass the physical and they wouldn't clear him so I'm like, "Oh great, now they won't even let him be in the movie!" So, I went to Lionsgate and they agreed to let him in to shoot as much as I could. Because, Sid and I had talked about this. He wants to be in the movie and the character is important to the story and the fans. So, I shot as much as we could and did my best to complete the journey of Captain Spaulding. But what it is is not what I was planning in the years leading up to it. But what can you do? You plan one thing but Life has another plan.

DC: As we speak, Sid Haig is in the hospital recovering from an accident. He's been upfront about the fact that his health has been declining over the past few years. Do you think Captain Spaulding would have had a bigger part in 3 From Hell had Sid been in better shape?

RZ: Oh yeah, he was through the whole movie. Richard Brake's character, Foxy, didn't exist in the original script. That was something I made up as I could see that Sid couldn't do the movie. So. in the last three weeks leading up to shooting the script was in a constant state of rewriting—constant chaos because of Sid's health. And I kept hoping for the best and it just didn't pan out. And I was happy when he came in and I'm happy with what we got because for a while I didn't think we were going to get anything. At the end of the day, I think everything worked out great. It wasn't what I had planned, but for all the chaos we endured, the film turned out great.

DC: What made you decide that Richard Brake was ready for a starring role in one of your films?

RZ: I had worked with Richard twice before. He had a small role in **Halloween II** *and a major part in* **31***. I love how he works, I love his vibe, we get along great, and he fits right in with everybody. The group of actors I work with all have a certain vibe and you either fit in or you don't. Richard totally fits in.*

When I called Richard to do the movie, I wasn't even sure if he was available. He works a lot. At that point, he was in Spain shooting a movie. I was like, "Aw, fuck man!" because if he couldn't do it, I didn't know what I was going to do. It was complete chaos. But it's funny because we were on the phone and he said, "Well, my hair's kind of long now and I grew a beard for this movie." I was like, "Perfect! Don't do anything! Just get to LA." So, he flew to LA as soon as he wrapped and got to work immediately. I think he read the script for the first time on the plane coming over.

DC: He definitely kills it (pun intended) as Foxy! Something Brake told me during our recent interview is that he'd love to do a Doom-Head feature film. What are the chances you'll make a 31 spinoff?

RZ: I haven't given that any thought, so who knows. Every movie I've ever made is a "who knows?" scenario. Every movie I thought I was making next isn't what actually happens. So, who knows!

DC: *3 From Hell* is more fun than *House of 1,000 Corpses* and *The Devil's Rejects*. There was almost

a celebratory tone to it. Was it more fun to film than the first two Firefly movies?

RZ: Not necessarily. For some reason, all of those movies have always been the most fun. I don't know what it is. Some movies are fun to make and some are... not! [Laughs] But these three movies were always a great time and that has everything to do with the vibe between the people. And even though a lot of people were new, I tried to bring back as many people as I could from the past Firefly movies, even in the crew department. It was part of my plan to recapture the spirit of **Rejects**. *And it's amazing how quickly that happened. As soon as the wig went on Bill Moseley and Sheri [Moon Zombie] was standing next to him with her hair all curly, I was like, "Wow, it doesn't feel like 15 years since the last time we did this. It seems like just yesterday."*

DC: Fantastic! So, what's next for the Firefly family?

RZ: I don't know! Maybe once this thing is out my mind will start thinking in that direction.

DC: Is there anything else you'd like to tell our readers before I let you go?

RZ: I've been trying not to say too much because it's hard these days not to spoil a movie. But I wanted to bring things full circle in a unique way. So, there's some of the vibe from **1,000 Corpses** *and some vibe of* **The Devil's Rejects** *creating a new vibe for* **3 From Hell**. *I wanted every movie to be its own journey but somehow they all work together. I never want to talk down to the audience and go, "Here are all those catchphrases you're waiting for and here's the same shit you were waiting for," because I think that's cheesy. It might seem cool the first time you see it, but ultimately it feels hollow.*

3 From Hell will reunite the Firefly clan (Bill Moseley, Sheri Moon Zombie, and Sid Haig); the film will also feature Richard Brake, Emilio Rivera, Danny Trejo, Kevin Jackson, Wade Williams, Jeff Daniel Phillips, Pancho Moler, Daniel Roebuck, David Ury, Sean Whalen, Austin Stoker, Dee Wallace, Bill Oberst Jr., Dot-Marie Jones, and Tom Papa.

Bill Moseley

ON 3 FROM HELL AND WHY "CHOP-TOP" NEVER
RETURNED TO TEXAS

Method: *Phone*

Originally Published: September 17, 2019

Dread Central was lucky enough to sit down with Otis Driftwood actor and horror icon Bill Moseley to discuss the Firefly Family's miraculous survival following the bullet-ridden finale of *The Devil's Rejects*, along with other details about *3 From Hell* (now playing in select theaters). Fans of the *Texas Chainsaw Massacre* movies will also learn why Chop-Top only appeared in one film. Read on!

Dread Central: When Rob Zombie first approached you about doing *3 From Hell*, were you as surprised as the rest of us to learn that the Firefly Clan had survived the conclusion of *The Devil's Rejects*?

Bill Moseley: I was certainly happy to get the call because it's a wonderful franchise and Otis is a great character. I was happy to hear that we had somehow, someway we had managed lurched our way into a third movie. For many years, Sid Haig and I sat next to each other at a host of horror conventions. And we would kind of joke with every-body, when somebody would ask if there was going to be a sequel [to **The Devil's Rejects**] *we'd say "No," and then in unison, "because we're fucking dead!" And so that's been the conclusion most of us drew.*

Then there was the question, "If there were a sequel, how would it work?" Would it be that we died and went to Hell and the Devil rejected us? Would it be the worst kind of Hollywood devices where someone wakes up and it was all a dream? And I think the way it came together was probably the best because if it were a dream, then that would be mean. And if we came back from Hell that would be supernatural and that would throw things into a different realm of reality. But the way this goes I think is the best of all possible worlds. And, of course, I was thrilled that the Fireflies were going to fly again!

DC: Hell yeah! I was amazed at how well Richard Brake became a part of the Firefly family, even though he wasn't in the first two Rejects movies. The chemistry was real and his inclusion felt very authentic. What was it like to work with him in *3 From Hell*?

BM: I loved working with Richard! I certainly thought he was an incredible force to be reckoned with in **31** *[as Doom-Head]. I'd since seen him in* **Mandy** *where he had a great scene—with the tiger! [Laughs]. He's a very solid actor. And when he came on the set he was very opened and humbled in the sense that he was very excited to be part of the family. Sometimes, actors coming into a situation like that will have some false bravado and can be tough to deal with. Richard came in opened and ready to play and was so much fun to work with. We really had a ball.*

The first time I got an eyeful of Richard's improv talent was when we're in the motel and Sheri [Moon Zombie] goes off to do her thing. I suggested we play Fish, so we got the cards out and started playing Go Fish. And through the course of that scene, Richard starts talking about his porno film ambitions. What he was saying was so wild! [Laughs] We really just had so much fun because I love doing that too, just going off. That was hilarious. Then I saw it again in the scene with Bill Obrest, Jr. and my wife (Lucinda Jenney), the two bounty hunters in the woods. And Richard just starts going off again and he does it in such a compelling way. Slow, smart, and just so funny. All in all, the Foxy character was a wonderful bonus. He and Sheri [Moon Zombie] already had a relationship from 31 and it didn't take long for me to really bond with him as a person as well as an actor and a character.

DC: I was surprised by the genuinely upbeat nature of *3 From Hell* (at times). It had aspects of a road trip movie and even a buddy flick. And then we see the Firefly family enjoying themselves without even raping or murdering anybody. It made me think Zombie was intentionally trying to show a brighter side of the Fireflies in order to turn you from villains to antiheroes. That's not really a question, but I'd like to get your thoughts.

*BM: That's a wonderful observation. As far as it went, obviously, with Captain Spaulding (who Rob always called "The Ronald McDonald of the franchise") not being part of the journey, that leaves a huge void. It's interesting that we do certainly enjoy mayhem and mischief, but I don't know. Probably because the Fireflies are missing Captain Spaulding, it takes the fun and the heart out of murdering and torturing people—at least for the time being. I think we're still trying to get on a new footing with Foxy. There are some genuine feelings and there's a great scene in a Mexican hotel room where we're missing Spaulding. So, there's kind of that sense of mortality which you don't see in the first two movies. There's a sense of growing older and wiser, but at the same time, there's really is no plan. I don't know if that somehow works into the perception of the characters. It's kind of like the ending of **Butch Cassidy and the Sundance Kid**. There's a kind of existential emptiness, like, "What do we do now?*

Do we just go shoot up the next people we find? Do we go back to the states?" If you think about it, the only one who really has a plan is Foxy.

DC: Whereas *The Devil's Rejects* felt like an ending, *3 From Hell* feels like the first chapter of a new beginning. I know that another Firefly movie depends on Zombie's schedule and creative urges, but in your mind, as Otis Driftwood, what should come next?

BM: You know, I don't know. We have a car and the film takes place in the 1960s or 1970s so it probably wouldn't be too hard for us to get back to the States. I don't know if we'd press on to Mexico City, but I don't really see us in a bungalow on the beach, just drinking tequila and sucking limes! But I don't know. As Otis, I'd certainly rather go back to "civilization" and fuck things up. Maybe even go back to the Firefly house. But I don't know what the plan is. The Fireflies are really good at acting and reacting in the moment. They had a plan to break Baby out of jail, but there was never a big plan. Maybe that's something for Rob to figure out.

DC: Switching gears for just a second, *Texas Chainsaw Massacre* fans know that there was almost a Chop-Top spinoff movie (tentatively titled *American Massacre*). Considering Chop-Top has remained iconic since the 1980's is there any chance we'll see that character again? And would you even be interested in reviving the role?

BM: Well I certainly would, because Chop-Top is still with me every day—no pleasure to my children necessarily, or the dog for that matter. I'm always going, "Dog will hunt!" It's funny because when we did **Texas Chainsaw Massacre 3D** *in 2013 I played Drayton Sawyer. And I remember when the producer called me up and said they were making a new* **Chainsaw** *movie, some kind of spinoff from* *the original, "and we want you to play Drayton". And I just thought that was like asking Curly to play Moe in a remake of **The Three Stooges**. Why wouldn't I play Chop-Top?*

*What I found out is that Lionsgate owned the rights to the characters and Chop-Top wasn't included because he was created for the sequel [**Texas Chainsaw Massacre Part 2**, released in 1986]. The sequel is owned by Sony so they didn't have the rights to Chop-Top. They would have had to negotiate for the character with Sony, which they didn't do. So that's why I ended up playing Drayton which was a great challenge and a lot of fun to do nonetheless.*

I would love to play Chop-Top again, but we'd have to rescue him from Sony's legal department.

DC: Let's start a petition!

BM: [Laughs] Yeah, let's start a petition!

DC: Do you have anything else you'd like to share with our readers before I let you go?

*BM: I did want to give a shout to David Daniel, the cinematographer on **3 From Hell**. He's been with Rob since **The Devil's Rejects** and he's a great cinematographer. Getting the gang back together doesn't just mean the actors in front of the camera but a lot of the crew. I want to give a shout-out to those who don't get as much of the spotlight as they deserve.*

3 From Hell will reunite the Firefly clan (Bill Moseley, Sheri Moon Zombie, and Sid Haig); the film will also feature Richard Brake, Emilio Rivera, Danny Trejo, Kevin Jackson, Wade Williams, Jeff Daniel Phillips, Pancho Moler, Daniel Roebuck, David Ury, Sean Whalen, Austin Stoker, Dee Wallace, Bill Oberst Jr., Dot-Marie Jones, and Tom Papa.

Ready for Some High Hell?

Method: *Email*

Reflections: It was the best of times, it was the worst of times.

If I ever do publish a memoir of my time at Dread Central, ***Chronic Horror*** will have its own chapter. In fact, ***Chronic Horror*** might get its own book. ***Chronic Horror*** was my baby, my brainchild. And I still have high hopes for the show, sincerely believing that it will manifest once again, someday, as something even better.

By October, 2019, I was living my wildest dreams. I had recently been promoted to Editor-in-Chief of Dread Central, I had just met the woman who would become my wife and the mother of my child, and I had my own talk show on the verge of being released. I was on top of the mountain. None of us had any idea that we were looking down the barrel of a previously inconceivable pandemic.

Patrick Ewald, CEO of Epic Pictures and co-owner of Dread Central had mentioned for a while that he hoped to create original streaming content for the site. So in late 2018, I dropped him an email, letting him know that I had a few ideas he might want to consider. He didn't respond, so I just went along doing my thing. So when he said he wanted to talk on the phone in March of 2019, I really had no idea what it would be about. I thought I might be getting fired, actually!

"So tell me your ideas for a show."

"Oh," I replied, relieved and somewhat surprised. "How about a video podcast?" I suggested, pitching something along the lines of **Shockwaves**, which was performing like gangbusters over at Blumhouse.com. But Patrick had no interest in starting a podcast.

"There are already a million horror podcasts out there. It's too late to get into that game." It's ironic because, in 2021, Patrick would double-down on podcasting, creating an entire Podcast Network beneath the Dread Central umbrella. This, at a time when the podcasting sphere had never been more inundated, the pandemic having encouraged everyone with a webcam to jump into the arena.

"What other ideas have you got?" Patrick inquired. Well, I did have this other idea, something that I'd been kicking around in my head for a while, something that would unite two of my passions, something that would benefit from my mad interviewing skills. But I was a bit nervous about pitching it.

"What about… a show about horror movies and cannabis?" At the time, I had no idea if Patrick was "hip". Sure, cannabis was now legal in California (and other states), but there were still negative connotations associated with the lifestyle. Patrick could have been "square" for all I knew—or in AA maybe. And even though folks immediately assume that a white guy with dreadlocks smokes cannabis, I had just officially outed myself as a "stoner". Had I damaged my reputation? Would Patrick now think I'm a slacker, or a bonehead?

He paused for a long time before finally responding: "Well, what would we call it?"

"*High on Horror*." I replied without missing a beat.

Another long pause. Sweat was literally creeping down my neck. "Let's do it," he said. "Let's have a meeting the next time you're down in Los Angeles." And that was it. *Chronic Horror* was born.

While researching, I discovered a prominent Facebook group called "High on Horror". Wanting to respect that they established the "brand" first, I brainstormed new ideas for the show's name before zeroing in on *Chronic Horror*, which I actually think is an improvement. There's a pun to it; "chronic horror" basically means "never-ending dread" while "chronic" alone implies all of the wonders of cannabis culture.

I'll be the first to say it: There isn't an inherent link between horror fandom and cannabis culture. But during my travels, I'd come to discover that many horror fans are down with the herb. Plus, I was already somewhat in the habit of conducting my interviews high, especially over the phone. Being high while interviewing made for more interesting conversations, and I imagined what it would be like actually sharing a joint with someone while I interviewed them.

First and foremost, Patrick set out to connect me with a director, someone with experience to help me flesh out this concept and bring it to fruition. While Mike Mendez (the director of *Big Ass Spider*, an Epic Pictures release) initially expressed interest, the job ultimately went to the dynamic duo of director Hank Braxtan (*Snake Outta Compton*) and his beautiful wife, producer Arielle Brachfeld.

Producer Arielle Brachfeld and Director Hank Braxtan

It was decided that *Chronic Horror* would take place in a spooky "Scare Lair". I would invite guests in for an interview before getting them high. Once fully imbibed, we'd be served grotesque delectables, courtesy of Kaci Hansen, the

Homicidal Homemaker. And then, high as kites, we'd watch a horror movie, riffing throughout MST2K style.

It took months of planning and organization before we were ready to film the first four episodes of a planned 12-episode "season" in September 2019. Our first batch of guests included Camilla Jackson, Dylan Reynolds, and Richard and Anastasia Elfman. We also shot a "field trip" episode where soundman Richard Trejo and I visited SOTA effects studio (where we raised jolly mayhem and drank fake blood).

A second batch of episodes (five through eight) were shot in November, including a "Live" reunion episode and a "paranormal investigation" at Cobb Estate. The plan was to finish the season by shooting the final four episodes in February 2020, but that never happened for obvious reasons.

By the time the dust settled and the worst of the pandemic seemed behind us, Patrick Ewald no longer had any interest in producing **Chronic Horror**. "Times have changed," he told me. The show was too expensive to make. I was invited to turn the show into a video podcast, but there would be no more sets, no more live guests or field trips, no more puppets, and no more Homicidal Homemaker. No more magic stash box, no more smoke machines, no more crew. In terms of releasing originals to stream, Patrick was now focused on acquiring completed content. This was near the end of my tenure with Dread Central, and it was definitely an indication that I was outgrowing my position.

I think Patrick missed the boat. I think combining the worlds of horror and cannabis creates a winning combination. And the cannabis industry is flush with money, so making forays into that industry would have been nothing but lucrative. And while Patrick may have cooled, I know that a revamped ***Chronic Horror*** can be a hit (pun intended!). Truthfully, I think the taboo nature of the show's content (the issues it posed on platforms like YouTube) gave him cold feet. I'm sure that's not how he sees it.

The intersection of horror fandom and cannabis culture is ripe for exploration. I hope those of you reading about ***Chronic Horror*** now for the first time will seek it out online (it's currently streaming on Tubi) because I'm incredibly proud of what we accomplished. And if you're a fan of cannabis like I am, we can dream together about a day when the smoke will flow freely once again!

The article below was indeed written by me, but we thought it would carry more clout if it appeared at least somewhat objective. That's why it's written in the third person, and why it was published under a different staff writer's name.

———

ORIGINALLY PUBLISHED: **October 1, 2019**

This isn't just the beginning of a new month, it's the beginning of a bold new chapter in Dread Central's history. In an effort to bring our readers the kind of exciting and original content they're requesting, we're proud to announce ***Chronic Horror***, our latest streaming series! What's ***Chronic Horror***, you ask?

Synopsis: ***Chronic Horror*** *is a short form interview series that crosses the streams of the worlds of horror filmmaking, horror fandom, and cannabis culture. Join our host Josh Millican, a cannabis and horror expert who takes you on a ride full of laughs and enlightenment.*

"When I was told Dread Central was looking for more streaming content in an effort to forge a new identity, I decided to pitch this idea I'd been kicking around for a while," Josh Millican explains. "Thankfully, Epic Pictures' CEO Patrick Ewald was confident enough to back me, and ***Chronic Horror*** was born!

"The next step in bringing this zany vision to life was finding the right director and producer. That's when Patrick hooked me up with the dynamic duo, Hank Braxtan and Arielle Brachfeld (***Snake Outta Compton***). I couldn't have done it without them!"

Says Hank Braxtan: "Josh pitched me the idea for ***Chronic Horror*** and I said 'Yes'.

"The first few episodes were a lot of fun to be a part of, and I think we've made a show that is cool, even if we still use the term 'lit'. Ha ha ha! But honestly, it's been a great experience and we've really tried to approach it with an open mind, embracing an evolving landscape where cannabis is being decriminalized more and more. One of the biggest challenges we've had in making the show is convincing the abundance of filmmakers, especially horror filmmakers, who regularly use cannabis, to admit to it on a TV show. I think there are a lot of folks who still can't get past the societal stigma, so they still prefer to keep it on the down low. I think one filmmaker told us 'My mom still doesn't know I smoke weed, so I'm trying to keep it that way'."

Arielle Brachfeld adds: "Through ***Chronic Horror***, Dread Central is yet again breaking new ground in the horror genre by allowing fans to interact with horror culture and filmmakers in a whole new way, while breaking through a stigma still present in our society."

Each week, Josh will be joined by his undead dummy/side-kick "Mr. Munchies"; Kaci aka "The Homicidal Home-maker" is also a fixture, producing the kind of gourmet, horror-themed treats that have already earned her thousands of social media followers. Our first batch of guests includes Los Angeles promoter Camilla Jackson, Dylan Reynolds (writer/director of *4/20 Massacre*), Richard Elfman (Mystic Knights of the Oingo Boingo, *Forbidden Zone*) and his Scream Queen wife Anastasia Elfman, filmmaker Richard Trejo, and special effects mastermind and SOTA co-owner Matt Falletta.

Josh is the first to admit: "You don't have to smoke or vape to be a *Chronic Horror* fan. The show is for anyone who enjoys getting high on horror!"

Los Angeles area horror fans will also have the opportunity to attend a *Chronic Horror* Live! event at the Arena Cinelounge in Hollywood on Saturday, November 16th. You'll be able to meet the cast and crew and enjoy some CBD-infused drinks, all while having a blazing good time! Full details will follow.

We hope you're just as excited as we are to embark on this spooky and stony adventure. If you enjoy *Chronic Horror* and want to see more, let us know—because we aim to please!

Sean William Scott

TALKS ABOUT BLOODLINE & PLAYING A SERIAL KILLER

Method: Phone

Originally Published: October 10, 2019

He got his big break playing a horny teen in ***American Pie***. Now, see Seann William Scott like never before in Blumhouse's ***Bloodline***, currently streaming on multiple VOD platforms. Scott plays a stone-cold serial killer who's so unnerving, you'll forget the actor ever played Stifler.

Dread Central was lucky enough to sit down with Scott recently to talk about Bloodline and what it was like playing such an intense and gruesome role. Check out our conversation below the film's synopsis.

Synopsis: *Haunted by dark memories of childhood abuse, Evan, a social worker and first-time dad, struggles to keep his need for revenge in check.*

Dread Central: You got your big break in *American Pie* playing a very funny character and most of the film's you've done are comedies. What made you

want to be a part of *Bloodline*, which is a very grim horror movie?

Sean William Scott: Well, I'm a huge fan of horror movies. I love the genre. I became an actor because I love movies, not because I had this crazy desire to perform. It literally came from fucking loving movies. I felt like this was something I could do and I wanted people get that same feeling when they watch a strong performance or see a great movie.

*I actually approached Blumhouse. I was like, "Can we please take a meeting because I would love to work with you and I think I can do something different than I've ever done before throughout my entire career." They believed in me and they sent over **Bloodline**. The script needed some work but I remember the character and the themes were really appealing to me. Then we ended up getting Henry Jacobson to direct. It's definitely something I've always wanted to do in my career. I love psychological horror and always wanted to do something like Jack Nicholson in **The Shining**. Or Malcolm McDowell in **A Clockwork Orange**. I watched **Henry: Portrait of a Serial Killer** and some other fucked up shit when I was young. So I was ready to finally do something like that.*

DC: What are some of your favorite recent horror movies?

*SWS: **Hereditary**. For me, I was like, "Holy shit!" I thought it was perfect, from beginning to end, every part of it. It was the first time in a while that something really fucked me up. I loved it! **Get Out** was also just incredible. Pretty much everything that **Blumhouse** has done.*

DC: How is acting in a horror movie different than acting in a comedy?

*SWS: My goal has always been trying to make people laugh. But in **Bloodline**, I was trying to be as grounded and believable as possi-*

ble. *Different thought process, but, ironically, I probably had more fun doing this one than any other film.*

DC: When I was watching *Bloodline*, your character (Evan) seemed like a bit of Dexter and a bit of Norman Bates. How would you describe him?

*SWS: You kind of nailed it. I've always loved **Dexter** and I knew there would be comparisons. But that's probably the best description I've heard. A little bit of Dexter, a little bit or Norman Bates. His relationship with his mom was so weird. I loved that open-mouthed kiss!*

DC: *Bloodline* has some really gruesome scenes. Were any of them difficult for you to film?

SWS: No, I enjoyed it. I mean, definitely there were days when I'd be mentally exhausted, but I really loved the entire process. I love the genre and the entire crew we worked with was young and energetic. It was a smaller crew and we only had four weeks to film. There were some scenes where I put a lot of pressure on myself, but I loved it. I loved it all, all the blood and violence!

DC: What makes *Bloodline* different than other serial killer movies?

SWS: It isn't just another violent serial killer movie. That would be dull. This violence is something Evan inherited from his mom. It's more complicated than most vigilante films. It's about a guy who can't accept that people can get away with hurting others.

Michael Beach Nichols

INTERVIEW WITH WRINKLES THE CLOWN
DIRECTOR/DOCUMENTARIAN

Method: *In Person*

Recollections: Fantastic Fest 2019 was the best time I've had covering a film festival, ever. First of all, the folks who organize the program really know how to treat journalists right. They have an entire boarding house that they offer to attending journalists free of charge. And there's a "Press Room" at the Alamo Drafthouse on South Lamar in Austin, Texas; a place for Journalists to snag WIFI and (relative) peace and quiet in order to bang out a review or some transcription.

I had attended Fantastic Fest the year prior a made a ton of friends. In 2019, I felt more established, more confidant. As opposed to being consumed with wonder, wandering the crowds slack-jawed, I felt like I belonged this time. Still, the event had an odd undercurrent swirling just below the surface for Team Dread Central.

Though I had attended previous film festivals with then Editor-in-Chief Jonathan Barkan, he had never let me conduct interviews or review films. He did all of that himself. Which is fine. As top dog, he's allowed to give assignments to whomever he believes is most qualified—even if it's himself. At Fantastic Fest 2019, however, Jonathan didn't do anything (meaning it fell on me to do everything). And while I worked long hours attending screenings and conducting interviews, Jonathan spent most of the festival holed up at his Air B&B with his girlfriend. What had changed?

In retrospect, I think it's safe to say that Jonathan had "quiet quit" Dread Central. We'd been hearing rumors that he was taking interviews with other companies. This was bolstered by the fact that Jonathan seemed to be purposely dodging Patrick Ewald, who was also at Fantastic Fest scouting potential releases. So in some ways, it made for a strange experience. And while I was a bit baffled, I enjoyed taking a front seat in terms of providing festival coverage for Dread Central. In the back of my mind I realized: "If Jonathan does resign, I'll be next in line to take over as Editor-in-Chief." And while I was perfectly content as Managing Editor, I would not waste the opportunity for advancement should it be offered. And, eventually, it was.

It turned out, Jonathan would go to work as Vice President of Acquisitions at The Horror Collective. It sent shock-waves through the company and put many of his actions over the past few months into question. But it was the end of an era—and the beginning of another.

As for **Wrinkles the Clown**, it's a great and vastly under-rated documentary, a deep-dive into a modern urban legend with surprising discoveries.

ORIGINALLY PUBLISHED: **October 17, 2019**

One of my favorite films out of Fantastic Feast 2019 was the documentary ***Wrinkles the Clown***. As opposed to Pennywise, Art the Clown, and the legion of grease-painted villains haunting the horror genre, Wrinkles is real. No seriously. You can call him right now at 407-734-0254 (although you'll most likely get his voicemail).

Wrinkles offers a unique service: Unlike your typical birthday clowns, he can be hired to scare naughty children. He's sort of like a modern, real-life Krampus, though not bound to a specific season. He advertises his services guerilla style: By tagging with stickers. Wrinkles went viral after nanny-cam footage of him emerging from under a sleeping child's bed hit the internet.

Dread Central was lucky enough to talk to ***Wrinkles the Clown*** director/documentarian Michael Beach Nichols about legend building in the Internet Age, the ethics of inflicting fear, and the viral fiend's future. Peruse our conversation below.

Synopsis: *In Florida, parents can hire Wrinkles the Clown to scare their misbehaving children.*

Wrinkles the Clown is now streaming on VOD.

Dread Central: I love the fact that you told a true story that still managed to have a really big twist. It's genius. Is that something you really struggled with: How tell a true story and still give the audience a surprise?

Michael Beach Nichols: Yeah, definitely. It was something that, because Wrinkles wanted to stay anonymous, we were sort of stuck in this position where, because that's a natural thing to do, right? You're with this person in a mask and you don't know who it is. But because he didn't want to be revealed we had to figure out a way to tell the story. It was an interesting process because you're shooting a film where you can't really show anyone's face, so it's a very different process as a shooter. So, you're in the film for about fifty minutes and then finally being able to show a face and have that sort of mean something, it felt really powerful. We thought we might do it but didn't know a hundred percent during production.

DC: I didn't know a ton going into it, and I'm in the horror community so I'm literally inundated with screeners and trailers. But creepy clowns will always catch my attention. Last night in the theater I sat down next to a couple of women and they were really excited and I was like, "So, is this a mockumentary or a documentary?" And they're all like, "It's a documentary, you can hire this guy to go and scare your kids!" I don't want to give anything away, and I understand the film is about legend building in the Internet Age, but does part of you feel like you're pulling the curtain too far back?

MBN: Parents have figured out a way to use Wrinkles to scare their kids. And so they're using a voicemail and these incredibly visceral and disturbing messages so their children think it's completely real, or their child thinks they're talking to the boogeyman! So the parents have figured out a way to make Wrinkles nightmare fuel for their kids. There's something really interesting about that, the power of an active voice mail.

DC: Are you a little bit worried that people are going to walk away from the film liking Wrinkles less after learning the "true" truth?

MBN: Yeah, I think it's interesting because Wrinkles himself was worried about that too. Any sort of exposure in terms of what he actually does or doesn't do, it was sort of taking away from his power. So yeah, I guess there is an element that people will watch this and it will be just a totally different relationship with Wrinkles. But to me it's sort of fascinating to be with someone in real-time as they're sort of orchestrating this myth but having it bolstered by children and random people on the internet and have them weigh in and have their say about what they think Wrinkles is. So I'm hoping there might be a little bit of grey area there for some people.

DC: So, let's talk about child abuse because that's another really interesting element of your film. We live in this era of "safe spaces" and I was kind of relating it to experiences in my own life. I remember, when I was in kindergarten, there was this older girl who told me that Dracula was her uncle and she was going to get him to come and suck my blood in the middle of the night, and I didn't sleep at all that night. But I didn't have a psychiatrist in my corner saying, "That girl abused you! She subjected you to mental abuse!" It made me realize most kids think monsters are real and figuring out they're not is a natural part of growing up. Do you think the child psychologist in your film is overreacting?

MBN: Yeah, it's funny. I'm not a father but I have a nephew and I love scary movies, and I loved being scared when I was younger. I sometimes scare my sister's kids more than she's comfortable with because I liked it when I was a kid and I feel like it helped me really appreciate horror things, scary things. But yeah, it's not for every kid but for me it may cross the line if it's done repeatedly. They're would be eight calls from the same phone number, over and over and over again and with the example of Antonio in the film, his calls were sort of spread out over six months. We met his daughter and she sort of thought it was funny but also, she's so young, I don't know what a three-year-old is thinking and how it's necessarily going to affect her. So yeah, I'm sort of more in the middle. I don't necessarily think its outright child abuse but I guess it also depends on how your child reacts. If your child is wailing in the background and absolutely losing it, I think that crosses a line. I think some kids though, I think I could have handled it. I would have been scared but would have gotten a thrill from it, so I think it's very much case by case.

DC: You talked to the one kid who was so afraid of Wrinkles, he took his box spring out of his room so no one could hide under his bed. But then he talks about how he faced his fears and now, he wants to be a filmmaker himself! That's fantastic because that's the story of so many horror fans who saw *Halloween* on TV when they were way too young, and now they love scary movies.

MBN: No, yeah. I was watching scary movies when I was too young. I just got such a thrill out of it. It fucked me up but I'm grateful for it.

DC: Yeah, you're saying it fucked you up and I'm telling you about experiences that fucked me up, but isn't being fucked up part of childhood?

MBN: Yeah, I definitely think there's a place for fear and darkness.

DC: One of my favorite parts of the film was when Wrinkles is just talking to some kids and they love him. They say, "I love you, Wrinkles," and you get to this point where Wrinkles isn't scary. Wrinkles

is just another misunderstood guy, making his way day by day. It's almost like Wrinkles doesn't know he's scary.

MBN: Yeah, we were so fortunate to get those recordings. We wanted to do a thing where we just filmed him and see what happens and it didn't take long for that to happen. Also, we found this one girl, her mother didn't allow her to be filmed, but she called Wrinkles like 36 times, or something insane. She just thought he was really cool, like would sing him songs that she wrote, would talk about her artwork. I got her to email me some of the artwork she's made of Wrinkles, so there's definitely this really sort of sweet thing happening, where a lot of kids weren't seeing the scary side. They were seeing the misunderstood, maybe kind of grouchy, funny old man…not really scary, just sort of fun. "I can talk to him, I can talk to his voice mail and he might hear it, he might text me back!"

DC: So I'm not going to press you on the identity of Wrinkles but is this a one-off or is he a working artist/filmmaker?

M: Yeah, he's definitely very much in the arts scene. I can say that. Big time, he's into making stuff.

DC: Well, I wish him all the best and I hope you can keep this going for years. How do you think your film will change Wrinkles' urban legend, or do you think it will?

MBN: That's a very good question and something Wrinkles is worried about. It definitely could take away some of the power. At the same time, the number is still there. I do think he is going to continue to make videos. It might just shift into this thing now where he becomes this famous clown because there is a movie made about him and, regardless of who's behind the mask and because he's anonymous. I think there's some power there. We really don't know who this person is. It might change that dynamic but I think it might still be fun and kind of creepy.

DC: I'm going to give you a gift here, a way to turn this into a franchise. I don't want any writing credit or anything. You have to make a meta-movie where the "real" Wrinkles is so pissed off he kills you, the actor pretending to be Wrinkles, and the entire film crew!

MBN: Yeah, I like that.

J.D. Dillard

TALKS SWEETHEART, SLEIGHT & THE FLY REMAKE

Method: *Phone*

Recollections: As a huge fan of David Cronenberg's ***The Fly***, I truly hope the now-in-limbo remake discussed in this interview someday comes to fruition. I think J.D. Dillard is a hell of a filmmaker and I'd love to see what he can do!

——————

ORIGINALLY PUBLISHED: **October 21, 2018**

Available tomorrow on digital, ***Sweetheart*** was one of the most outside-the-box films to screen at Fantastic Fest in Austin last month. Dread Central was lucky enough to sit down with the film's director and co-writer J.D. Dillard to discuss this unique tale of isolation and survival. We also discussed his first feature film, ***Sleight***, and plans for an upcoming remake of ***The Fly***.

Give our conversation a spin below the synopsis for ***Sweetheart***.

Synopsis: *Jenn has washed ashore a small tropical island and it doesn't take her long to realize she's completely alone. She must spend her days not only surviving the elements, but must also fend off the malevolent force that comes out each night.*

Dread Central: I'm a big fan of *Sleight*, which came out in 2016. Now fast forward to 2018 and everyone's talking about Black Panther and saying, "Finally, there's a superhero African-Americans can relate to". Do you ever sit back and go, "Damn, I created an African-American superhero years ago and no one seemed to notice?"

*J.D. Dillard: I'm happy and glad we got to build a character but you know, Marvel has their movie playing on a thousand screens world-wide. It was funny to see in a couple of pieces that came out around that time being like, "Don't forget the little guys", and gave us some love around when **Black Panther** came out.*

DC: That's good to hear. You know, something else that I was considering as a journalist: When *Sleight* came out, we were still in the Obama administration, with people were talking about a "post-racial society". Now that Trump is in office all these issues surrounding racism have simmered back to the surface with a vengeance. Do you think that *Sleight* might have been seen as more important or better received if it had been released during the Trump administration?

JDD: It's sort of like catching up for lost time with this medium. So, no matter what, we continue to have more stories that feature people of color, in terms of my own personal crusade, stories within genres. While I wouldn't say my work is only this, there's definitely a part of me that wants to go back to all the movies I've always loved and remake them with people like me. So, I am curious, existentially, how

Sleight *would be received right now. But regardless, the issue was always urgent regardless of the environment.*

DC: Very well said. You know, I've been in this horror journalism game for a minute and I remember being very excited a few years back when I heard you were going to potentially remake *The Fly* and that you were working on a script. Can you tell me what happened with that?

JDD: I'm not necessarily shooting that film tomorrow but we have a script that we're very, very happy with. We're really looking forward to moving forward and taking steps to bring that story to life.

DC: Fantastic. I grew up in the '80s and *The Fly* was one of those films that made a huge impact on me so I'm really excited. I'm glad to hear that it's not dead, just in this limbo. I know you want to keep things close to your chest but can you just tell us a little bit about how you plan to make *The Fly* relevant again for the 21st century?

JDD: Yeah, all I want to do is start these genre stories with a character and look, ***The Fly*** *is such a remarkable film and regardless how you look at it, whether it's technological, performance, direction…I mean, I was even joking with some friends the other day, it's one of the most efficient stories I've ever seen. You start the movie and five minutes later it's the main cue. Seven minutes later it's "Let me show you something". 15 minutes later an exciting incident has occurred and it's remarkably efficient. You know, what's so fun about it being 2019, looking at the opportunity to do that one first, with the technology to tell a body horror story is just so exciting. Looking at what we're doing today, it's certainly a bit more difficult thirty years ago, it's certainly an exciting prospect. That said, just sort of socially looking up. Women's right to their own bodies, this whole gender thing, the sort of threshold of pain that doctors assume people of color or African Americans can* stand. *There are a lot of things in that headspace so* **The Fly**, *should we get to make that, it will be done in a way that excites me. It collides a lot of interest and a lot of love, even a lot of social issues in this day and age.*

DC: That's exciting, and I'm even more excited about it now than before. I'm keeping my fingers crossed and hoping that it comes to fruition. Let's talk about *Sweetheart* since that's the film of the hour here at Fantastic Fest. What were your inspirations for that film?

JDD: My writer is Alex Hyner, and we wanted to create a smart genre experience. We wanted to see what it would be like to reset the vocabulary a little bit and grew to know our character through action and not necessarily labor, like a complicated backstory. So, on one side, there's that. On the other side, loving **Alien**, *loving* **The Fly** *and wanting to take a swing at a practical creature feature and all that comes with that. Lastly, and probably most importantly, half of what I do is making movies I think my sisters will want to see. Jumping into that and not necessarily the movie being a social statement. I really like to make movies where people who don't usually get to do the cool things do the cool things.*

DC: Was it difficult to do a film that had very little exposition? Did you find it more challenging or less challenging?

JDD: I think in some regard you do have to reset your vocabulary. The way I shoot her is a tool of productivity, in a strange way back to basics to tell the story. Obviously it's a moment in the film where exposition is more of the story. In that way it actually ended up becoming a little harder working with exposition because you have been, for forty-five or fifty minutes, not using it as a tool at all. So, then the words are so much louder and so much older because there's been so much discus-

sion up to this point. So, it really felt like we had to choose our words even more carefully to have access to the dialogue.

DC: A buddy of mine and I were talking about the film last night and he was like, "Ask him what the title means".

*JDD: We could have called it **Deep** or **Not Alone**. We had a plethora of options on that side but you know honestly, it made sense that we center it on her journey and it should not necessarily sound like a horror film. Honestly, I have to counter-program that a little bit. It has been kind of fun to put a creature feature out that doesn't have a creature feature name.*

DC: Fantastic. It's been a real pleasure. Like I said, I've been a fan of *Sleight* since day one, and I'm really excited for what you've got cooking. I hope people love *Sweetheart* as much as I did. Congratulations!

JDD: I appreciate that.

Bong Joon Ho

TALKS PARASITE & UPCOMING MYSTERY PROJECTS

Method: *In Person*

Reflections: So, yeah, I interviewed an Oscar-Winning Director about his Oscar Winning film, and thank God I had the presence of mind to snag a picture. You can see I'm absolutely beaming. Bong Joon Ho was Belle of the Ball at Fantastic Fest in 2019 (The Alamo Drafthouse even renamed a theater after him).

When I first heard that Bong had created a film called **Parasite**, I assumed it was somehow connected to his 2006 monster movie, **Host** (as hosts and parasites are natural companions). I was stunned to experience, instead, a film about class struggle and poverty. And, while far from your conventional horror movie, **Parasite** was captivating. The film's haul from Oscar Night 2019 (Best Foreign Film, Best Director, and Best Picture) proves I'm not the only one who thought so.

There's an almost mystical quality about Bong. He's slightly detached but incredibly intelligent and thoughtful. I'll always treasure the fact that I was able to hold court with this talented filmmaker and can't wait to see what he comes up with next. (The "mystery projects" discussed in this interview were no doubt sidelined by the pandemic).

———

ORIGINALLY PUBLISHED: **October 23, 2019**

Parasite, written and directed by Bong Joon Ho, was one of the best received and reviewed films to screen at Fantastic Fest in Austin last month. While promoting the film, Director Bong (whose past films include **The Host**, **Snowpiercer**, and **Okja**) spoke to journalists (including myself) about what makes this particular film so special.

Synopsis: *All unemployed, Ki-taek's family takes peculiar interest in the wealthy and glamorous Parks for their livelihood until they get entangled in an unexpected incident.*

Parasite stars Kang-ho Song, Yeo-jeong Jo, and So-dam Park.

Bong Joon Ho: A lot of people say this is a film about class struggle, but actually the working class don't struggle against the rich in this film. They fight amongst themselves and there's a line that's being drawn and the rich always stay beyond that line. Mr. Park always stays beyond that line and whether or not it's intentional or natural, he doesn't know what's going on and doesn't even try to figure out what's going on amongst the have nots. It's almost as if, for Mr. Park, it's something that happens in outer space. In the film there is one instance where that line is crossed (during the climatic sequence) and I think you can look at their relationship in that context. And so, you have the poor father, and the rich family. They are so nice, and so kind on the surface, but underneath, within that character, something is being built up towards Mr. Park and in the end it all explodes. So, this film, it doesn't have a clear villain. No one is the bad person, but we reach this disastrous tragedy in the end and I think that in itself is the fear that this film delivers."

Dread Central: After having seen *Snowpiercer* and *Okja*, I hear you've made a film called *Parasite* and immediately my expectation are that it's a movie about an infection, potentially something that turns you into a zombie, takes over your body. But "parasite" can be slang for somebody who leeches off of you but in a scientific sense, the most successful parasites are the ones you never notice because it's a symbiotic relationship. So, I'm wondering in Korean, is it the same kind of double meaning with "parasite" and were you intentionally trying to play with people's preconceived expectations about what your follow up to *Okja* would be?

BJH: In Korea the word parasite doesn't have any "sci-fi" connotation. A human parasite, that would carry a lot of disdain if you were leeching off someone else. So, when we first brought up the title with the

Korean marketing team, they were quite hesitant. They thought it was kind of a risky title. I explained to them that all the characters are mutually parasites. You could say the rich family was leeching off the labor that the poor family provides, so it's not just the poor family that's being the parasite.

DC: After *Snowpiercer*, which was completely in English, and *Ojka* which was fifty/fifty, was there a lot of pressure for you to make another film that would have more of an international appeal? Were people saying, "No, no, no...don't make a strictly Korean movie. Make sure there's English in it..."?

*BJH: That wasn't really the case. I started working on **Parasite** during the post-production of **Snowpiercer**. That's when I started talking to the production company. I just followed the ideas that occurred to me at the time so even before **Okja** I had already started working on this project. **Snowpiercer** at that time, nobody pushed me in regards to doing something bigger in an English language movie. One day I just found out about this French graphic novel and I was fascinated by it. The stories about the human survivors in the "running train", the human survivors. If all the people on the train were from North Korea and South Korea, it's going to be very awkward, so we have to do some international cast and the movie goes to some English language or something. But it truly is quite a mix. Some Korean actors there, a Japanese character, I mixed almost all English language. But it wasn't as if I had a specific plan or strategy to work on Hollywood or American film. I was just very into the original graphic novel and the process was very natural and even for my upcoming projects. I have one in Korean and one in English, that I'm currently working on.*

DC: Can you tell us a little bit about them?

BJH: Yes [laughs]. So, it's a horror film and it can only work in a relatively homogenous society like Korea, rather than a multi-racial society like the States. So, the fear would only work if people had a similar skin color, maybe that's even more confusing.

DC: So that's the Korean one, what about the English one?

BJH: The English one is based on a true case from 2016, inspired by a CNN article I discovered last year. Sorry, I can't discuss anymore.

Paola Nuñez

TALKS THE PURGE SEASON 2

Method: *Set Visit*

Reflections: I can't thank the folks at Blumhouse enough for bringing me out to New Orleans in 2019 to visit the set of ***The Purge*** Season 2. I was joined by just a few other journalists and influencers. We got to interview the show's stars and even got to see them set a school-bus on fire. Best of all, we all got to be extras in the Season 2 finale. No spoilers, but if you look really closely, you might see a dude with dreadlocks at a political rally! For the scene, I was put in costume and even given a boss "tattoo" on my neck.

The fun actually kicked off the night before when my colleagues and our Blumhouse rep crawled the French Quarter. Sure, it wasn't Mardi Gras (or even a Friday night) but that district is always hopping; there's a pervasive sense of sin and danger.

Of course we all probably drank too much, but leave it to me to get ripped off! Earlier in the evening, a street dealer had pulled me aside to offer me as assortment of party favors, from cannabis to cocaine. I declined (as he took me off guard) but later (and drunker) I began to wish I had taken his up on his offer for a few choice nuggets. So when another less reputable dealer popped up, attracted to my dreadlocks, I decided to go for it.

I gave him $40. He put a small plastic baggie directly into my pocket and shuffled off down a dark alleyway.

The party continued when we got back to the hotel, with everyone convening in my room. It was there that I surprised my peers with the "cannabis" I had procured. Except it wasn't cannabis. It was white.

"Holy shit! Did I accidentally buy cocaine?" was my initial thought and, while it wasn't what I had planned to consuming, cocaine isn't something to be wasted. Plus, several of my compatriots were interested in the booger sugar. Except it wasn't cocaine either. When I opened the bag, it turns out I had paid $40 for a wadded piece of napkin. It was embarrassing but hilarious!

"Anybody want a line of napkin?" I offered.

———

ORIGINALLY PUBLISHED: **November 1, 2019**

The Purge Season 2 is three episodes deep on USA, with new episodes dropping on Tuesdays through December. If you haven't gotten in on the action yet, take my word for it: You're missing out!

During a set visit last September, I had the privilege of interviewing series star Paola Nuñez. She plays Esme Carmona, an employee of the New Founding Fathers who monitors activity on Purge Night. When something unusual catches her eye, her curiosity sends her down a rabbit hole of intrigue and mystery—one that will test her core values and moral center.

Synopsis: *Based on the hit movie franchise,* **The Purge** *revolves around a 12-hour period when all crime, including murder, is legal. Season 2 explores how a single Purge night affects the lives of four interconnected characters over the course of the ensuing year, all inevitably leading up to the next Purge. Hailing from Blumhouse Television and UCP, this season of the anthology series opens on Purge night but dives deeper than ever before into what the Purge world looks like the other 364 days of the year.*

Enjoy our conversation below!

Dread Central: For our readers who may be meeting you for the first time on *The Purge* Season 2, can you tell us a little bit about how you got into acting and your journey thus far?

Paola Nuñez: Yeah sure, I'd love to. My name is Paola Nuñez. I'm Mexican and I started acting when I was nineteen. I'm from a little town in Baha called Tecate. When I was 19, I moved to Mexico City and studied acting there. I've lived in Mexico my whole life until five years ago when I decided to move to the States. I started working and the first thing I did was **The Sun** *for AFC. after* **The Sun** *I did* **Queen of the South**, *and I just finished* **Bad Boys 3**. *Now I'm here working on* **The Purge**.

DC: Gigi Saul Guerrero directed some episodes this season. She's making a great name for herself as a Latina female director. What was it like working with her?

P.N: It was great. We didn't know each other, but it was great to be together. I can't believe she's that young and super focused and she knows exactly what she wants. She's super confident on set, being surrounded by men, older people. And, you know, you have to have that confidence, especially when you're that young and a woman. You have to come to set with an energy and hold your ground which she did, and I admire that.

DC: I was on the set of *Culture Shock* when she was filming that and I was surprised at her style of directing because she's actually yelling directions to the actors from behind the camera, whereas you always imagine everyone being silent. Was she like that with you as well, yelling directions to you while you were acting?

PN: Yeah, totally. She was having fun, so much fun, and you can tell that. What I admire most about directors, it's weird, when you have a director that you sense doesn't know what he's doing. Automatically you just don't trust him and his point of view and you don't respect him and think, "Well, I guess I'm on my own". But when you see that clarity, that's what happened to me as an actor. I'm going to do whatever you tell me to do because you know what's up, and Gigi was like that. She gained my respect on the first day. I was like, "Yeah, I like you!"

DC: Let's talk about *The Purge* specifically. The whole concept behind *The Purge* is that you take this one night to get all your aggression out and you'll be great for the coming year. When we meet your character in the first episode, you're a proponent of The Purge. You're a part of the system and you come to the conclusion that it's ok. You separate yourself emotionally, but it feels like that is changing for your character. You're starting to think The Purge might not be the answer it's sold as, am I correct?

PN: I don't remember where I discovered that something was wrong.

DC: I think it was around episode two, looking into Professor Adams, retracing her steps...

P.N: Ok, perfect. So, I think before Professor Adams [played by Avis-Marie Barnes], I think my character was completely involved and a believer in the system. She dedicated, not her entire life, but a part of her life to this, because the interesting thing about Esme is, she's not just coming from a place where she's doing this for people because it's what she believes in. She's coming from a place that's full of guilt and she needs something to make her feel better. And because I didn't protect people in the past, I need to do this to make me feel better. So really, she's not coming from a healthy psyche and that's why she's here. So, as soon as she sees something that's not right, she's scared because it's like, "Oh, maybe this isn't what I thought it was." So, she feels betrayed and she's like, "I hope this is not what I think it is..." But a part of her knows something is not right, and maybe this father figure that she has is the end of her faith. It's just going to betray her again like it did in the past. Like I said, it's not coming from a healthy place, it's coming from her past, and that's why she reacts that way because, the way she reacts is not even healthy. It's like I have to get him, and now she wants the truth and now she wants to avenge the system after she finds out.

DC: Let's talk about the system because, thematically, catharsis seems to be a huge tent pole of The Purge. The whole idea that when you get your violence out, it actually makes you a better person. But it seems like the Professor's research is pretty much the opposite, that when people participate in The Purge it actually opens the door for even more violent behavior. If we lived in a world where The Purge was real, what do you think would actually happen? Would it make society better or would it send us tumbling into complete anarchy?

PN: I definitely do believe that violence creates more violence. I don't think I'd be able to kill another person but I'm not a mother and I've heard a lot of people say, "Yeah, if someone hurts my kid I would be able to kill that person". I kind of understand that but I do think that if we start killing people, that's not going to start anything and yeah, that would create something that is unhealthy in our society. Also, that's definitely not the answer because we would be destroying our whole existence, right? Let's be honest, if we think about it, we start creating a list of all the people that shouldn't be in this world, that should be purged, you start with one person and then you start thinking about it and realize someone is going to want to purge me, someone is going to want to purge you. So, on the first night everyone is just going to purge each other and destroy the world. That's a stupid answer but at the same time it's so real, it's talking about intolerance in general.

DC: I don't think that's a stupid answer at all. Especially in the last couple *Purge* films, I think they are making it very clear that it's the rich targeting the poor, and I haven't seen that stated as overtly in Season 2. It seems like everyone is dangerous, kind of what you were just talking about. So, I don't think that was a stupid response at all. Have you seen all the other *Purge* movies, and season one?

*PN: I've seen a few and what I really liked was the first time I saw the original **Purge**, what I really like about movies is after seeing a movie it becomes a conversation. You know when you go see a movie and you're walking out of the theater talking about how hungry you are and you don't even mention the movie? I think that's a bad sign. I think movies should be conversations and **The Purge** does that. You ponder if purging is something that will fix the world, fix it by violence, and what you might do. It's funny to think, if I purge on this holiday, what do I do for the rest of the year? Would I be scared about being on someone else's list, and would that help me behave better as a human* *being? Those conversations make you talk about our reality. I mean, we are getting to the point now where we are so intolerant and insensitive to everything. You can't think a different way or I'm going to attack you. Social media and all that power, just because you have a different thought. Stand-up comedians can't even make jokes like they used to because everyone is digging up things from their past. What was said fifteen years ago. And they're going to want to hate you and destroy your entire life because of it.*

DC: The pendulum swings both ways. Things will probably normalize, but right now we really are in a sensitive state.

*P.N: I always think we're going to come to a better understanding but right now everything is so drastic and intolerance. I think the theme of this decade is intolerance in general, and I think that's why **The Purge** is so important right now. It's such an interesting movie, such a subject to touch, like how intolerant are we are feeling so much separation between us that we can't even sit down and say, "I don't understand but I get it." But now you can't sit down with friends and have a normal conversation without it being super-heated up...politics, right?*

DC: Well, Dread Central is a horror website so I'm curious: Do you like horror movies in general and what are some of the first horror movies that made an impression on you?

*P.N: **Evil Dead**, is one. It's one of the first movies that I saw. And of course, I remember **Child's Play**. I couldn't sleep after **Child's Play** for a week, so I decided I didn't want to see more of that because I got really scared. And so, when a horror movie comes out, I just prefer not to watch it, because I have insomnia. I know everything that disturbs my nerves a little bit, that's just going to prevent me from sleeping. So, I respect that genre so much that I don't even watch it.*

DC: What's the last horror movie you saw that gave you nightmares?

P.N: **The Others**, *I think. And two years ago I saw* **The Exorcist** *again and it's an amazing movie. The acting is incredible, the photography is great, it's so good. Now that I saw it again, I think it's my favorite horror movie ever.*

DC: If someone asked "What makes Season 2 of *The Purge* so special?" or, "Why is this worthy of my time?" how would you respond?

P.N: It's so special, even if you're a fan of the franchise, you get to see what happens between Purge nights. It's the first time you get to see how people behave in this alternate world between purges. So, what happens after you've gone and purged someone? Who cleans the city after Purge night? Think about it. Those little things are so cool to watch. It's like, "Oh right, I never thought about that!" And there are repercussions: What happens to people that purge? How are they able to handle the fact that they purged? Are they ok or not ok with it, and what happened if someone wanted to purge you and couldn't and you had to live with that for the year, until the next Purge night? Should you be scared or not? Those questions, people are going to get answers throughout the other 364 days of the year.

DC: Well Paola, thank you very much for your time! It was really nice talking to you, I enjoyed your insights.

Rochelle Aytes

TALKS VOYEURISTIC VIOLENCE IN THE PURGE SEASON 2

Method: *Set Visit*

Originally Published: November 22, 2019

We're midway through *The Purge* Season 2 on USA, with new episodes dropping on Tuesdays through December. If you haven't gotten in on the action yet, take my word for it: You're missing out!

During a set visit last September, I had the privilege of interviewing series star Rochelle Aytes. Horror fans probably remember her as Maria in Michael Dougherty's elite horror anthology, *Trick 'r Treat*. On *The Purge*, she plays Michelle Moore, a woman whose complex marital status has potentially deadly consequences come Purge Night. Give our exclusive interview a spin below the show's synopsis.

Synopsis: *Based on the hit movie franchise,* **The Purge** *revolves around a 12-hour period when all crime, including murder, is legal. Season 2 explores how a single Purge night affects the lives of four interconnected characters over the course of the ensuing year, all* *inevitably leading up to the next Purge. Hailing from Blumhouse Television and UCP, this season of the anthology series opens on Purge night but dives deeper than ever before into what the Purge world looks like the other 364 days of the year.*

Dread Central: For some of our viewers who might be seeing you on *The Purge* for the first time, can you just tell us a little bit about how you got into acting and how it felt to get this role on Season 2?

*Rochelle Aytes: How did I get into acting? Well, I used to be a professional dancer. I grew up in New York, and I had a quick career in dance. But I did a Broadway show where I had to act, sing, and dance and I got the bug. I left the tour and I started studying acting in New York to even see if I could do it; to see if I would even like it. And within two years of really focusing and solid studying I got a film called **White Chicks**. It was amazing, and I've been acting ever since. That was like 16, 17 years ago. And since then, I've been on the grind. I've worked consistently. Then I got this audition for **The Purge** in May. I'd seen one of the many **Purge** movies so I knew what it was about, I knew it was intense and I was excited I got the part.*

DC: I've been watching The Purge Season 2 and I'm loving it! Without getting into specifics, can you talk about your character's story arc throughout the season? How things start isn't how things end, right?

RA: Michelle is married to Marcus [played by Derek Luke] for a solid amount of time. They've got a really comfortable relationship. Everything seems to be great between them. But then someone attempts to "Purge" him and it really changes our life because we're trying to find out who did it. It then opens up a can of worms of "Who are these people?" and "What has their relationship really been like?" And we get to see it's not the perfect life viewers thought it was. He's not there as much. He's not focused on her and some secrets are revealed about her past; specifically, she had an affair. So, she's looking guilty. It's going up and down but towards the end they become united. He doesn't trust her and she's feeling guilty but then they become united as one and it seems like these two are more in love with each other than they've ever been, and this kind of tragedy brings them together and changes her I think a great deal. She becomes a person who is so brave and strong. She's willing to lay her life on the line to prove to her husband that she is there for him and their family.

DC: You said you've only seen one of the *Purge* movies. Does that mean you're not a huge horror fan?

RA: Honestly, I'm a huge horror fan, mostly from the eighties and nineties.

DC: Can you tell me some of your favorites from the eighties and nineties growing up?

*RA: Every **Friday the 13th**. I've seen every **Nightmare on Elm Street**, every **Halloween**. I saw **The Exorcist** when I was 8--too young to watch it! I fell asleep and the bed jumped and I was like, "Oh my God!" My mother let me watch all of those horror movies.*

DC: How does acting in horror differ from acting in other films? What's it like on set or how does it make you feel?

RA: Acting in horror is different, depending on which side of the horror you're on. Whether you're the murderer or murderee. [Laughs] There could be a lot of screaming, and a lot of acting up terror, which is exhausting emotionally, as opposed to something else that could be emotional but it's just different. I think it's just more physically exhausting to do horror.

DC: Now let's imagine we live in a world where Purge Night actually happens once a year. Do you think there's any truth to the concept that it would actually make society more peaceful because we'd get it out of our system, or is it just a pathway to complete chaos?

RA: I think it's so great, the way they're doing this season. They're showing you that The Purge, this society, this government, saying that it helps… But you get to see it through the eyes of a regular person, and it doesn't work. It really makes you go crazy. I think it desensitizes you from things that are just horrific and terrible. It takes away from all empathy. So no, absolutely not. I don't think it would work in our society.

DC: Do you think anything that's happening in Season 2 is a direct reflection of our current political state in America? I mean, I heard the words "fake news" in the scene that was just shot. Are there any more parallels that illustrate where we are today?

RA: You know, what's interesting is this Purge world that shows them making money off of it. You can take Purge vacations. They're selling consumer products and masks. It's becoming a money market and I think that's very similar to our world. I don't know, maybe our social media: How powerful it is, how it's just wrapped up in recording and watching people fight and then publicizing it for more likes and tweets, when you should have put it down and helped. Like, where's the empathy?

DC: That's really interesting. I never even thought about the whole idea of the voyeuristic aspect of it, as opposed to the good Samaritan aspect of it. So, what has been your biggest, most satisfying

moment so far and what has been your biggest challenge so far on *The Purge*?

RA: This is probably going to be weird but I'd say the most satisfying thing is feeling tough and picking up that gun. In this episode where we're ready to throw down, we've got each other's back. Marcus's ex-wife and husband come to the house and I hadn't worked with them yet, and we'd just become a family. And they're like, "We've got your back", and we've got those guns and we're ready to protect each other. It's so brave. For me, Rochelle, it's fun because that's not me in real life. I'm not picking up a gun but I will pretend. So that was fun. The most challenging thing for me in this whole season was shooting the scene where I had to confess that I had the affair. As an actor it was hard for me to do it. I don't know, it's just like, going to that place, remembering that I've ever cheated, what was that like. It was a challenging scene as an actress to portray.

Peter Block

TALKS THE SHED, FRIGHT NIGHT & CONFIRMS BIG NEWS COMING ON PUMPKINHEAD REMAKE

Method: *Phone*

Originally Published: November 28, 2019

Peter Block's IMDB page reads like a Greatest Horror Movies of the 21st Century list. The prolific producer has been involved in some of the biggest and best-received genre films of the past two decades. His most recent film is ***The Shed***, is a chiller that flips vampire tropes on their head while incorporating timely and important social commentary. Check out the synopsis for ***The Shed*** below. Our exclusive interview follows.

Synopsis: *Stan lives with his abusive grandfather and tries to protect his best friend from high school bullies. When he discovers a murderous creature has taken refuge inside his tool shed, he tries to battle the demon alone until his bullied friend discovers the creature and has a far more sinister plan.*

Dread Central: You've produced a ton of horror movies over the years, including some of my

personal favorites. What attracts you to the horror genre?

Peter Block: It's quite interesting. I've worked on quite a few but more importantly, the things I'm proudest about are not necessarily the ones I produced but the ones I found. I started out kind of in the acquisitions business and when a lot of people were ignoring the horror genre generally, and things I found more interesting specifically. I had the greatest sandbox in the world. I could just buy them and market them myself.

*So getting to find these cool little films, whether they were English speaking, like **May or Hard Candy**, or foreign language stuff like **High Tension**. Filmmakers I'm not sure anybody would have found if they didn't get a break, like the **Spirit Brothers**. That was fun for me. I was always very interested in films that were off the beaten path so horror was interesting. I was always a fan. The films I grew up with and reading [Stephen] King and [Clive] Barker. But when I started in the film business, I was working for a company that did mostly art house films and we had to increase the number of films we could handle each month. And I said to the guy, "We just have to do more horror films because it's not cast dependent."*

*When somebody goes into the rental store like my parents who will go every two or three months and rent one movie, they'll go in every week and rent three. So that was how we grew the video business. When I was at Lionsgate, I kind of used the exact same approach. I was running video and TV stuff at the time and when we were trying to branch into commercial films, and basically talked about the publicity benefits of films like **House of 1,000 Corpses**, **Open Water**, **Saw**, and **Cabin Fever** as being the driving force that opened those films. It worked out really well.*

DC: Fantastic. As someone who's been in this game for a while, can you talk a little bit about how the industry has evolved over the last decade-plus, especially how it pertains to horror movies?

PB: Yeah it's funny. Horror is always that thing that everyone wants to take advantage of but nobody really wants to tout. It's changed a little bit obviously recently but in the eighties, they considered it those schlocky movies. Even the studios didn't want to touch the slasher films and that's where it allowed independent cinema to come from. No one would dabble in the horror thing. They would always play it safe.

By the way, some of my favorite horror movies came out of the studio, so I wouldn't say without exception, but to a large extent. Just as horror started to get a nice resurgence in the nineties, everybody wanted to kind of make it PG, and start to go where nothing was objectionable and for me it just left a huge hole for hard R films. Not that I'm drawn to those specifically. Actually, I'm probably not. But there was an opening there. What people failed to understand was the horror audience wasn't new. The horror audience hadn't gone anywhere, they just didn't always necessarily invite them to the party. But they were always having a party on their own.

What I like most about the horror genre is people love to talk about it. I go to the movies as a social activity and you find you can agree on a movie to love. It may not be for the same reason, or even if somebody didn't like the movie and you did, there's probably some common ground in scenes you didn't like. So, I find that it kind of lends itself to comradery and social activities that other types of movies don't have. Plus, I think, for a guy who likes horror films also, the ability to translate a foreign film to a horror audience is essential because if you get your sound and your lighting right, you don't have to necessarily have to understand exactly what's going on for the benefit of that movie. So, I think it translates very nicely and allows people to explore new types of films and filmmakers. I also think the horror audience is also willing to indulge itself in a movie they didn't like. Even a bad movie has great moments, and sometimes a bad movie, there's nothing better than a movie that's really, really bad. You want to watch it again. It's so bad and there's a fun part. I think the general mainstream audience doesn't appreciate the entertainment value as much as a horror audience does.

DC: Very well put. So, let's talk about _The Shed_. What attracted you to that film?

PB: Well, it's interesting. I get submitted a lot of things and [director] Frank [Sabatella] submitted me **The Shed** back in 2012 or 2013. I just remember when I read it, I didn't know him at all but thought, "A vampire in a shed. That's interesting! I can see artwork..." The old nineties horror guy in me was like out in full force but I kind of just put it in a drawer and didn't think much about it. I had other films I was working on and other businesses I was doing.

About two years ago I guess, I was thinking about my favorite movie at the time. So, I was thinking about that and watching a news program about a kid who was bullied and went home to his dad's closet, got a gun and went back to school, and I just had this epiphany. And I just said, "What if he didn't have a gun? What if he had a vampire in the shed?" And I immediately had to go back to my old files to figure out, "What was that guy's name?" So, I called up Frank and said, "How would you like to work on that script a little bit?" and then we really put that element in there, the whole "dollar twist". And we kind of paired it down to a bunch of locations and things, and I just got happier and happier with it as we went along. I always like being entertained while there is some additional subtext to it. And working with Frank, as a writer, I got to appreciate how he would be as a director. So, it made the decision to go out and make the movie a lot easier. Sometimes you just write for writing's sake just to see the creative outlet and sometimes you're writing to see if you're going to make the movie. And this one I kind of felt well right and it worked out great.

DC: Fantastic. You know, _The Shed_ reminded me a lot of Tom Holland's _Fright Night_. Like that film you have a protagonist, and his girlfriend, and his best friend caught up in the terror, not to mention the high school setting, the themes of sex and

bullying... Was that film an inspiration to you and Frank?

*PB: 100% it was an inspiration to Frank. I even think in the initial letter he wrote to me, he said, "This is my valentine to **Fright Night**". He loved that movie and I love it to so it was easy to kind of see what he was after. And it got me thinking, back in 2012, I'm like, I like the **Fright Night** aspect, but let's inject a little **Twelve O'clock High** into it (and I realized how old I was talking about **Twelve O'clock High**). It kind of evolved a little bit, but without a doubt, **Fright Night** and **Near Dark** were films we talked about through the writing and shooting process.*

DC: Fantastic. I've seen *The Shed* so I can attest that it's a great film but I'd like to hear from you: What makes this film extraordinary and what sets it apart from the pack?

PB: I think what sets it apart from the pack is it's just fun. It's entertaining. I think it's fun, I think there are moments to laugh. but I wouldn't call it a horror-comedy. There are moments to joke but I'm not going to say it's the scariest movie out there either. But sometimes an audience just wants to be entertained.

*You look at a mainstream audience and a movie like **Peanut Butter Falcon** that does $25M and you go, "Why?" And sometimes you just want to relax, enjoy and have a smile, and I think that's what **The Shed** is. It's not overly dreadful. It uses elements that people can relate to as outsiders trying to either get along together as Stan and Dommer do or take advantage when they feel they have to break outside of that, as Roxy tries to do. At the same time, we put it in the context of a pretty sure of itself horror film. We both use the tropes and shine a light on the tropes at the same time. Obviously, the little conversation before they are going to go upstairs, it's all about what usually happens in a horror film. But at the same time, we have fun when Roxy wants to get nostalgic and wants to look at photos when we know she should* *be looking in the closet. So, we were trying to let everyone know that hey, especially in this day and age, it doesn't have to be uber-serious, just be fun.*

I think this film works really well on that level, but what I think is best about it, truthfully, is the casting unknown kids who are all great. You just don't know who's your hero and who's your villain. We consciously said, "We're not going to have actors in here just for the sake of filling up some screen space. We want to give everyone something good to do so not only do they have motivation throughout the film, it's constantly changing". We hope we had something to say about anti-bullying and people can kind of say "Oh, there was a leap, a reason for it and they weren't just looking for the buck, they had something to say". So hopefully that all comes through and you found some of that, that can be your experience as well.

DC: I saw in your IMDB page that you're producing the upcoming *Pumpkinhead* remake. It's been a while since we've gotten any news about that project and I know our readers would love to know what's up.

PB: There is new news, but I'm not at liberty to share it at this time. But I'll be more than happy to when were able to, and I hope it will be in the not-so-distant future.

Tristan Risk

PROMISES HER CHARACTER IN RABID WILL CAUSE "SLEEPLESS NIGHTS"

Method: *Phone*

Reflections: I'll go to my grave defending 2019's ***Rabid*** as one of the most underrated horror movies of the 2010s. And not because I love Jen and Sylvia Soska. The film is nothing if not a homage to David Cronenberg (the original ***Rabid*** and the filmmaker's legacy). And it hits at every level. It's packed with subtext, important explorations regarding the pathology of beauty and transhumanism. The special effects are top-notch and gruesome—perhaps too gruesome.

As the Twisted Twins were gearing up to promote Rabid's UK premiere at Fright Fest, a screenshot from the film shared on Twitter was deemed so extreme, their account was suspended. It's ironic, because the same image had already been shared by others (including the organizers of Fright Fest) without repercussion. So, in a sense, the Soskas were prevented from giving their version of ***Rabid*** a full-court press in terms of promotion.

Whether this has anything to do with why the film failed to resonate like it should have is impossible to deduce.

But I'm a huge fan of **Rabid**, and I was honored to be given access to so many of the film's key players. I did everything I could to get folks to check it out, and if you're a long-time follower of mine, I hope you did. If not, **Rabid** 2019 still has the potential to be a huge sleeper hit—and Tristan Risk's role at the film's climax should already be iconic.

I've had the pleasure of meeting "Little Miss Risk" in person on a few occasions. She's exactly the manic pixie you might imagine; a beautiful and complex soul inside and out.

———

ORIGINALLY PUBLISHED: **December 9, 2019**

To my fellow entertainment journalists and bloggers, take this advice: Don't let the ink dry on your "Best Horror Movies of 2019" lists until you've seen **Rabid**, the remake of David Cronenberg's seminal body horror classic by Jen and Sylvia Soska (aka The Twisted Twins). It's not only the first (and so far only) remake of a Cronenberg movie, it's a gruesome and engaging romp that will leave moviegoers rapt and devastated.

Rabid arrives in US theaters and VOD this Friday, December 13th. Peep the synopsis below.

Synopsis: *Horribly disfigured after a freak accident, doctors perform a radical medical procedure on an aspiring young fashion designer. But when the bandages come off, the side effects soon cause her to develop an insatiable appetite for human blood.*

Today, Dread Central is launching a full week of **Rabid** coverage with an exclusive conversation with Tristan Risk, a famous actress/model/burlesque artist/filmmaker who's been in the Soska's inner circle since she appeared in **American Mary** back in 2012. We discussed her relationship with the Twisted Twins, her role in **Rabid**, and what makes the film definitively Canadian. Read on!

Dread Central: I've heard the story about how you met Jen and Sylvia Soska at the Vancouver premiere of their first film, *Dead Hooker in a Trunk*. Your working relationship looks like a genuine friendship. True?

*Tristan Risk: Yeah, I mean, I don't know if I'd have a career without them. **American Mary** was the thing that got me started, and then to also be in "T is for Torture Porn" [in **The ABCs of Death 2**]. When this opportunity with **Rabid** came along and they were, like, "We've got these places where ok, it's going to take a certain someone to pull this off. Let's see if Risk will do it". I was very excited to be part of that because yeah, as a Canadian, it's a source of pride to be included in one of the great works of cinema, and this was a double-barreled one: A Soska's film and based on a Cronenberg film.*

DC: Are you as much of a Cronenberg fan as the Soskas?

TR: I'm not as rabid a fan as they are [laughs] but it's really hard to top. Their knowledge and academia about him as an artist is incredible so I don't think I can even scratch that surface. I definitely appreciate his films and what he's contributed to Canadian cinema. I'm incredibly into his style of body horror. But when I think when it comes to number one fans, no one is going to beat the Soska's.

DC: You play several roles in Rabid, and one of them is a secret/spoiler. Without revealing too

much, what can you say about this mysterious character?

TR: I got to play something that is going to make people really grossed out, and not just because of the visual aspect of it, but the implications of what the character is and what she represents. And I think there are going to be some people who have some sleepless nights. And when I was putting this character in that moment, that's what I was thinking about. Just kind of how people are going to take this and I'm like, "This is going to weird a whole lot of people out and if a kid sees this at too young an age, that kid is going to have some serious questions later in life, I feel."

DC: You've been conveying a real sense of Canadian pride when it comes to *Rabid*.

*TR: It's nice to see more Canadian stories and supporting other Canadian crews and performers and just a lot of the homegrown talent that goes into it. And **Rabid** was very much made in Canada with Canadian content. And despite having all this talent we mostly wound up working, obviously in Vancouver for a lot of American productions. But as far as the remake, we didn't get farmed out to the Americans and the corporations, we kept everything in Canada and we used a lot of the same crew that David Cronenberg himself used. That was pretty cool for me. That was a cool part of the process. It was like, "Oh, I wonder how this is going to hold up for the OG crew, this?"*

In addition to Risk, **Rabid** stars Laura Vandervoort, Benjamin Hollingsworth, and Ted Atherton.

Ted Atherton

EXPLAINS THE PATHOLOGY OF BEAUTY IN RABID

Method: Phone

Originally Published: December 10, 2019

Synopsis: *Horribly disfigured after a freak accident, doctors perform a radical medical procedure on an aspiring young fashion designer. But when the bandages come off, the side effects soon cause her to develop an insatiable appetite for human blood.*

Yesterday, we shared an interview with the incomparable, multi-talented Tristan Risk, who explained what makes **Rabid** truly Canadian, and promised one of her three roles will lead to sleepless nights for many! Today, we continue our Week of **Rabid** with an interview with Ted Atherton. Atherton plays Dr. William Burroughs (a nod to the American Beat Poet of the same name—and Cronenberg's adaptation of **Naked Lunch**). Give it a read below.

Dread Central: Let's talk about the preparations you made for playing this character, Dr. William Burroughs, in *Rabid*. Did you look into the current

state of human cloning and transhumanism in science?

*Ted Atherton: Yeah, the Soska's sent a number of research bits regarding that, that were really wild about that particular sort of rabbit hole. And then I pulled it down on the internet a little bit. Although, what I really found kind of interesting about the movie, like all good horror movies, it's about some deep, dark truth about the human psyche, and **Rabid** has it. And I also watched the original Cronenberg movie and in this re-imagining, as conceived by the Soska Sisters, this cultural obsession with a certain standard of beauty leads to a kind of pathologizing of anything that falls short of that standard, do you know what I mean? As if to not be beautiful or fit means you're in need of a cure. And I found that particularly interesting from the character I was playing, Dr. William Burroughs, (with that nod to Cronenberg's obsession with William S. Burroughs of **Naked Lunch** fame).*

The fact that Laura Vandervoort's character Rose works for a fashion designer (really played beautifully in a darkly comic way by my friend Mackenzie Gray, whose new line is called Schadenfreude, the German word for the dark pleasure we take in another's misfortune) really dramatizes the moral sickness at the heart of this obsession with physical beauty, particularly physical beauty that's competitive. And Rose is not a model but she's not ugly. She's average looking, or as average looking that hair and makeup can make you when you're starting with Laura Vandervoort! But average isn't good enough and it actually holds Rose back in events in her career. When this horrific traffic accident that drives Laura Vandervoort's character into the hands of Dr. William Burroughs, it's seen as a kind of good fortune because it provides the occasion for a complete physical transformation—a cure for the sickness of her mediocre looks and the cost, of course, becomes a growing and unknowing hunger, a special diet.

She gets transformed from a human being, a member of society with all the connections of human society, into this solitary predator. That's

345

what I found most interesting. Dr. Burroughs, he comes across as very kind, sort of paternalistic, a kind of a father figure. And Rose is ultimately his creation, his child in a way. But he's transforming her into this child that's going to have no connection with anything else in the world, because anyone that gets anywhere near her, who comes close enough to care about her, she's going to destroy and turn into that same kind of lone predator.

DC: You've done a lot of sci-fi and drama but is it safe to say that *Rabid* is the most gruesome, brutal movie you've been in?

TA: Oh my God, absolutely. I've seen all of those prosthetics and practical effects close up and I have to tell you, they were absolutely disgusting.

Mackenzie Gray

EXPLAINS "SCHADENFREUDE" IN RABID

Method: *Phone*

Originally Published: December 11, 2019

Synopsis: *Horribly disfigured after a freak accident, doctors perform a radical medical procedure on an aspiring young fashion designer. But when the bandages come off, the side effects soon cause her to develop an insatiable appetite for human blood.*

On Monday, we shared an interview with the incomparable, multi-talented Tristan Risk, who explained what makes **Rabid** truly Canadian, and promised one of her three roles will lead to sleepless nights for many! Yesterday, we continue our Week of **Rabid** with an interview with Ted Atherton. Atherton plays Dr. William Burroughs (a nod to the American Beat Poet of the same name—and Cronenberg's adaptation of **Naked Lunch**).

Today, we're talking to Mackenzie Gray who plays thorny and flamboyant fashion designer Gunter. Give our conversation a read below.

Dread Central: First of all, I think people are going to love Gunter. Your character, when we first meet him, is so intimidating, so mean. But by the end of *Rabid*, we love you! What was it like playing this over-the-top character and who were your influences?

Mackenzie Gray: Well definitely [German fashion designer and artist) Karl Lagerfeld was one. I used his tone of voice, his phrasing, and we did actually put some of Karl's actual statements into Gunter. He's a guy who absorbs fashion and makes it his own in his own way, so you have loads of guys dressed like sluts and they do these beautiful clothes. So, we came up with the scarves and scar on his face, the clothing, the big shoes. We came up with a look to make him his own design.

The Soskas were totally open to anything I came up with. So, when I said, "I think he should have had a facelift but he keeps his scar, whereas Rose hides her scar", the gals loved that. He loves his scar, wears it like a badge, and she hides hers. Right away you've got a duality there.

DC: Gunter created a line of clothes called "Schadenfreude". I think most of our readers are probably familiar with the term, but can you briefly talk about what it means and how it works for both the clothing line and the themes of Rabid?

MG: Well, Schadenfreude is one of those beautiful German words, to take the place of a lot of words, and basically it means laughing at other people's misfortune. When you find other people's downfall or misfortune funny and have a chance to ridicule them and enjoy that, it's called Schadenfreude. Schadenfreude right now, if you think about Donald Trump and the things happening in his life, there's a lot of humor in it. A lot of people laughing at it, calling him ridiculous because they don't like him. So, there's Schadenfreude present in American pop culture and talk shows right now.

Schadenfreude, in the case of Gunter, he's laughing at fashion, laughing at people's conformity and that everybody who thinks they are doing something new, starting a new trend, blue suits with bad shoes and stuff, it's not original at all once everybody is doing it. It's laughable because they think they're being original and hip when in fact they're not. And so, the idea for me with Schadenfreude was who's laughing at who. It's on the billboards. He's ripping up fashion and doing different stuff and eventually, he does rip up Rose's dress and shreds it. So, he's tearing up fashion and he's laughing at the conformity of fashion. That's how I took it, anyway.

DC: What makes working with Jen and Sylvia Soska so special?

MG: I think they're original. I think they're a hit. They're smart, I think they're driven... It's not been easy for female directors and they don't listen to that bullshit. They go, "Who cares, we're doing it and we're making it!" and I really love that energy. Working for them was a treat. It was absolutely fantastic. They run a happy, courteous set. A thoughtful set. There's no yelling and shouting at anybody. They are open to suggestions and get excited by it. You say, "Hey, can I try this?" And they say, "Yeah, yeah!" and get excited by it.

When I was studying to train as a director, I was given a great piece of advice which was, always take responsibility for inspiring people. Because I was getting a little uptight about people saying, "Oh, can we try this, can we try that?" like they were trying to run away with my vision. And the mentor that I had, a great director named Ken Gas, he said that to me, "Always take responsibility for inspiring people". If you take their idea, it's yours. You chose it. And if you don't at least they've been heard and are still part of the process, and the Soskas live by that. They completely try to inspire you and get you to create and rarely say no. They say, "Yes, let's try it!" and that's a beautiful freedom. I love them for that. And it was also a lot of fun. They're fun gals!

The Soskas have huge respect for David Cronenberg, not just a Canadian and horror icon but as a great director. He has never let anyone remake any of his films so there's great respect that they had. Every day it was, "How can we keep this film our own but respect David every stage of the way?" And I think they really, really did that and the whole crew and cast were on that same page. Playing Gunter, playing an over-the-top character, you can go too far. But I tried to ground him in a sense, in his own purvey and his own arrogance, that he's aware of. So, all of those things allow you to heighten a performance were there but a lot of it was because of their respect for Cronenberg.

I will finish by saying it was also a crew that was all women. Objective photography, our first and second camera, key grips. There was a huge female presence on the set and they didn't just do that to make a point. There was a really different energy on set because of that presence and I really loved that presence. It was a delight. Even when we were under pressure, the day was running away, it was a totally different energy. And I really love that they create that and they do that, and that is something worth noting for anyone who sees the film.

Stephen Huszar

EXPLAINS RABID AS METAPHOR FOR THE
ENTERTAINMENT INDUSTRY

Method: *Phone*

Originally Published: December 12, 2019

Synopsis: *Horribly disfigured after a freak accident, doctors perform a radical medical procedure on an aspiring young fashion designer. But when the bandages come off, the side effects soon cause her to develop an insatiable appetite for human blood.*

On Monday, we shared an interview with the incomparable, multi-talented Tristan Risk, who explained what makes ***Rabid*** truly Canadian, and promised one of her three roles will lead to sleepless nights for many! Tuesday, we continued our Week of ***Rabid*** with an interview with Ted Atherton. Atherton plays Dr. William Burroughs (a nod to the American Beat Poet of the same name—and Cronenberg's adaptation of ***Naked Lunch***). Yesterday, we talked to Mackenzie Gray about "Schadenfreude" and today, we're thrilled to grill Stephen Huszar who plays soap-opera actor Dominic. Read on!

Dread Central: I interviewed Ted Atherton and Mackenzie Gray and what I found interesting was they each play archetypical characters in *Rabid* and they were both able to talk about the film from those perspectives. Ted gave me a kind of thematic exploration of *Rabid* from a medical standpoint and Mackenzie was able to talk about *Rabid* and the fashion world and how the themes are intertwined. You also play a type of archetypical character: A soap opera actor. So, how would you explain *Rabid* through the lens of the entertainment industry?

Stephen Huszar: Wow, that's a really interesting question. Let's see… You know, **Rabid** *explores how we can literally transform from an outside perspective. Entertainment relates a lot to the way you look, the way you react, but also, there's a deeper connection to things when we're talking about actors and performances. So, as a soap actor star, playing someone who is actually an actor in the movie itself, you're kind of like breaking that fourth wall a little bit. It's interesting to see the transformation that my character Dominic goes through. He's getting a bit of work done so to speak, on himself. But by being [in the hospital] he connects with somebody who's going through a real challenge in Rose from an emotional standpoint, from what she's going through, and it's something that's passed on to Dominic. And then he goes through a similar thing. I often feel like this happens in the entertainment industry, where you get passed on certain energy or issues and we have to be careful in how we connect in certain ways because it can have a pretty drastic effect on the end result, if that makes sense at all.*

DC: Everyone else I've spoken with loved working with Jen and Sylvia. What was your Soska experience?

SH: Yeah, phenomenal. We hit it off right away. They're very giving and open directors and I feel like they're very much actors' directors because they give us a lot of freedom on set. A lot of times sets are very controlled and there's a preconceived notion of how you want scenes to go. Of course, there is preparation but also on the day, it's wonderful to be on a set where there's freedom to explore and that's really my experience with them, from a professional standpoint. I think a lot of the magic that came from the scenes is because of that freedom they afforded to us as actors. From a personal standpoint, they're amazing. It was nice I could meet all the other lead and supporting actors before we started shooting, which was very helpful. A lot of times you don't have that opportunity on films. And they're Hungarian, and I'm also Hungarian blood so we have that connection as well, so that worked out well!

DC: Is there anything else you want to tell us about *Rabid* before I let you go?

SH: I feel a lot of times people ask me, or are curious, about how actors can play different kinds of roles. I'm known quite a bit for my romantic comedy roles. I see a lot of that, and I enjoy making people laugh. But on the other side of the equation, I love the opportunity to be challenged as an actor, to really go there, emotionally, psychologically and even physically in this instance, and really see a transformation. Like, when you're introduced to the character to when the last time you see him on screen. This is an awesome opportunity to do that and a great challenge and I really appreciated the opportunity. I just really enjoyed that and I think as actors we are always really pushing each other, or ourselves, no matter what roles we have, so it was a pretty awesome experience to be able to do that.

Richard Stanley

DISCUSSES "CAGE RAGE" IN COLOR OUT OF SPACE

Method: *In Person*

Reflections: Of course I've seen ***Hardware*** (1990) and ***Dust Devil*** (1992), but I really began to love Richard Stanley when I saw the documentary ***Lost Soul: The Doomed Journey of Richard Stanley's Island of Dr. Moreau*** (2014). As wacky as that film ultimately turned out to be, it pales in comparison to the behind-the-scenes lunacy. Stories of epic ego clashes between Marlon Brando and Val Kilmer are legendary. Most intriguing are insinuations that Stanley never really left the production after he was canned as the film's director. Instead, it's rumored that he "went wild" and continued to lurk around the island set, even going so far as to secretly appear as an extra in some scenes.

I wish I could have grilled Stanley for hours about that experience, separating truth from conjecture. But our meeting was in support of ***Color Out of Space***, which was greatly lauded at Fantastic Fest in 2019. I've never interviewed Nicholas Cage, but interviewing directors who have worked with the intense actor is always a joy. I love jawing about how awesome that man is while simultaneously addressing the phenomenon known as "Cage Rage".

In this interview, I was most impressed with how Stanley discussed the problematic legacy of H.P. Lovecraft.

ORIGINALLY PUBLISHED: **January 24, 2020**

I was lucky enough to catch ***Color Out of Space*** when it premiered at Fantastic Fest in Austin, TX last September. I was even luckier to have a chance to sit down with the film's legendary director, Richard Staley, for a one-on-one.

Color Out of Space is now playing in theaters nationwide. Read the synopsis below. My exclusive conversation with Stanley follows.

Highlights of our conversation include: "Cage Rage", young actor Julian Hilliard, and H.P. Lovecraft's problematic legacy.

Synopsis: *After a meteorite lands in the front yard of their farm, Nathan Gardner and his family find themselves battling a mutant extraterrestrial organism that infects their minds and bodies, transforming their quiet rural life into a technicolor nightmare.*

Dread Central: Your movie is based on the H.P. Lovecraft short story "The Colour Out of Space". I'm just curious why you axed the "The"?

Richard Stanley: I think as it comes around it will be put easier on the marques. It also shows that we're not the short story, we're an adaptation. We dragged it kicking and screaming into the present day. The slight change of spelling in the title indicates that. It's faithful but not completely faithful.

*DC: Fantastic. Let's talk a little bit about Nicolas Cage. Cage is kind of enjoying a renaissance right now. What I loved about **Mandy** was they put him in a situation where his over-the-top freak out was understandable. He's just seen the love of his life murdered right in front of him, you see him go ballistic, and it doesn't seem outlandish. Similarly, in **Color Out of Space**, you've got some great scenes of "Cage Rage" but in situations where you can't really under-react to what's going on, so it seems very fitting. Do you want to talk about what it was like working with Nic? Was this type of over-the-top performance something you were going for, or did you have to rein him in?*

RS: Well, I think this whole project only happened because of Nic. We noticed there was a Lovecraft script flying around and [producers] managed to put the two of us together. He's got tremendous potential.

DC: I think horror is a great genre for him.

RS: Yeah, he absolutely adores what he does and brings an incredible energy to it. It's all planned in advance. It's not nearly as chaotic as people think. We went through the script weeks before we shot and highlighted different areas he could cut loose. "So, I'd thought I'd do something with this scene here? Do you mind if I run amok and try and milk the alpacas?" *Which was a scene that was subsequently cut out–hopefully it makes the Extended Cut at some point. The level of hysteria on display in a part of the movie that was toned down considerably. Once that's locked in, once the sequences are decided on and we know what we're doing, Nic will repeat that same performance with the same timing and inflection again and again from every camera angle. So, it's not as out of control as people think. There's quite a lot of method going into it. The volatility in his performance, for me, is thoroughly entertaining to watch, never knowing when he is going to blow up or how he is going to react, which I think just keeps it a lot more interesting.*

*I notice people have been having trouble with the sense of humor coupled with the dark subject matter which for me seems bizarre because, in real life, no such generic distinctions are apparent if something really terrible happens to me. At the same time, on camera, I was channeling a lot of emotions connected to my mother's death from cancer. She was a huge H.P. Lovecraft fan so that bleeds across the terrible relationships, across the family members in the movie. Nic is, in the later part of the movie, doing the same, largely channeling his father, who was the basis for the strange accent and hand movements and things. And I think that last time he did that was on **Vampire's Kiss**, also a point of recreation of his dad. Not a lot of people know that. They think his just chumming around. But to an extent he's actually working through baggage and trauma from his own past.*

DC: So, one of the things you always hear in regards to filmmaking is "Never work with kids or animals". I'm wondering what it was like to work

with the youngest cast member (Julian Hilliard) and I'm really curious to what it was like to work with alpacas.

*RS: Both were incredible, so don't believe what they say. Young Julian Hilliard, who was the youngest member of our cast, was having a ball. I think if he survives growing up he'll be a genre directory, probably. He's super observant and very smart; constantly watching, seeing what we're doing, checking how it was coming out, fully aware of what was coming next. His mom had to sit next to me and I briefed her and had her cover his eyes and ears, mostly due to language. No sex. There is some body horror but not your conventional violence. I don't want to give away too much. There was body horror, so it was difficult to shield him from that. But his habit of drawing monsters the whole time we were on set, drawing creepy creatures with crayons, really helped. We incorporated that into the movie. He was constantly running up to me with completed drawings of creatures and their different dimensions, how large they would be in real life and what they would sound like. Between this coming out and **The Haunting of Hill House** he's going to be with us for a while. He was a joy to work with.*

*As for the alpacas, they came in very early in the draft. We knew the story had been adapted a number of times before, most notably **The Farm** from the eighties and "The Lonesome Death of Jordy Verrill" in the original **Creepshow**. The original story is from the 1930's and had a huge impact on 1950's B movies. Every single movie where a meteorite comes from outer space, it seems to be descending from the same source material. So, I knew going in we couldn't do that. We had to find a different way of doing those key sequences. I didn't want to show a meteor come down and hit them in a long shot. I knew it couldn't be a conventional farm family that would come out and poke it. At the same time, I didn't just want cows or chickens. So, one of the first decisions was, "Ok, what are they farming?" and I think it was a toss-up in my mind between ostriches and alpacas. Ostriches can be a* *little dangerous and hard to get a hold of whereas alpacas are pretty user-friendly and valuable.*

DC: We live in an age now where your past sins are going to come back to haunt you and, recently, I've noticed some backlash against Lovecraft because of the racism of his era. Do you think H.P. Lovecraft is problematic in any way for modern audiences?

RS: I would like to think that Lovecraft should be problematic. I'd be sorry if he wasn't. Lovecraft has always been problematic and I would hope that he still retains the power to shock and unsettle audiences. I think Lovecraft is an author who generally had the power to destabilize the sense of what grounds you—if you read too much into it. Lovecraft was obviously almost unknown during his lifetime and from the time his works started appearing in paperback in the sixties and seventies, those had a strong core following. About fifteen years ago it was at the point where he was almost inducted into the pantheon of American literary elite and they started putting up bronze statues to him in Providence, Rhode Island. They named town squares after him. And, of course, when that happened people started examining his life more closely and it was the letters he wrote which pointed to his racism and his sympathy towards the Nazis.

In full context, I think Lovecraft's racism is symptomatic of his overall worldview. If you read him long enough, you'll realize he kind of hates everyone. He's as insulting towards Italians, Irish people, Polish—pretty much everyone. There are a number of stories, notably "The Outsider" and "The Shadow over Innsmouth" where he looks himself in the mirror and realizes that, the writer realizes, that he too is a monster. I think in one of those stories the character was looking too close to his own reflection and ends up dosing himself in gasoline and setting himself on fire.

So, I think Lovecraft's racism is his dislike for the human race on the whole. In a way it's part of his hatred of life. I think his has mistrust of anyone who is enjoying themselves too much. Life is such a terrible thing, surely if you are enjoying it too much there must be something wrong, something off about you too. I would recommend a more careful approach to reading his material but on some level, he is the American Kafka. It doesn't rob him of the fact that he is still a major figure to be dealt with.

DC: I'd like to hear your thoughts on *Color Out of Space* and what people are going to get out of it.

RS: Well above all else, first and foremost it's a heck of a ride. I tried to make a movie that is very carefully paced…intentionally funny and horrible. I'd like to think that people who are looking for something suitably mind-bending, something that works well at the midnight hour. **Color** *delivers on all of that. It is a psychedelic movie as well. It contains some psychedelic aspects that I think improve the later in the evening you watch it. I think it also improves with the larger audiences. I'd hate to watch it alone or in the morning. It would probably hurt my head!*

Osgood ("Oz") Perkins

DIRECTOR DEFENDS PG-13 GRETEL & HANSEL: "DOESN'T AFFECT SOPHISTICATION OF HORROR"

Method: *Phone*

Reflections: This one is a heartbreaker.

I'm a huge fan of Osgood ("Oz") Perkins, especially his 2018 psychological *horror The Blackcoat's Daughter*. I was really excited to interview him. Unfortunately, I had technical issues with my recording device. No sooner had he and I said our goodbyes when I realized I hadn't actually captured a single word discussed.

In a panic, I banged out this "interview" as quickly as I could. Unfortunately, it was difficult for me to remember much beyond our final topic, that being the PG-13 rating of *Gretel & Hansel*. While I think the point about horror audiences and ratings is both important and interesting, I'll always lament the loss of our 15-minute conversation. On reflection, all these years later, I can't even remember all of what we discussed, and it still kills me.

Oz, if you're reading this, I apologize for my blunder. Hopefully, I'll have another opportunity to interview you again in the future.

It's also worth noting that January 2020 was the first time many of us heard about a flu-like disease causing a stir in the Chinese province of Hubei, specifically in a city called Wuhan. Still, I don't think anyone could have possibly foreseen how utterly and completely the world would be shaken up. This was the cusp of a new era, and things will never be the same again. I caught Gretel & Hansel when it played theatrically. I wouldn't attend another public theater screening again for more than two years.

———

ORIGINALLY PUBLISHED: **January 30, 2020**

Arriving in select markets tonight in advance of a nation-wide release tomorrow (January 31st), ***Gretel & Hansel*** is the third film from Osgood Perkins (***The Blackcoat's Daughter***, **I Am the Pretty Thing That Lives in the House**). The filmmaker's previous efforts aren't for the faint of heart and Perkins wants genre fans to brace themselves for an impactful experience—despite the film's PG-13 rating (something that's seen as a curse to many hardcore horror fans).

"[The rating] doesn't affect the sophistication of the horror in ***Gretel & Hansel***" Perkins assured me in a recent interview. At the same time, the filmmaker is indeed targeting younger viewers for what may seem a surprising reason. Check out more of our conversation below the film's synopsis.

Synopsis: *A long time ago in a distant fairytale countryside, a young girl (Sophia Lillis, IT: Chapter 2) leads her little brother (Sammy Leakey) into a dark wood in desperate search of food and work, only to stumble upon a nexus of terrifying evil.*

While **Gretel & Hansel** isn't likely to disappoint today's discriminating horror aficionados, Perkins sees the film as something of a primer for the next generation of rabid genre fans:

"This PG-13 film is really quite dark, and the kids who go through this darkness and come out of it will, hopefully, say, 'Ah! I made it!' I think that breeds self-importance, self-power, and resilience. And I think these are all great things to have. If a weird little movie like this can do that for a couple of kids who go in thinking, 'This might be too much' but come out feeling 'I'm okay,' well, I think that's a win."

Tommy Chong

TALKS COLOR OUT OF SPACE & CANNABIS, MAN

Method: *Phone*

Reflection: Those waning days of January 2020 were bliss. I had met the woman of my dreams (my future wife), I was getting into the groove of my new position as Editor-in-Chief at Dread Central, and we were gearing up to release the next wave of **Chronic Horror** episodes. I was at the top of the apex, looking down at the world, and feeling both hopeful and confident.

Even though I was extremely proud of those first four episodes of **Chronic Horror**, I had dissected them with a critical eye. I'm not an actor, so this was the first time I saw myself "on TV". I realized I was fidgety, that I sometimes had a stupid grin on my face, and that I had been excessively sweaty. (We couldn't run the AC while filming, and we'd go for long stretches—and it was fucking hot!)

I knew what I liked and what I wanted to change, and the next batch of episodes was even better! A "Live" episode filmed at Arena Cinelounge on Sunset Blvd, a paranormal investigation of Cobb Estate, and in-studio guests Sadie Katz (***Wrong Turn 6: Last Resort***) and Australian musician/comedian Hairy Soul Man (Kai Smythe).

Before the Pandemic came and ruined everything, the plan was to shoot the final four episodes of ***Chronic Horror*** Season 1 in late February or early March of 2020. I had a "Dream List" of potential guests, and of course it included Tommy Chong. So, when the opportunity to interview Chong in support of ***Color Out of Space*** came along, I jumped at the opportunity.

Notice how I got Chong to agree to make an appearance on ***Chronic Horror***. While there's no way of knowing if this connection would have actually manifested, I'd like to think it was a done deal!

Someday perhaps, I will write an entire book exploring the intersection of horror fandom and cannabis culture. And I honestly think ***Chronic Horror*** will rise from the ashes, manifesting in a new and improved format. It's just a matter of time.

ORIGINALLY PUBLISHED: **January 30, 2020**

I was lucky enough to catch ***Color Out of Space*** when it premiered at Fantastic Fest in Austin, TX last September. I was also lucky enough to score (pun intended) a sit-down with one of the film's stand-outs, the irrepressible Tommy Chong! For a guy who has his own talk show about horror movies and cannabis, it should come as no surprise that it was a bucket-list interview for me!

In **Color Out of Space**, Chong plays Ezra: A sage (and stoned) hermit living in the woods. The film is now playing in theaters nationwide. You can read the synopsis below. My exclusive conversation with Chong follows.

Highlights of our conversation include: The evolving "stoner" archetype, the (literal) trials and tribulations of being one of the world's most famous cannabis users, that rumor John Carpenter wanted to cast him as the sheriff in **Halloween** (1978), and "hidden messages" in **Color Out of Space**.

Synopsis: *After a meteorite lands in the front yard of their farm, Nathan Gardner and his family find themselves battling a mutant extraterrestrial organism that infects their minds and bodies, transforming their quiet rural life into a technicolor nightmare.*

Color out of Space is directed by Richard Stanley and based on a short story by H.P. Lovecraft; in addition to Chong, the film stars Nicolas Cage, Joely Richardson, and Madeleine Arthur.

Dread Central: I was born in the 1970's so I've been watching you my whole life, and it's amazing, in retrospect, how the stoner archetype really evolved. In *Up in Smoke* you were so high you were basically impaired. But now, in *Color Out of Space* your character is sage and wise. Can you talk a bit about how the archetypical stoner has evolved over the decades?

Tommy Chong: You know, marijuana has always been a religious sacrament, since the beginning, since the burning bush in the Bible. So, the weed thing had come around in a big, big circle. It has been an illegal substance, used by law enforcement as a racist tool to keep the Mexicans in line. Over the years the hippies got involved. That was all the white people with long hair, and it was still illegal. Now it's 2020 and it's legal and old ladies are smoking it and hippies are barely existing anymore. It's just a new world. It's lost its notoriety, its racist 'law', and now it's accepted as what it was many thousands of years ago: A medicine and religious sacrament.

DC: Right on, I totally agree. I don't think kids today realize how risky it was for you in the 70's and 80's to basically come out as a famous pot smoker. It really put a target on your back, didn't it?

TC: Yeah, in the 1990s, [then President George] Bush wanted some kind of excuse to go after the hippies because of his Iraq war. It spawned Operation Pipedream, [a federal sting operation] that took me down. I was in jail for nine months, but it was all ordained. It was all meant to be. And it changed my life. Look at us now: The biggest problem is what to do with all the money. That's a good problem.

DC: Yeah, now that cannabis is being legalized and decriminalized across the country, have you seen artistic representations of the herb and cannabis smokers changing?

TC: Oh yeah, totally. As far as the criminality thing, now you've got old ladies talking about what strain they'd like. One would like to sleep, another one wants to create. They like the sativa, so it's really fun to hear. I go to parties, a lot of billionaire parties, and I bring chocolate and I'm like the candy man. As soon as I walk in the door, they are all over me for my marijuana infused chocolate!

DC: Do you act in films while imbibed?

*TC: It depends. It depends on the bit, you know? In **Up in Smoke**, we weren't always stoned. Sometimes it's relaxing if you know what you were doing, but if you don't it probably isn't the best idea to get too* *blazed. I have little breath mints that I sell and they are infused with about 20 mg of some really good THC and that's all I've been doing lately. Just these breath mint strips.*

DC: In your opinion does being stoned enhance the experience of watching a horror movie?

TC: Absolutely. I would not watch any movie without being stoned—especially horror. It's too scary. When you're stoned you see the humor beyond the horror.

DC: What's a horror movie you like to watch stoned?

*TC: Well, **Christine**. You know, the car.*

*DC: That reminds me of something I read on IMDB. John Carpenter directed **Christine** but he's most famous for **Halloween**. I heard you were actually considered for the role of the sheriff in that flick. Is that true?*

TC: Possibly, possibly.

DC: Hey, have you heard of this new talk show called *Chronic Horror*?

TC: Yes, I have.

DC: I'm actually the host and creator of that show.

TC: You are?

DC: Yeah, that's me with the dreadlocks. I have guests come on and we get stoned and have some gourmet munchies and watch movies. I'd love to get you on the show or come out and check out your company (Pipe Dreams) on a field trip or something.

TC: Anytime, anytime man. You know how to get a hold of me.

DC: Fantastic! Let's do it! Is there anything else you'd like to tell me about *Color Out of Space* before I let you go? Anything about the film that no one's asked you yet that you'd really like to discuss?

TC: There's a hidden message, especially in my performance, and if you see the movie it will affect your life to a point where 'things' will happen to you for no reason. It has that effect. There's a little mantra I did in the movie and if you see it enough times it will make sense.

Ant Timpson

TALKS COME TO DADDY & TURBO KID 2

Method: *In Person*

Originally Published: February 6, 2020

One of my favorite films that screened at Fantastic Fest in Austin last September was **Come To Daddy**, the directorial debut of Ant Timpson (best known as the producer of films like **Turbo Kid** and **Housebound**). Give the film's synopsis a read below.

Synopsis: *A privileged man-child arrives at the beautiful and remote coastal cabin of his estranged father, whom he hasn't seen in 30 years. He quickly discovers that not only is his dad a jerk, he also has a shady past that is rushing to catch up with him.*

Come to Daddy stars Elijah Wood, Stephen McHattie, and Garfield Wilson.

I was lucky enough to sit down with Timpson at Fantastic Fest last September. Give our exclusive conversation a read below.

Dread Central: I remember how you tweeted out one time about how *Turbo Kid* was the most pirated film of 2016 or something like that. I've always been a real proponent of anti-piracy.

Ant Timpson: It felt like that. It felt like we got screwed big time at the time. But overall, we're making the sequel. The sequel hasn't been held up because of [piracy] but because the guys have been busy. It's like [there is] an entire generation that doesn't understand [the effects of piracy] and they don't care, really. That's what's lame.

DC: I'm in my 40s and I've seen the change. I'm still a collector of physical media and I love paying my twenty bucks to support a film I love and then own it, as opposed to just code.

AT: There was an idea I came up with: An "Uber tip". If you're watching Amazon, any player form, you can tip the filmmaker a dollar. There should be an interface there. It doesn't affect their revenue stream.

DC: You're well known for producing some great films and this is your directorial debut. What made you want to get into directing? Did you feel like people were screwing up your films?

AT: That thought there has never passed through my mind because my thought there is finding new talent. Really, that's my whole background. Through the "48 Hours" thing I do with Peter Jackson in New Zealand, it's all about finding the new talent, watching the pipeline go. When I've seen the films, I've never been like, "Oh, I would have done it like this". That's a crazy game to play. Like reading a book and saying, "Oh, I wanted that character to do this". It's ridiculous.

For me, I started off as that crazy, weekend, filmmaker. Me and my brother and friends went out and shot, like, a movie every weekend. So I started off being that kid, making horror movies every weekend. And then I got serious with arty farty black and white 35mm shorts, to get these art grants. I was working towards being a serious filmmaker and then I got sort of derailed man. I got hooked into Film Festivals, which became this huge thing in my life. It just blew up and I got so much energy from it, just being surrounded by friends and doing the thing that we loved most: watching crazy movies together at big old cinema palaces and then introducing this new material to the populace. It's such a rush and that was a decade that, boom, it was gone. And I was kind of like still supporting other filmmakers on the side. Basically, I hadn't changed. I always wanted to be that director but it took my dad dying in front of me to say, "Fuck, life's short. Get trying or get dying." I think that's the line.

DC: That's a good dovetail into my next question. Come to Daddy is based on a story by Toby Harvard. How much of the original concept of the story did you change as the film's director?

AT: Toby did a shitload. I gave him a skeleton structure of what I wanted the beast to be, and that's already when it was a low-fi, a kind of film I thought I could just pull favors and shoot the thing. And he just ran with characters, took that, blew it out and expanded the idea. The main ideas with the characters are all Toby's invention. It was just like archetypes and he just wrote little flavors. We have a process where we just bounce stuff back and forth, and I could never do dialogue as good as Toby. But it's more about us finding the balance of time. Sometimes he really pushes it. There were nibbles of breeziness in it originally, and I was like, it's going to be a really fine line in this film in terms of the tonal balance. It's going to be absurd but let's not point it to cartoonish. So that was a process of tweaking everything through it. When I got to the location and sorted through the geography, scans and sending it back saying "Hey, we're going to have to shift things." And so he was writing live as I was on set and pre-production, more like the scout, and we tweaked it to the exact location. I wasn't really evolving, it was all there. Just fine-tuning.

DC: For me, you've got Act One, where you think you know what's going on. There's this huge Act Two twist, and then there's a Third Act that goes off the rails.

AT: Mine was way more straight horror originally. And then when this came back it was way more in line with… It was a tribute to my dad, is what I wanted to do with it. And he was never a horror guy but he was a throwback, dark comedy, gallows humor. So it just worked out that Toby went down that path, so it was kind of beautiful.

DC: It's a movie about fathers and sons and you mentioned that your father passed recently.

AT: Yeah, so he passed and that kick started the whole thing. At that point the project kicked into gear and there was the whole thing about unfinished business, which is: What if your father's dark history came back into your present, and his unfinished business became your present-day business? So, the things that pass on, the sins of the father, all of that, the way we set it up was so on the nose, that's why we undercut it with humor. Because it's so serious and I hate those sort of quotes at the start of films. So, we thought we'd have some fun with that start in.

DC: You know, Elijah Wood was such a great score, not just because of how famous he is for being in *Lord of the Rings*, but it's been so fun watching him go from being Frodo to being a real cutting-edge advocate of horror movies. He's got his own distribution thing going on and he's got a lot of friends that work with him.

AT: He's incredible, and that supersedes his desire for acting in a way. That's his focus: All those sort of Spectrevision projects. I think he loves supporting crazy geniuses like Richard Stanley, or new originals like Jim Hoskins. That's his vibe. They are doing so many things now: Gaming, whatever they can expand into. Music… But his love of genre has a pretty wide taste, even though it feels like he's the horror guy. His taste is pretty eclectic and he's got a lot of passion and I know him as a mate. We met through here, through Austin, so I've known him for a long time. And Toby and I were talking and said it would be amazing if Elijah did it, this character. He's from Los Angeles, he's a DJ...

DC: That's what I was going to talk about. It's such a great skewering of hipster culture. The Elton John bluff! Was anything improvised?

AT: It was all written. It was actually cut down. I remember being on set, it was during the read through. And I remember we cut that whole passage down. And I remember I started thinking, just when I was hearing Elijah actually in the room with McHattie doing it, I was like, "Oh man, he's fucking nailing it!" I wanted all that other shit in there because we went through that thing where we were like, "Maybe it's too on the nose?" But we just chucked it all back in. He's so good in the film and there was a lot of concern with Elijah because he brings this huge likability as well, and you kind of want him to be that pretentious twat. You didn't want that guy to be totally accessible and likable to the audience, There had to be some sort of distance to it and not just be a cartoon, so I think he did a really good job of being that. That essence of that certain type of individual, but also shows some empathy for the audience to connect to as well. He's just really clever. He's just very aware of where he needs to be. He's usually the most experienced person on the set. For me, being the first time with him, it was pretty fucking great to have someone hit the marks and beats every single time.

DC: You mentioned Stephen too who I also think was a great coup for the film. He's one of most underrated genre actors in my opinion. Everyone has seen a movie he's been in but no one knows his name or recognizes him in just a straight-up picture. Did he and Elijah have some great chem-

**istry? I mean, some of the scenes they had were
intense.**

*AT: That was their chemistry, it really was. Stephen is really stoic.
He's not one to overshare right away. He's not someone you meet for the
first time and then it all comes out right away. There was a barrier in
the beginning. Like when we first met, it was like a starring contest in
silence between us and you can lose yourself in those goddamn eyes. He
doesn't have to do much really. And he had fun with it and got looser as
he went on. He really loved the experience. I think he sometimes turns
up places as the bad guy, like a lot of those people do. It's weird
because he was super handsome and now, he's got this sort of craggy,
sort of borderline villainous persona. But he was a handsome lead in
some of the films that I saw that came out in the 70's. He brings
what, like sixty years of experience working, man. And he's the type of
guy, like a Jack Palance type of guy. Before his big scene he went down
and did fifty press ups. The dude was in shape, so he was an imposing
presence, which was pretty cool. It helped man. You wanted that. You
wanted the elements of Elijah's stature versus McHattie so we could
have these ominous sort of distinctions between them. And when things
get dark you feel like shit can really happen to them.*

**DC: I'm just curious, and we can wrap it up with
this: Can you tell me a little bit about what it's like
being a filmmaker in New Zealand? You're about
as far away from Hollywood as you can possibly
get, so how does a filmmaker go from New
Zealand to some of the biggest international film
festivals?**

*AT: A lot of Kiwi's have bailed and jumped to Hollywood but the
New Zealand landscape is like: You have Peter Jackson's empire and
the Hollywood films that come in, and the actual film commission only
has a small amount of money to make these films each year. Really
relatively small, like the size of one middle Hollywood movie in the*

entire industry. So, filmmakers grow up during the film and then they go through the grant process. It's like this thing where you put your cap out and say "Please, may I have a nickel?" And to me, that's what I love about the US: It's fucking do or die, dog eat dog. There's a passion and hunger for making shit over here that doesn't exist usually [in New Zealand] because we've got decades long drip-feeding mentality in getting a little bit of government money. It's like, don't wait in line. If you want to make something then you should be fucking making something. That's no excuse.

DC: I think that's good advice for anyone, no matter where you're from. Now that Steven Soderbergh released a feature film made on an iPhone [Unsane], what's your excuse?

AT: Exactly, and that's what I've noticed. There's these people who do the 48 thing that I do each year and that's the only thing they do each year. Some of them have other gigs and it's just a fun side project, but for the ones that are really interested, you should be doing that every weekend. If you want to hone your craft you've got to get out there and do it. I'm a bit bummed there's not more independent stuff coming out. There's a lot, and there's only a very few things that pop up, like **Mega Time Squad** *by Tim [van Dammen], which I thought was an amazing self-funded feature. I want to see about twenty of those every year coming out of New Zealand. It's changing, thank God. Like people are suddenly realizing. "Yeah, maybe I shouldn't wait in this big queue of people for a handout, I should just go and do some shit."*

DC: One more thing I'd love to end this on: Just tell us as much as you can about *Turbo Kid 2*.

AT: There's a script, and it's pretty amazing. It's had a few rewrites for the team to get it where they wanted it to go and now it's the amazing laborious process of getting money for it. But it's on the way. It was announced really early and the guys got really excited but we literally just got the new rewrite and it was fresh. So it's usually from that point, by my math, it takes about a year to get everything signed, contracts done and then let's get into it, so it still feels a ways away.

DC: The fan base just keeps growing. I mean, when we sell Dread DVD's at horror cons *Turbo Kid* sells out every time. We can never bring enough copies of that. It's one of things where people say, "Oh, I saw this before it dropped off Netflix, now I've got to have it!"

AT: Yeah, it's massive, and the fan base has been so great. They are insanely supportive and keep the fires burning during all the downtime, before something else comes out.

Come to Daddy arrives in US theaters tomorrow (February 7th).

Tommy Chong

Method: Phone

Reflections: Dread Central has a sister site. *Dread XP* is devoted to spooky video games, so, technically, an interview in support of *Bud Farm* should have appeared there. But when Tommy Chong is involved, I'm greedy! *Bud Farm* isn't even a horror game, but since Chong has genre cred, I made an exception.

There really wasn't much to talk about this time. I'm not much of a video game guy, and Chong admitted that he isn't either. And, even though I never played the game, I get the feeling *Bud Farm* is more basic than the kind of advanced, character-driven horror games Dread readers love best. You'll notice how quickly our conversation devolves into, basically, "So what have you been up to?"

And, of course, I got him on the hook once again regarding a future appearance on *Chronic Horror* (at the time, merely "on hiatus" as opposed to "cancelled").

But it's worth noting how, in the few months since my first interview with Tommy Chong, the entire world had been turned upside down. Nothing was "normal", including being a cannabis smoker.

———

ORIGINALLY PUBLISHED: **May 7, 2020**

Tommy Chong is a pop-cultural icon, a comedian and actor who horror fans loved in films like ***Evil Bong*** and Richard Stanley's ***Color Out of Space***. It was only inevitable that Chong would bring his classic, 1970s-era stoner persona into the world of video games.

Cheech & Chong Bud Farm (coming soon) is created by LDRLY Games, the world's largest publisher of cannabis games. The developers of ***Pot Farm***, ***Bud Farm: Grass Roots and Bud Farm: Idle Tycoon*** have been developing weed games for a decade. LDRLY Games are leaders in the cannabis industry being first to market on Facebook, Android and iOS.

Game Description:

Cheech and Chong find themselves stranded in the tiny hamlet of Hierba Verde. With no dope to be found, they start growing their own, and stumble ass-backwards into a lucrative business empire. With the crooked mayor in their back-pocket, the boys are on their way to striking it rich and living out their days lying on a beach like sun-kings. Unfortunately for them, Sgt Stedenko is hell-bent on putting them in jail for life. With the help a freaky cast of supporting characters, Cheech and Chong will chase their dreams of fame and fortune, while staying one step ahead of the law.

As the host of **Chronic Horror**, I'm always down to chat with Chong about his projects. You can read our recent **Bud Farm** interview below.

Dread Central: Let's talk about *Cheech & Chong Bud Farm*. Tell me a bit about what makes it so special.

Tommy Chong: Well, it's about making money selling weed…you don't have to do a whole lot, but it's just a lot of fun. It's so much fun and so addicting. Like at casinos: You can play your favorite slot machine or whatever it is, hours can go by, if not days.

DC: What are some of your favorite video games?

TC: I'm not a video game guy, never have been. This is really the first game that I've really been involved in. You know, when I've got time on my hands I don't want to have to work. I want to sit there and be entertained, which is why I'm not the greatest video game guy in the world. I think this is why it took so long to make a video game. Our fans had to grow up and become video game makers. I mean, I had a hard time switching from a land phone to a cell phone, but I made it.

DC: So how did you spend 4/20?

*TC: I was on Zoom. We had a big cluster of people, you know… we're quarantined. We had Wilmer Valderrama from **That '70s Show** and I laughed because when I met him, he was so young he couldn't grow hair on his face!*

DC: Do you still hang out with those guys from That '70s Show?

TC: Yeah, not really. It's events like that when we hook up, that sort of thing. Craig Robertson was also there, a bunch of people. And before that I was on with Willie Nelson. Yeah, he was singing away and Willie is great with jokes. He loves jokes, so we were trading the best dirty jokes that he had.

DC: What was the best one? Share with us.

*TC: Well, we were talking about whorehouses and the one that came to mind was, I told Willie: This guy knocks on the door of a whorehouse, and here's this guy standing there. He's got both his arms and legs in a cast. And the lady says, "What the hell do you want?" and he said, "Well I rang the bell, didn't I?" Willie laughed. He hadn't heard that one, even though it's an old joke. We had a great time. I love Willie. What is he now, 87? And he's still as powerful, singing away, like a young guy. Somebody asked me, "How do you build your lungs, with this pandemic?" and I said "Singing!" When I was on **The Masked Singer** I took singing lessons and it's all about breathing and getting powerful lungs, learning how to control your breathing. So yeah, if you're worried about that take up singing.*

DC: That's fantastic, that the cannabis community was still able to rally together during these unprecedented times of quarantine. Let me ask you: Do you think the Coronavirus is going to change the way stoners socially imbibe? No more sharing joints?

TC: Probably, for the short term anyway, until they find a vaccine. It's weird you know because the pandemic, if you do time in jail like I did, it's kind of what you do in jail. I mean, you definitely don't hang out with anybody close, you keep your distance the best you can, except for the sleeping quarters. We used to have our distances. But yeah, it's quite a trip to see what we're going through and it's all because of Trump. When you put people in jail like he did, innocent kids, there are some terrible things that are going to happen to you, in retaliation, and I think this is one of them. I think the whole pandemic is curing the planet anyway, because we're not burning fossil fuel like we were, and we're not creating plastic like we were. So I think in the long run it's going to be ok.

DC: Good perspective. So you and Cheech Marin are reunited here in the video game, so I was curious: When is the last time you guys smoked cannabis together?

TC: I think when we were on tour. We do a lot of casinos and we always have a celebratory smoke at the end of the show. I do it halfway through the show and sometimes before the show but Cheech usually waits to the end of the show because he has a lot more to remember.

DC: Are there any plans for a new tour or a new movie together?

TC: Not right now and it's weird how this happened because almost a year ago, Cheech hurt his knee and he had to get a knee replacement. So, he shut down for a year and then this pandemic came down and everything died anyways. It's weird how it happened like that, everything got shut down and we were already shut down. Yeah, so, when we get out of this I don't know, I don't know what's going to happen. We're just going to have to play it by ear. Right now, I'm enjoying it. I enjoy being under house arrest.

DC: Better than your last arrest I take it?

TC: Oh gosh, yeah. But that's the other thing: It's emptying the jails. Everybody is crying about prison reform, now we're getting all the nonviolent types out of prison.

DC: We're getting a kind of recalibration here on a lot of things that need fixing. What's your favorite way to get high these days?

TC: A little homemade pipe. I make my own pipes out of different things. I did a podcast for somebody, he gave me a little pipe, and it's an all in one, with lighters built in. You just fill up the bowl, hit the lighter that's right next door to the bowl. And that's ok, but I like my own homemade pipe because I know what I'm smoking then.

DC: What are your favorite munchies when you're imbibing?

TC: Well, anything. [Laughs] I've been making my own. What I did, I've got oranges growing on my roof so what I did was I pulp them. I don't get rid of the pulp or the juice I just squeeze them until they're all mushy, then I put them in the freezer with a popsicle stick and then I have a frozen orange. It's really good. What it does is it doesn't put all that sugar into you, it gives you a nice taste with the cool and gives you something to do, too.

DC: You make your own pipes and munchies...a great way to do things.

TC: My wife has been making bread, cookies, banana bread...man.

DC: You've already accomplished so much in your life. What are the goals for the future?

TC: I've got some really good plans about how we can save the planet. One giant plan is I would like to have my own movie studio and then I could create employment for everybody, hiring everybody either as an extra or the crew or an actor.

DC: Well you know, I'm going to be knocking down the door looking for a writer job when you get that up and running.

TC: What we're going to do, in order to bypass the immigration problems, we'll have casting people in the interviews, get all the information and then get them in on a movie permit. Yeah, so I've got some big, big plans and thanks to smoking. That's what the pipe does for me.

DC: Well whatever you've got going on you know we're going to support you one hundred percent at

Dread Central. As soon as this lockdown ends I'm going to be hitting you up about getting you on *Chronic Horror*.

TC: Ok man, let's do it.

Robert Englund

FAVORITE NIGHTMARE SEQUEL, FREDDY KILL, ONE-LINER & THE REASON JOHNNY DEPP WAS CAST

Method: *Phone*

Reflection: As the actor synonymous with Freddy Krueger, interviewing Robert Englund is on every horror journalist's Bucket List. My conversation with the living legend did not disappoint.

———

ORIGINALLY PUBLISHED: **May 8, 2020**

JJ Villard's Fairy Tales is a new, twisted, fun take on the classic Brothers Grimm fairy tales like ***Cinderella*** and ***Snow White***. The charm and cuteness of the original stories remain, but now they've been updated and packaged into a ball of raw, visceral, gross weirdness. The animated quarter-hour series is created, and executive produced by JJ Villard (***King Star King***) and produced by Cartoon Network Studios.

Look for *JJ Villard's Fairy Tales* to premiere Sunday, May 10th at 12:15 a.m. ET/PT

Voice talent this season includes Linda Blair, Warwick Davis, Corey Feldman, Alan Oppenheimer, Jennifer Tilly, and Robert Englund, who we were lucky enough to chat with recently.

While we start off talking about *JJ Villard's Fairy Tales*, the conversation inevitably turned *to A Nightmare on Elm Street* and Freddy Krueger. So, what could he tell me that hasn't already be reported before? Read on to find out!

*Robert Englund: This is my favorite addition to my resume. Keeps you humble. If you go way, way back on my resume, I think in the theater I was "Robot #2" in a production of **R.U.R.** [**Rossumovi Univerzální Roboti**], a famous Czech play that sort of coined the word robot. And that's one of my favorite resume inclusions, like "Bad Guy #2" on **Charlie's Angels**. In my "Goldilocks and the Three Bears" episode of JJ Villard's Fairy Tales, I'm one of the bears with his head stuck in the beehive because he was trying to get to the honey. I'm also a character called "Porridge Daddy" who is really a gob of snot. I'm Goldilocks's father and I've been turned into a gob of snot, and I'm also a toilet. So on my IMDB, my resume is going to be saying "Porridge Daddy", "Hive Head" and "Toilet". It'll be there for the rest of my life, and that will keep me humble, I think.*

Dread Central: So, I think I know the answer but I'd like to hear your take: What do you think makes Fairy Tales so appealing to horror fans?

RE: Well, you know, Fairy Tales originally, before Walt Disney and politically correct parents got a hold of them, were really dark stuff. They were cautionary tales, warnings about things in life that could happen, telling us there was evil in the world and cloaking it in a story and narrative.

*You think about **Hansel and Gretel**, they were a product of the Brothers Grimm. There was a huge famine in Germany, and one later on in Ireland, and to keep the children in line and well-behaved they would threaten them with evicting them from the house. And, of course, there was very little food in the house, but they knew if they were kicked out of the house they would starve to death. What's the first thing that happens if you're beginning to starve? You hallucinate. And if you were a child and you were starving and hallucinating, you'd hallucinate a house made of cake and ice cream and candy and sugar and icing and of course that's Hansel and Gretel. That's the dark element, the cautionary tale. Wes Craven uses it in **Wes Craven's New Nightmare**. Instead of bread crumbs being left in the woods by Hansel and Gretel, the little boy uses sleeping pills as a trail for his mother to find. But it's that great darkness that is the root and origin of Fairy Tales. Even though the **JJ Villard Fairy Tales** are more in the world of satire, of the old Jay Ward **Fractured Fairy Tales**, from the **Rocky and Bullwinkle** days but still, they're also kind of fun. **Bevis and Butthead**, **Rick and Morty**, the same kind of rough, raw, twisted kind of gross humor. And I think more than dark, it's really deconstructed and gross, which is what I really like.*

I got to work actually with the pencils, storyboards of the show and it was really helpful but kind of strange, Josh. Usually they have a picture of the character. It's the best they can do if you're doing voice work early. But it was really fun seeing these rough little pencil drawing, the storyboard sequences. They gave me a sense of the style and the energy and just how off the wall the show was.

DC: It really is off the wall. I've seen the first three episodes and it's just nuts. Talking about animation some more, Mark Hamill made a huge splash as the voice of the Joker in the *Batman* animated movies. Are there any iconic animated characters

that you'd be interested in providing the voices for?

RE: Speaking of Batman I'm the voice of The Riddler on the **Batman** *TV series and I'm The Vulture in* **The Spectacular Spider-Man**. *That show was so good and I'm so disappointed it got cancelled because most of the time I got my ass kicked by Spider-Man. I was just yelling! I really didn't get to my big giant Vulture episode yet, only flying around, barking out a couple lines. I didn't really get into the character in terms of lots of dialogue. That was a disappointment. But I love animation.*

A couple of years ago I got lost in Burbank near Hollywood. It was at the new branch of Walt Disney Studios. But they brought me in there for some weird project that had never been made but it was such a great idea. It reminds me a little bit of the guy who does the Funko Pop toys, and this was sort of a movie about all of the retired characters from television and advertising, hanging out together. They were kind of like combating something. So Snap, Crackle and Pop from Rice Krispies, Tony the Tiger, Speedy Alka-Seltzer and all those characters were together in this movie. And I can't remember what part I was up for, but it was just such a great, strange, bizarre idea and I was always hoping that thing would get made. All of our pop culture ideas and advertising coming together for some reason. They had to stop something, I can't remember what it was, but I just loved it. I'm sure the problem was they couldn't get the rights to all of those characters.

DC: Do you think *Nightmare on Elm Street* would make a great animated series?

RE: I think **Nightmare on Elm Street** *done as a dark, graphic novel style movie would be great. A 90-minute graphic novel. What I would do is, I would do that, then I would do a prequel movie. And then I would go into rebooting the rest of the franchise, using new special effects and technologies, new casts for new versions of the franchise for a new audience. But I think it would be great to start it out* *with a great graphic novel,* **Nightmare on Elm Street 1**. *That would be fun. In that great, graphic novel style, kind of noir style.*

DC: You mentioned a *Nightmare on Elm Street* prequel. How do imagine a prequel unfolding?

RE: There was a great script going around, I think it was called **Kruger: The First Kills**. *I'm not sure if I'm right about that, though. At one time they wanted John McNaughton to do it and it was Freddy as a killer and the cops have to catch him. So, it's the two bumbling police detectives that finally catch him, but then here's where it gets interesting: The whole middle and ending of the movie is the courtroom. It becomes a courtroom drama with Freddy in jail, and Freddy going to court every day. And then the two courthouse lawyers, the ambulance chasing lawyers, they get Freddy off, and those are the best parts. Freddy's in the courtroom, and he takes the stand, and the parents of the victims take the stand with the lawyers blaming the parents for alcoholism and opioid use. It's crazy. And in the end, the parents just taking the law into their own hands and burning Freddy alive. I heard about that at a Monster Party a few years ago, from a guy working at New Line and I thought that's the one. It's a little bit like what Tobe Hooper did for the pilot on the television series. When* **Freddy's Nightmares** *still had money and the original producers, they took ten days to shoot them back then and they gave Toby free reign. That's why the pilot is so good for that show.*

DC: I want to switch gears a little bit here. You were a really huge proponent of Mark Patton's documentary *Scream, Queen! My Nightmare On Elm Street*. I was wondering what you think of *Freddy's Revenge*'s reputation as "the gayest horror movie ever made" and that film's evolving legacy?

RE: I don't know if it's the gayest. Maybe **The Hunger** *with Susan Sarandon, David Bowie and Catherine Deneuve. That's pretty* great gay horror. But I feel that was definitely a subtext. If you were to remake **Nightmare 2** now you could further. And you could see the fun of Freddy manipulating Mark Patton's character, and knowing subconsciously Mark was gay and playing with him, playing with that. And playing with the Robert Rusler character because Freddy knows their subconscious; he knows their dreams and that's what we were doing. We were hinting about that in the movie.

What was amazing to me about Mark's documentary was I didn't know any of that stuff about AIDS and what had happened to his partner and everything and what he went through. He was just ahead of the curve at that time because AIDS had just hit in Hollywood. Everybody was kind of "Don't Ask, Don't Tell" and I think it was very frustrating for Mark at that moment in time. I knew about Mark before, as a little theater actor. I'd heard great stories about Mark in the wonderful **Come Back to the Five & Dime, Jimmy Dean, Jimmy Dean**. He did the play before he did the movie with Cher and the great Sandy Denis. So I knew he was in this great play and, you know, maybe Mark should have gone back to New York after **Nightmare 2** and done another play. Maybe that would have been the wisest choice. He was so involved with his partner and his illness in LA and I didn't know any of that, and it was just really eye opening, that documentary.

My wife and I, one of our great regrets, is that we never got down to Puerto Vallarta which is where they shot that great movie **Night of the Iguana** with Richard Burton and Elizabeth Taylor, directed by John Huston. But my wife and I never got down there and apparently Mark had this great art gallery in the lush, beautiful foothills of Puerto Vallarta. Mark knew everybody down there, all the secret B&B's. I just wish I had gone down and share the time with Mark. I kept meaning to. I just never got down there. I would have loved to see that town through his eyes.

DC: Since we're talking about *Nightmare on Elm Street* sequels, I'm just curious: What's your favorite *Nightmare on Elm Street* sequel?

*RE: Oh, I think **Wes Craven's New Nightmare** is the best. It's meta, it's deconstructed, and he made it for the fans. You can watch it over and over again and it holds up. It's really good on DVD and Blu-ray and there's some great hidden Easter Eggs in it. I tell people, watch Heather Langenkamp playing Heather Langenkamp. Watch her go to visit her husband's set, the Wes Craven movie, with her husband doing special effects. Watch her costume: It slowly shifts and it's really interesting to watch her wardrobe. It's kind of like the kid in jeopardy; that's a real Guillermo Del Toro troupe, to have a child in jeopardy. A kind of child witness through the horror. He does it in **Mimic**, he does it in a lot of his films. He has the child witness and I think it's a great troupe, a great hook, and Wes does it in **New Nightmare**.*

DC: What's your personal favorite Freddy Kruger kill?

*RE: I think it's the boy in part six [**Freddy's Dead: The Final Nightmare**] with the hearing aid. That's a good one. It's so politically incorrect.*

DC: What's your personal favorite Freddy Kruger one-liner?

*RE: Well, I like mine, the one I came up with, which was, "Welcome to prime time, bitch!". There were some good one-liners in **Freddy vs. Jason** too.*

DC: Speaking of *Freddy vs. Jason*, we've all heard that there were storyboards for a final scene that would have included Pinhead from *Hellraiser*. Who do you think would win in a fight between Freddy and Pinhead?

RE: Oohh…you know Doug Bradley's an old pal. We did a couple of movies together and we did some CD projects of H.P. Lovecraft together. I really like Doug. I don't know…I think the baseline is if anybody has to sleep, even the sleep of stupidity like Jason, even a dumb, passed out monster sleep… If they encounter Freddy and they sleep, at some point in whatever their world is Freddy can get to them. So that means Freddy would win, if he can get to you and manipulate you and exploits something that scares you or hurts you or that you're afraid of or that can kill you.

DC: Robert, it's been great talking to you. I'm a journalist so I'd like to get something unique and juicy. Can you tell me something about ***A Nightmare on Elm Street*** **that's never been reported or that you've never told anyone before?**

*RE: I think I've told all the secrets… Oh, maybe you don't know this: I think the reason Johnny Depp got the part [in the first **Nightmare on Elm** Street] was Wes Craven's daughter threatened her dad. She was like "Dad, if you don't cast him, I'm leaving home!" So, I think she was the real selling point for Johnny getting the role: Wes Craven's daughter.*

Kevin Bacon

REVEALS HOW HE WOULD HAVE REBOOTED FLATLINERS & GUSHES OVER ONE CUT OF THE DEAD

Method: *Video Conference*

Reflections: I remember playing 6-Degrees of Kevin Bacon with friends in the 1990s. So having the opportunity to talk to this iconic actor was a real thrill. For kicks, you can play yourself, connecting Bacon to everyone else that I interviewed in this book. And… Go!

Since he played Jack in the original ***Friday the 13ᵗʰ*** (1980), it's not exaggeration to say that Bacon has been part of horror history since the genre's heyday. And while he's not a horror actor exclusively, he's no stranger to terrifying tales, having appeared in ***Flatliners***, ***Tremors***, ***Stir of Echoes***, and more. And he continues popping up in horror today, having recently appeared in ***You Should Have Left*** (discussed below) and 2022's ***They/Them***.

By June 2020, it was painfully obvious that the Pandemic wasn't going to go away in a matter of weeks (or months). Not only that, the summer months signaled the beginning of a terrifying surge. But being told to remain indoors as the weather got hotter was a maddening endeavor, and cracks were beginning to show as COVID became increasingly politicized.

Films take years to complete. So, while the producers couldn't possibly have intended this, *You Should Have Left* felt nonetheless apropos of life at that moment: Trapped indoors.

———

ORIGINALLY PUBLISHED: **June 22, 2020**

Kevin Bacon struck up a lasting friendship with David Koepp over 20 years ago on the set of *Stir of Echoes* (where the later served as screenwriter and director). The duo recently re-teamed on the twisty supernatural shocker *You Should Have Left*, now streaming everywhere.

Dread Central was lucky enough to score a sit-down with Bacon. In addition to *You Should Have Left*, we got something of a career retrospective, touching on *Friday the 13th*, *Tremors*, and *Flatliners*. Dive in below the synopsis for *You Should Have Left*.

Synopsis: *In this terrifying, mind-twisting tale, a father fights desperately to save his family from a beautiful home that refuses to let them leave. Theo Conroy (Bacon) is a successful middle-aged man whose marriage to his much younger actress wife, Susanna (Amanda Seyfried) is shredding at the seams, frayed by her secretiveness, his jealousy, and the shadow of his past. In an effort to repair their relationship, Theo and Susanna book a vacation at a stunning, remote modern home in the Welsh countryside for themselves and their six-year-old daughter, Ella (Avery Essex). What at first seems like a perfect retreat distorts into a perfect nightmare when Theo's grasp on reality begins to unravel and he suspects that a sinister force within* *the house knows more than he or Susanna have revealed, even to each other.*

Dread Central: In *You Should Have Left*, your character is married to an actor and what sets off all the drama hearing her in a sex scene. It got your character thinking, "If she can fake it with him, she can fake it with me." Since you ARE married to an actor I was wondering if that was something you and Kyra Sedgwick can relate to?

Kevin Bacon: Yeah, I mean, I think being married to an actor has its challenges. Now if it's specifically faking it in a sex scene, I think that's a way to kind of drive home how it's a little more complex than that. When you go off to work, as you know, you work in these very intimate settings, you're there for really long stretches of time, you're in emotional types of situations and close contact with a lot of people. Sometimes you're on location in hotels, and on top of that, everybody always refers to the crew like "family". You hear that a lot. So, if you're in a marriage and you happen to deal with that, it can be challenging. You don't know these people, you don't have the same kind of relationship with them. The person comes home and says, "Oh wow, I can't believe Jimmy said that," or whatever. That's why we very specifically wanted [the character of my wife, played by Amanda Seyfried] to be an actor, to lay in that paranoia, as well as the fact that she's younger than him, way younger. And he is a man filled with a lot of doubts, paranoia, at this point in their lives. He clearly loves her, and it seems like she loves him, but these nagging doubts are eating away at him.

DC: It's almost impossible not to see aspects of *You Should Have Left* as a metaphor for the Coronavirus pandemic, right?

Kevin: We certainly didn't know there was going to be a pandemic when we made the film, but the idea that people are stuck in a house, and the amount of time you spend in the house, the house can kind of take on its own character, it's certainly something I think people can relate to at this particular time.

DC: Yeah, it makes it very timely, whether it was intentional or not. *You Should Have Left* was a reunion for you and David Koepp, 20 years since you two did *Stir of Echoes* together. What made you guys want to work together again and did you have the same chemistry this time around?

*KB: I wanted to work with David from the day they said "wrap" on **Stir of Echoes**. He was busy with a lot of other stuff, I was busy with stuff. But we did stay friends which is pretty unusual in this Hollywood life, where you keep a real friend long after the movie has wrapped. I was always saying, "Come on man, let's go make something contained, in the same kind of genre as **Stir of Echoes**. We did it well the first time around." One of the blessings of this project was developing it with him. He's such a fantastic writer, and to work and collaborate with him is amazing. I love his eye, his attention to detail and it was a great process. I think we have a real shorthand that comes from both having made one movie but also being friends for so many years. He just wrote a great book, a short story I guess you would call it, or novella, called **Yard Work** that I read for Audible. It's a creepy, fun, scary kind of thriller and I got to do the audio book for it, so that was fun.*

DC: Let's do a little career retrospective while I've got you here. *Friday the 13th* is celebrating its 40th anniversary this year. When you made the film in 1980, did you have any idea you were participating in what would become a cultural phenomenon?

KB: Absolutely not, no. Look, in 1980 I needed a gig. It's not like I had a lot to choose from. I was doing a lot of theater in New York and I got this audition, got the part and the film was shot in Blairstown,

New Jersey, which was on the other side of the George Washington Bridge. And for the most part I was able to shoot and run back to the city, to the village, to do plays. I kind of thought it would come out, find its little niche on the first weekend, the horror audience, and bang, it was so successful. And you could tell me how many **Friday the 13ths** *they made. A lot.*

DC: 12 if you count *Freddy vs. Jason* and the remake in 2009. So, let's jump to the 90's and *Tremors*, another franchise that is still kicking out sequels. We all heard in 2018 that you made a pilot or made for TV movie but we never got to see it. Can you tell us a little bit about what happened?

KB: I looked at that character [Valentine McKee] and thought to myself, "You know, this is probably the only character I have ever played that I want to really go back and see what's happened to him." He was such a fascinating character to me because he's such an ordinary man. Not that smart, not that special, and yet he had this extraordinary circumstance that he had to sort of step up to the plate for. I thought to myself, "If you take that away, if they just went away, those worms, what does a guy like that do? The rest of his life has now really become uninteresting," so exploring that I thought would be fun. We made an excellent pilot outside of Albuquerque, recreated the town, had a really great cast, director and writer. And to this day I still don't understand why they didn't want to move forward with it. It's a real head scratcher for me. If I honestly thought the pilot was shit then I'd say we just didn't crack it. But it was cool, and that's a really hard balance to get, between funny and scary. As you know, that's the sweet spot. **Tremors** *was good at that, as were* **Shawn of the Dead** *and* **Get Out***. But yeah, it was for a series, not a TV movie.*

DC: Well, hopefully something else will come of it. We're all huge fans and we'll keep our fingers crossed that it will see the light of day. Let's stick

in the 90's for a second because I've always been a huge fan of *Flatliners*. We recently did a little expose for film's 30th Anniversary. It was a great film, had such great aesthetic, but they really bungled the reboot a couple of years ago. I was curious, if someone came to you and said they wanted you to produce a legitimate sequel to *Flatliners*, what approach would you take?

*KB: That's a really good question. I don't know but I could tell you that to me, the most interesting element of it was having things in your past you regret come back. And we also deal with that in **Stir of Echoes** and **You Should Have Left**. Those are interesting topics so I think I would probably lean into that. But it's been a very long time since I've seen **Flatliners**, probably since it came out, so I'd have to see it again first before I'd have a really good take on it.*

DC: You should look back on it! You don't have anything to be ashamed of there. I think it's aged very well. It's definitely of an era but story wise it's solid and the acting is top notch all around.

KB: I seem to remember there was a lot of hair.

DC: All of you guys had a lot more hair back then! So, let's circle back to *You Should Have Left* a bit because one of your most recent horror flicks was *The Darkness*, and that film was also about a family facing off against a supernatural power. Are you attracted to that kind of story, a family in peril sort of horror troupe?

*KB: I like family movies. I like family dramas, movies like **Ordinary People** you know. There is actable stuff there. The reason that horror excites me is you have these life-or-death situations people are in and there can be a lot of room for emotional extremes. Also, as* *an actor, you have the challenge of trying to temper and modulate your level of fear and terror. It can't be all one note and that can be a real challenge. Challenges are something that draw me as an actor and certainly that is what these films have afforded me, these challenges.*

DC: You mentioned *Shawn of the Dead* and *Get Out*. What are some other recent horror movies that have made an impression on you?

*KB: One of my favorites is pretty obscure but if anyone has ever seen it it's probably you. It's called **One Cut of the Dead**. The thing about **One Cut of the Dead** is that, I don't think I've ever seen anything quite like it and it works on a few different levels. The friend of mine that turned me on to it said, "Ok, whatever you do, you're going to think I've recommended the worst movie ever for you... but, I don't want to spoil it. Just hang in there!" And I'm so glad that I did. I would say it's a little more funny than it is scary maybe but it's also this really kind of a loving look at the genre and low budget film making, things that I can really relate to. So I think that's a pretty cool one.*

DC: It was fantastic, I'll agree with you there. So, is there anything else you'd like our readers to know? Anything you'd like to share specifically about *You Should Have Left*?

*KB: I guess just that I also want to mention the child, Avery Essex, who is in it: She's amazing. David did a great job with the little boy who was in **Stir of Echoes**. He's very, very good with kids and is able to create a safe working environment for children, which I think is much more important than making a good movie. But also getting this amazing performance out of her and kids. She'd never acted before, been in a movie before. She might have done some commercials or something like that, but she was pretty remarkable.*

DC: Well, that's great to hear. They always say, "Don't work with animals and kids," but I've heard plenty of examples of people saying that the opposite is true, that with a great director and great young actor you can really do some amazing things. And you're absolutely right, Avery was fantastic. Well, thanks again Kevin, I really enjoyed *You Should Have Left* and I hope everyone checks it out.

KB: Thanks man, appreciate it.

David Arquette

Method: *Phone*

Reflections: David Arquette comes from a famous Hollywood family, has an absolutely wacky filmography, and has
lived a truly wild life (just look into his career as a wrestler if
you don't believe me). Still, he was incredibly down to earth.
Talking to David was like striking up a fantastic, genuine
conversation with a person you just met at a dive bar.

The main topic of conversation was ***Spree***, a film that terri-
fyingly satirizes social media obsession and the quest for
internet fame. I loved getting David's perspectives. It was
really eye-opening to hear him discuss how even celebrities
with established careers are being pulled (sometimes kicking
and screaming) into the social media sphere. In fact, it's
increasingly seen as essential.

Don't get me started. I abhor social media obsession. I hate
Twitter and Instagram (and Tik Tok and whatever digital
Hydra comes next). And yet, I too acknowledge the power
of these platforms. It disheartens me that we're in an era

where having tons of followers is somehow more important than having skill/talent/knowledge. I hope this is merely a blip in history, that it won't be long before we look back and laugh at how much credence we gave so-and-so, just because they had X-number of followers. End diatribe.

Just days after this article was published, my girlfriend and I eloped to Las Vegas and got married. When it felt like planet earth was on the brink of going up in flames, we retreated into our love and made hopeful plans for a bright future. It wouldn't be long until we had relocated to Los Angeles (back to my roots). I had decided that returning to Southern California after a 20-year absence was the best thing possible for my career. Yes, the entertainment industry was still, basically, on lockdown, but I wanted to be where the action was as soon as doors started opening again. These were crazy, unpredictable times when nothing was certain and anything seemed possible.

———

ORIGINALLY PUBLISHED: **August 17, 2020**

Now in theaters, digital, and On Demand, *Spree* is directed by Eugene Kotlyarenko (*Wobble Place*, *0s & 1s*) from a script co-written by Kotlyarenko and Gene McHugh. The film features an all-star cast led by Joe Keery (*Stranger Things*) in his first film feature leading-role, Sasheer Zamata (*Saturday Night Live*), and David Arquette (the *Scream* franchise).

Spree is executive produced by award-winning rapper and record producer Drake ("Toosie Slide," "Hotline Bling").

Synopsis: *Meet Kurt, from @KurtsWorld96 (Joe Keery). He dreams of sitting atop a social media empire, but for now he drives for* the rideshare company *Spree*. *Fortunately, Kurt has come up with the perfect way to go viral: #TheLesson. He's decked out his car with cameras for a nonstop livestream full of killer entertainment – murdering his passengers. In the middle of all this madness, a stand-up comedian (Sasheer Zamata) with her own viral agenda crosses Kurt's path and becomes the only hope to put an end to his misguided carnage.*

Follow @kurtsworld96 on Instagram to learn more!

We were lucky enough to score a sit-down with David Arquette during which we discussed **Spree** (and his character Kris Kunkle) at length. We also tried to squeeze him for new details about the recently announced **Scream 5**. Enjoy!

Dread Central: I'm about your age and what *Spree* really brought home for me was just how much fame, and the idea of being famous, has changed in the 21st Century. I remember as a kid wanting to be a rock star or an actor, but now it's like everyone is an "influencer" and the only thing that matters is how many followers you have. Do you feel like being famous means something different today than it did in the 80's and 90's?

David Arquette: Yeah, I do. It's interesting: I think it comes down to the fact that everyone really wants to be loved. They want to be appreciated, understood, and it's a social media world where people can actually make a living off of being these social media influencers. So, on top of it, there's a financial component. One thing people will learn from getting famous is that there are a lot of drawbacks to it. When people invade your privacy, monopolize you, you have to watch what you do and say. There are a lot of things you have to be careful of. But the best thing about it is you can lend your name to charities, which is pretty much the most positive aspect of being a celebrity. But yeah, for me, I'm kind of lost when it comes to the social media world. I don't really know how to deal with it. I tolerate it, I try to use it to promote things that I'm doing. I try to stay in touch with fans. But I don't get too caught up in reading comments, take things too personally, or block people and all this stuff.

DC: Another thing that *Spree* really illustrated for me was how the line between being famous and being infamous has almost completely disappeared. It's like talent doesn't matter and nothing is off limits. Do you think the drive to become famous, or "internet famous", has become dangerous?

DA: I think it's just a misguided understanding. You know, there's an aspect to [Joe Keery's character] Kurt [Kunkle] that's sociopathic. He doesn't have an understanding of empathy for the pain that he is going to cause all these people. So, that's' something we need to be aware of, as far as society goes. I like the fact that society doesn't typically say the name of mass murderers now, not spread their name. But it's a crazy world right now. In general, we have a lack of empathy, a lack of being kind to one another and a lack of a social construct in being polite to each other. It's all a big reflection of what we are going through.

DC: Very well put. You kind of hit on this already but in *Spree*, you play a Gen-X'er like myself, we're about the same age, who is trying to adapt to this new millennial model of fame and being famous. It's funny because your character is kind of a man child who never grew up, but it also illustrates how he's bought into this idea that everyone needs to play by these new rules. I'm curious: You're famous and have been famous for several decades now, so has social media changed the way you quantify your own fame or relevance?

DA: It's definitely changed because studios and producers, they look at how many followers you have, and if it comes down to you and another actor and you don't have a strong social media base, you may lose a job because of it. It's pretty important as far as that goes but it's also important to be able to communicate with fans to let them know what's coming out. But the character [I play in **Spree***], Kris, is just so lost in that world. He's still holding onto his dream of being a DJ, a musician in some way. He's definitely lost and doesn't know how to do it all. He's not very responsible in terms of having a job and being a loving father. That was interesting to sort of discover that.*

[Director] Eugene [Kotlyarenko], Joe and I went out in Los Angeles before we started shooting, to have a night of bonding, and shoot some behind the scenes clips that are up at kurtsworld96 on Instagram, because they built this whole Instagram site, as if it was Kurt's. And it's really impressive what they've done. They've created memes, product reviews… They really took a deep dive into influencers that didn't have a lot of followers. So why were they doing it? Why would they continue to do it when only four or five people are watching? It's just kind of fun. It really helped me an understanding of the world we were in and during that whole process. The Kurt character would say something and I would think to respond as the father, which I am, in a fatherly way. But then I'd have to check myself instantaneously, before I improv, what a bad father would do. A bad father would make it about himself, belittle his son, not be supportive or understanding. So, it made for this really interesting exercise where we kind of ended up feeling like, "Oh, ok. I mean, my character is not a sociopath, like Kurt is." So, I have feelings. I want my son to love me, but I feel like my character is more of a narcissist, where he wants him to love him for himself because he's so great, anyway.

DC: **Spree** **really seems to represent this new model of filmmaking as well, where we get an approximation of a social media experience, something normally confined to phones and laptop**

computers. Do you think we'll be seeing more of films in this style?

DA: Yeah, absolutely. I think it's just part of our culture now, part of our world, part of our communication with each other.

DC: I write for Dread Central and I know that our readers would kill me if I didn't ask about *Scream* 5. Is there anything you can tell me about *Scream 5* that hasn't been reported yet?

*DA: We're really excited about the filmmakers [Radio Silence]. I had a conversation with them and they are fans of [**Scream** mastermind] Wes [Craven]. They want to honor Wes and his legacy. I'm really excited that Courteney [Cox] is on board, we've all got our fingers crossed that Neve [Campbell] joins as well. And it will be great to just bring everyone back together and be able to play these characters again. I love playing the role of Dewey, growing my moustache out, and I don't know when the film is going to go but hopefully it will go soon.*

DC: Fantastic. Is there anything else you want to tell our readers before you go?

DA: You guys have been really supportive and I appreciate it.

Crispin Glover

SAYS HIS CHARACTER IN SMILEY FACE KILLERS COULD BE CONNECTED TO RIVER'S EDGE

Method: *Phone*

Reflections: Did you know that Crispin Glover's middle name is Hellion? No, that's not a joke and, yes, it's a totally fitting moniker. For a while, Crispin was on track to become my generation's Andy Kaufman. His feverish, unhinged appearance on ***The Late Show with David Letterman*** in 1987 got him temporarily banned, but it also made him a legend. People are still wondering to this day: Was it all an act or is he really crazy? Hellion, indeed.

Sometimes, though not often, there will be certain off-limits topics. In the case of Crispin, a rep told me I was not to ask him anything about ***Back to the Future***. As a horror guy, I didn't even know what the deal was, so I had to do some research. While I won't claim to be an expert, there was an apparent dust-up between Crispin (who played George McFly) and the film's writer/director and writer/producer (Robert Zemeckis and Bob Gale respectively). There's also a rumor that Crispin demanded equal pay with the franchise's lead star, Michael J. Fox. In the end, Crispin was replaced in both **Back to the Future** sequels by an actor wearing George McFly prosthetics. Crispin sued. The story actually goes on and on, making a quick summary of the scenario impossible. It isn't difficult to find mountains of details online; look for the article "Why Crispin Glover Wasn't in Back to the Future Sequels" on **80s Kids**, for starters. The ironic part of it all is, in this case, is that I had absolutely no interest in discussing **Back to the Future** in the first place

I was excited to talk to Crispin Glover about the horror movies he's appeared in throughout his career, along with some of the other iconic villains he's played. Because anyone who's seen the guy on a movie theater screen knows there's something special (and potentially maniacal) about this fellow.

So, was Crispin the nut everyone thinks he is? Not in the slightest. Crispin is a talented, complex, passionate artist who approaches every project with serious intensity. He's an intelligent, thoughtful person and I thoroughly enjoyed making his acquaintance.

I've been lucky enough to interview Crispin twice: Once for the written interview below and once as part of an online showing of **Smiley Face Killers**. That one was a live-streamed roundtable with Crispin and the film's co-stars, Ronen Rubinstein and Mia Serafino. In that instance, he was just as professional and genuine. He made certain not to overshadow his co-stars, knowing that the opportunity meant more for them than him. Class act all the way.

I saw **River's Edge** when I was in high school and it absolutely blew my mind. My favorite part of the interview below was discussing Crispin's portrayal of Layne—and the possibility that **River's Edge** and **Smiley Face Killers** are connected.

On a personal note, my wife and I had officially relocated to Los Angeles by the time this interview was published on Dread Central. Even though there wasn't really an end in sight where the pandemic was concerned, I was poised for the industry's re-opening. Everything was changing and I was exactly where I needed to be.

———

ORIGINALLY PUBLISHED: **December 2, 2020**

From novelist Bret Easton Ellis (**American Psycho**) and director Tim Hunter (**River's Edge**) comes the terrifying true-crime-inspired horror movie **Smiley Face Killers**. Look for it in Select Theaters and on Digital and On Demand anywhere you rent or buy movies on December 4th and on Blu-ray and DVD on December 8th.

Dread Central is hosting a virtual screening and Q&A with **Smiley Face Killers** cast members Crispin Glover (**River's Edge**), Ronen Rubinstein (Fox's **9-1-1: Lone Star**) and Mia Serafino (NBC's **Crowded**) on Tuesday, December 8th at 4 PM (PST).

Dread Central was lucky enough to score a sit-down with Glover, who discussed the process of transforming for **Smiley Face Killers** and how his character may be connected to Layne from **River's Edge**. Give our conversation a read below the synopsis!

Synopsis: *As a strange wave of mysterious drownings of male college students plagues the California coast, Jake Graham struggles to keep his life together at school. Finding himself stalked by a hooded* *figure driving an unmarked van, Jake fears he may become the next victim in the killers' horrific spree.*

Dread Central: One of your first breakout films was *River's Edge* (released in 1986) and now you're appearing in *Smiley Face Killers*, both directed by Tim Hunter. What was it like to work with Tim again after all these years and how have you evolved as an actor and an artist?

*Crispin Glover: Well, Tim is the reason I'm in the movie. It's great working with Tim. I've been friendly with him since all the years we shot **River's Edge**. He approached me to do it and I was in the middle of a film. I make my own films as well; a filmmaker that's been toying around for fifteen years. My first film **What Is It**, this is the fifteenth year I've toured [with it]. I actually did a tour at the beginning of the year before everything shut down. I perform hour-long live shows of books that are profusely illustrated and projected behind me, then I show my feature film, then a Q&A, and then a book signing at the end. I've been doing this for fifteen years now. I've got two feature films that I've completed that I've been touring around with all this time.*

*I'm currently working on a third feature film, which is actually not part three of what will be a trilogy that the first two are part of. It's a film with my father. He's an actor, Bruce Glover. He's in films like **Diamonds are Forever** and **Chinatown**. He and I had never acted together before so I developed this project for he and I to act in. I've been developing it for many years and was in the middle of shooting, or preparing for a production segment, shooting different production segments over the years, unlike most feature films where it's done in one increment. But I've done smaller production segments for many years, and I was just about to do this production segment when Tim approached me about this film and my whole concentration was on my own filmmaking.*

When I do a production segment, I don't have a big team around me. I'm really doing it myself. On the days of the shoot, I have a whole production team but I do everything so it's a huge amount of work. I looked at the script and I knew Bret Easton Ellis. He's an excellent writer, and I had experience working with Tim, so I looked at it. But I just looked at the character to see what it was. I read through that very quickly because I was in the middle of other stuff with my own film, and my feeling was it did not need an actor. It just needed an interesting looking person.

I turned it down at first and Tim was really quite insistent. So I got on the phone with him and he said he really thought I would add something to it, and then he mentioned a prosthetic. Something has happened with contemporary prosthetics in that they look very much like a mask and I said, "Well if we could do something that was like what Lon Chaney was doing in the 1920s..." where you really see the facial features. And that is done with hooks, that are pulled in various places, and it's not particularly comfortable, part of the reason they really don't do it anymore. But Tim said he was ok with it.

So I said, "You like the script, you think this is something you can do, make something interesting?" And he said, "Yes" and I just trusted Tim. So I said, "Alright, I'll do it, I'll go in and meet with the fellow..." who did a great job with the prosthetic. He knew all the tricks with what Lon Chaney had done. We didn't do the same thing as Chaney but that kind of technique which as I said has a hook up here and then a hook in the mouth that is pulled by a latex piece. I had to physically have the cords tied to a loop in my belt and it was a complicated and not normally done procedure, but it does have a great effect and it is a bit uncomfortable. My enormous respect to Lon Chaney because compared to what I did he had way more stuff. The binding of his arms and legs; he did incredible performances on top of the fact that he designed the makeup himself. What he did was amazing. I just had a very small amount of screen time really, but even that small amount of time, it hurts after just a little while, which is why they stopped

doing it. But I asked for it myself so I couldn't complain and it's effec-
tive so I'm glad.

DC: Before we get back to *Smiley Face Killer* and
your career as a whole, I wanted to talk about
***River's Edge* a bit because I'm a huge fan of the**
film and your performance is so compelling. I
wanted to ask about Layne, because we've all had
friends like him growing up, people taking things
way too seriously and lose their perspective. At the
same time, there is something so genuinely
endearing about him like he's genuinely doing it
for his friends because he thinks, in my interpreta-
tion, that friendship is extremely important. I just
wanted to ask you, and maybe you could talk about
Tim's direction, but what made Layne tick? What
were the character's motivations? Where did you
draw from to get that performance?

CG: Well, you know, there are multiple things. First, one of the more
evident elements is I speak with a bit of a dialect in it, which is kind
of an extreme Southern California west coast dialect. I grew up in the
area so I can sort of naturally get to that but it is an extreme version of
it. When I read the script, I remember that it was a fairly quick thing
that I realized would be good for it but there was a more nuanced
aspect.

You mentioned it even with what you were saying, when you said there
was an endearing quality in that he was doing it for his friends, which
is on the page in the script. However, that actually isn't what I was
playing. Maybe that's not the right way to phrase it. Maybe it is what
I was playing but to me what was important for the character was the
character actually wanted attention which is actually insincere. Layne
says, "What I'm doing is for my friends," but, in fact, it's really quite
self-serving.

There's an adage: "Play comedy like tragedy and tragedy like comedy" and this film was essentially a tragedy. And yet there is an element of playing it like comedy. There are performances like that but it doesn't happen in the United States that often. It happens, but not often. That's part of what I like about the character, and the film. The film has a dark quality but there are elements of humor throughout so it has a dynamic that I think is compelling. I'm proud of that movie and I'm always glad it came about. I always enjoy talking about it, but that's what my interpretation would be.

DC: That's very interesting. Where do you think Layne would be today if he was a real person?

*CG: I was joking with Tim Hunter about it, that **Smiley Face Killers** was the obscure sequel to **River's Edge** and that my unnamed character is Layne. He got arrested, got into drugs, and then in jail he had some kind of pipe accident and got burnt. That's where Layne went to, but of course, that's a joke.*

DC: Your filmography is really extensive, but in the villains you've played specifically, you have this ability to be very scary by saying very little. Obviously, I'm talking about *Smiley Face killers*, but also I don't think you say a word, also the Thin Man in *Charlie's Angels*, and it's not something everyone can do. How do you make silence scary?

CG: I'm not sure if I'm necessarily concentrating on it being scary but I do love silent film. We've been talking about Lon Chaney, and there is a different art form, not necessarily in the acting, but in the actual film-making. And I think silent film, when it's good, is more powerful because you're looking at it visually and there's no interpretation of language. Visual is our primary source of interpretation. Even if there is a millisecond, language has a slight delay and there is a bit more consternation that the mind has to go through.

413

So, if something can be purely visual it's that much more powerful. I always, if I can get away with it, say as little as possible. I think it is more powerful generally. Sometimes with certain characters, it's very important that they speak and have a lot to do verbally. I love it when I don't have to say anything but in the same way as anything you're concentrating on that is important for the character to get accomplished, what the character needs to do, and that's the same whether there are words or not. Even when I was in acting classes as a young teenager I always tended to like characters that were a bit unusual, strange, crazy or whatever. I'm attracted to that artistically but I enjoy all kinds of characters as well. I have no issue with playing a scary or creepy character. I find it fun.

DC: Are there any final words about Smiley Face Killers you'd like to leave us with?

CP: December 4th it's going to be available [on VOD], and it's going to open in certain theaters and On Demand. And then, like I said, I'm completing my own film. I believe in January or February of next year I should have it completed but where I'll be touring with it or releasing it that I don't know. There's more information on CrispinGlover.com, Instagram, Facebook, those kinds of things.

*Also, **American Gods** Season 3, I'm in that, which is also out in early January and I'm working on a new thing right now, I just started a new production. I'm just grateful I'm working right now. I was not expecting it, but that just started so I won't talk about that too much. Other things are coming up and people can find out about them on online.*

Adam Wingard

GODZILLA VS KONG DIRECTOR EXPLAINS WHY NO POST-CREDITS SCENE

Method: *Video Conference*

Reflections: We were more than a full year into the pandemic but there were reasons to be cautiously optimistic. We had a vaccine and a new president. Still, no one had seen a movie in an actual theater with an actual audience since lockdown. The pain was real for cinephiles and entertainment journalists.

So it was a thrill to be invited to a drive-in style advanced screening of **Godzilla vs Kong** in March of 2021. The folks at Legendary passed out some amazing gift bags with T-shirts and action figures. While there was no interaction with anyone else in attendance (everyone stayed in their own car), it nonetheless provided a much-needed sense of community.

Godzilla has always been a hot topic at Dread Central. In fact, one of the best performing articles in the site's history (written by me) was about **Godzilla: King of the Monsters**, released in 2019. So that's why we really milked my interview with *Godzilla vs Kong* director, Adam Wingard.

We had been discussing strategy during weekly staff meetings, and someone suggested breaking longer interviews down into smaller, more digestible segments. So, even though I only spoke to Adam for 10 minutes, we spread the coverage out over five articles. Ultimately, this brought in a lot more traffic than a single, long-form interview ever could have. So there you have it: A peak behind the curtain of horror journalism.

————

ORIGINALLY PUBLISHED: **March 22, 2021**

For films that are part of cinematic franchises, post-credits scenes have become all but expected–nay demanded! This is certainly the case for Legendary's last three films in their MonsterVerse. But when early critical responses to *Godzilla vs Kong* (the 4th film in the MonsterVerse, arriving March 31st) hit the internet over the weekend, it was revealed that there is no post-credits scene this time.

We've seen *Godzilla vs Kong* and can confirm that this isn't a rumor or a marketing gimmick. It's true: There is no post-credits scene in *Godzilla vs Kong* (or a mid-credits scene, in case you think we're being coy); nada, zip, zilch. While this doesn't affect our enthusiasm for the film (which left us wanting for nothing) it was certainly unexpected.

So, what made *Godzilla vs Kong* director Adam Wingard decide to buck the norm in this case? And was it always the plan to release the film without a post-credits scene? Here's what he told us during our exclusive interview.

"We actually did shoot a post-credit scene," Wingard explains, "but we ended up using the footage in the movie itself. We never actually edited it as a post-credit scene. It kind of got cannibalized and ended up sort of being the end of the movie. We used it in a slightly different context than it was originally shot for."

"The MonsterVerse is at a crossroads now," Wingard continued. "It's really at the point where audiences have to kind of step forward and vote for more of these things. If this movie is a success obviously, they will continue forward. But I actually think it's good that there's not a post-credit scene because, you know, the MonsterVerse is different from the Marvel universe. Just because you have a [shared] universe it doesn't mean you have to do all the things that Marvel does. And ultimately, I think it's better with sequels to not pigeonhole yourself.

"I think some of the best movies are films that work completely independently and you can go into the sequel or the movie can stand alone. But if a movie is totally contingent on a sequel, then you are just talking about the next thing that is coming up and you can't totally enjoy that ride. But yeah, we did shoot [a post-credits scene] but didn't end up using it."

We'll be sharing more of our exclusive interview with Adam Wingard in our lead-up to ***Godzilla vs Kong***'s release! Look for the film in US theaters and on HBO Max beginning March 31st.

Synopsis:

Legends collide in Godzilla vs. Kong as these mythic adversaries meet in a spectacular battle for the ages, with the fate of the world hanging in the balance. Kong and his protectors undertake a perilous journey to find his true home, and with them is Jia, a young orphaned girl with whom he has formed a unique and powerful bond. But they unexpectedly find themselves in the path of an enraged Godzilla, cutting a swath of destruction across the globe. The epic clash between the two titans—instigated by unseen forces—is only the beginning of the mystery that lies deep within the core of the Earth.

Adam Wingard directs **Godzilla Vs Kong** from a script written by Eric Pearson and Max Borenstein. Terry Rossio, Michael Dougherty, and Zach Shields penned the story based on **Godzilla** by Toho and **King Kong** by Edgar Wallace and Merian C. Cooper.

Godzilla Vs Kong stars Alexander Skarsgård (**The Stand**), Millie Bobby Brown, and Rebecca Hall. Brian Tyree Henry co-stars with Shun Oguri, Eiza González, Jessica Henwick, Julian Dennison, Kyle Chandler, and Demián Bichir. Mary Parent produced with Alex Garcia, Eric McLeod, and Brian Rogers.

Adam Wingard

STILL WON'T EXPLAIN THE ENDING TO 2016'S BLAIR WITCH & HERE'S WHY HE NEVER WILL

Method: *Video Conference*

Originally Published: March 22, 2021

I said it four years ago and I'll say it again today: I'm a huge fan of 2016's ***Blair Witch***, directed by Adam Wingard from a screenplay penned by his frequent co-collaborator, Simon Barrett. The creative use of metaphysics and a shocking conclusion were pure delight, and I'll never understand why the third entry in the ***Blair Witch*** franchise (launched by Daniel Myrick and Eduardo Sánchez in 1999) wasn't a major hit.

Synopsis: *A young man and his friends venture into the Black Hills Forest in Maryland to uncover the mystery surrounding his missing sister. Many believe her disappearance 17 years earlier is connected to the legend of the Blair Witch. At first the group is hopeful, especially when two locals act as guides through the dark and winding woods. As the night wears on, a visit from a menacing presence soon makes them realize that the legend is all too real, and more sinister than they could have ever imagined.*

Blair Witch stars James Allen McCune, Callie Hernandez, and Corbin Reid.

When you listen to Wingard and Barrett's commentary on the *Blair Witch* DVD (which I've done more times than I care to admit) you realize that there are a lot of secrets contained in the film—and the creative duo was holding their cards close to their chests. Specifically, there's been a lot of debate about what we saw at the film's conclusion. Was the long-armed, pale figure Elly Kedward? Fans thought so, but Wingard and Barrett assured us it wasn't. Of course, the actual identity of this monstrosity was never divulged.

So during my recent sit-down with Wingard to discuss *Godzilla vs Kong*, I couldn't help but steer the conversation back to the Black Hills Forest of Burkittsville—if only for a bit. Since so much time has passed, would he finally be willing to shed light on the mysterious conclusion of 2016's *Blair Witch*? Here's what he told us:

"I just have to kind of reiterate, if I was going to reveal what happened I would have revealed it in the movie. That's part of the *Blair Witch*. I have my own interpretation of what's going on there but the mystery of *Blair Witch* is what is so interesting. *The Blair Witch Project*, that's what I always loved: there's never definitive answers. I think it's always important that the filmmakers have an answer, that we're not just like J.J. Abrams. I think he's a very talented director, don't get me wrong, but you always feel like he does this thing where he tees up all these mysteries and he doesn't really have an idea what the mysteries are. He just kind of comes up with really cool ideas and they never quite pay off, and it's always a little disappointing. I do have an idea what was going on in *Blair*

Witch. There are definitely definitive concepts there. But I think unless they were explored in another movie it will just always have to be a mystery."

Don't get your hopes up, horror fans. There's less than a snowball's chance in Hell that Wingard will ever helm another ***Blair Witch*** movie.

"I would never do another ***Blair Witch*** movie," Wingard states definitely. "Making found footage films are a fucking nightmare. It's awful. The most ungratifying type of film-making. It's very difficult. I'm very proud I made that film. I learned a lot doing it and I love that it's like '***Blair Witch: The Ride***'. But yeah, I don't think I'd make another found footage one again. Simon just recently did a segment for ***V/H/S 94*** and he tried to talk me into going down there and doing one. It was during this period where I kind of had an opening and I thought about doing it. But then I was I just like, 'No, I just know where that found footage road leads…' I can't let myself do it."

Unless he experiences a change of heart, it looks like Wingard intends on taking his ***Blair Witch*** secrets to the grave. You're killing us, Adam!

Adam Wingard

EXPLAINS CHARLES DANCE'S ABSENCE IN
GODZILLA VS KONG & REVEALS PART HE WANTED
HIM TO PLAY IN THE GUEST

Method: *Video Conference*

Originally Published: March 23, 2021

Yesterday, we talked to ***Godzilla vs Kong*** director Adam Wingard about the film's lack of a post-credits scene.

We also took a detour into the Black Hills Forest to revisit the controversial ending of 2016's ***Blair Witch***.

For today's exclusive, we're talking about Charles Dance and his notable absence from ***Godzilla vs Kong***. Wingard also reveals how he hoped to cast the actor in a major role in 2014's ***The Guest***! Enjoy our conversation below the synopsis for ***Godzilla vs Kong***!

Synopsis: *Legends collide in Godzilla vs. Kong as these mythic adversaries meet in a spectacular battle for the ages, with the fate of the world hanging in the balance. Kong and his protectors undertake a perilous journey to find his true home, and with them is Jia, a young orphaned girl with whom he has formed a unique and powerful bond. But they unexpectedly find themselves in the path of an enraged*

Godzilla, cutting a swath of destruction across the globe. The epic clash between the two titans—instigated by unseen forces—is only the beginning of the mystery that lies deep within the core of the Earth.

Godzilla Vs Kong stars Alexander Skarsgård (The Stand), Millie Bobby Brown, and Rebecca Hall. Brian Tyree Henry co-stars with Shun Oguri, Eiza González, Jessica Henwick, Julian Dennison, Kyle Chandler, and Demián Bichir. Mary Parent produced with Alex Garcia, Eric McLeod, and Brian Rogers.

Dread Central: I wanted to ask you about Alan Jonah [played by Charles Dance]. He emerged as the main villain in Godzilla: King of the Monsters but then he's nowhere to be found in Godzilla vs. Kong. I was just wondering where he went?

Adam Wingard: That's a good question. I don't know, he's out there somewhere. Presumably, he sold that Gidorah skull to Apex but he's not a part of the plot going on at this point. So, he's out there presumably, somewhere.

DC: Interesting. So maybe he'll pop back up again if Legendary continues the MonsterVerse?

AW: Yeah, could be. My editor was always really pro Jonah. He was like, "I don't understand why he is not in this film! We've got to bring him back!" But it just didn't fit. He was always pushing for him but there wasn't really space for him.

DC: Charles Dance is fantastic, it's hard to imagine any movie where there's no space for him.

*AW: I love Charles Dance. I don't know if you caught my film **The Guest**?*

DC: Only about... six times.

AW: Charles Dance was my first choice to play the Lance Reddick role [playing Major Carver] but he was doing something else, maybe **Game of Thrones**. *He was busy so I couldn't get him, but originally I was like, "He's got to be my 'Loomis' in this movie."*

Wingard directed **The Guest** (released in 2014) from a screenplay written by his frequent collaborator Simon Barrett; the film stars Dan Stevens, Sheila Kelley, and Maika Monroe.

If it's been a while, or if you've never experienced the horror of **The Guest**, check out the film's synopsis below.

Synopsis:

A string of mysterious deaths leads a teenager to become suspicious of a soldier (Dan Stevens) who showed up on her family's doorstep and claimed to be a friend of her dead brother.

Adam Wingard

SUSPECTS BARBARA CRAMPTON ACTUALLY IS A VAMPIRE!

Method: *Video Conference*

Originally Published: March 23, 2021

We got a lot of mileage out of our 10-minute interview with Adam Wingard during a recent press junket for ***Godzilla vs Kong***! We talked about the upcoming film's lack of a post-credits scene, as well as the absence of Charles Dance (who played the main villain, Alan Jonah, in 2019's ***Godzilla: King of the Monsters***).

But we also took a detour out of the MonsterVerse to discuss Wingard's past projects, including 2016's ***Blair Witch***, 2014's ***The Guest***, and we even touched on 2011's ***You're Next***–specifically, that film's star, Barbara Crampton.

Crampton, who was a leading lady in the 1980s, credits Wingard for revitalizing her career in the 21st Century for casting her in ***You're Next***. She's already had an incredible year in 2021; ***Sacrifice*** was a hit and her latest film, ***Jakob's Wife***, got rave reviews out of SXSW.

You can read our full exchange about Barbara Crampton below the trailer and synopsis for *Jakob's Wife*.

Synopsis: *In Jakob's Wife, Anne is married to a small-town minister and feels like her life and marriage have been shrinking over the past 30 years. After a chance encounter with "The Master," she discovers a new sense of power and an appetite to live bigger and bolder than before. As Anne is increasingly torn between her enticing new existence and her life before, the body count grows and Jakob realizes he will have to fight for the wife he took for granted.*

Directed by Travis Stevens (***Girl on the Third Floor***), he co-wrote the film with Mark Steensland (***The Special***) and Kathy Charles (***Castle Freak***). ***Jakob's Wife*** stars Barbara Crampton (***Re-Animator***, ***You're Next***), Larry Fessenden (***Habit***, ***Stake Land***), Nyisha Bell (***Coming 2 America***), Mark Kelly (***The Hot Zone***), Sarah Lind (***Wolfcop***), Robert Rusler (***A Nightmare on Elm Street 2***, ***Vamp***), Bonnie Aarons (***The Nun***, ***The Conjuring 2***), and Phil Brooks (aka CM Punk, ***Girl on the Third Floor***).

RLJE Films plans to release the film in theaters and on Demand on April 16th, 2021 and Shudder will premiere the film on its platform later in the year.

Dread Central: We love Barbara Crampton at Dread Central, and she's had such a great year with *Sacrifice* coming out and *Jakob's Wife* getting all of these wonderful, rave reviews at SXSW. As someone she credits for really revitalizing her career, how does it feel looking at her, enjoying this creative renaissance?

*Adam Wingard: I'm just so proud of her. She's such a great person and such a great actor. I'm glad to see she's really getting into the swing of things. You look at that new movie that she's in, **Jakob's Wife**, and* *you're like, "Is Barbara Crampton maybe a vampire in real life?" Because she's just as gorgeous as she was in the '80s. She's literally not aged at all. So, you kind of have to wonder about it. She's an executive producer on that film, so is that her subtlety disclosing to us that she is an immortal vampire woman? I don't know.*

Adam Wingard

REVEALS HIS FAVORITE KAIJU (WHO ISN'T IN GODZILLA VS KONG)

Method: *Video Conference*

Originally Published: March 24, 2021

In the latest from our exclusive interview with Adam Wingard, we discuss his favorite Kaiju–and it's a weird one!

Read the latest in our conversation with Adam Wingard below the synopsis for ***Godzilla vs Kong***. The film arrives in US theaters and on HBO Max simultaneously on March 31st.

Synopsis: *Legends collide in Godzilla vs. Kong as these mythic adversaries meet in a spectacular battle for the ages, with the fate of the world hanging in the balance. Kong and his protectors undertake a perilous journey to find his true home, and with them is Jia, a young orphaned girl with whom he has formed a unique and powerful bond. But they unexpectedly find themselves in the path of an enraged Godzilla, cutting a swath of destruction across the globe. The epic clash between the two titans—instigated by unseen forces—is only the beginning of the mystery that lies deep within the core of the Earth.*

Godzilla Vs Kong stars Alexander Skarsgård (***The Stand***), Millie Bobby Brown, and Rebecca Hall. Brian Tyree Henry co-stars with Shun Oguri, Eiza González, Jessica Henwick, Julian Dennison, Kyle Chandler, and Demián Bichir. Mary Parent produced with Alex Garcia, Eric McLeod, and Brian Rogers.

*Dread Central: In the press notes I got, you talked about going back and watching all the **Kong** and **Godzilla** movies chronologically. So, I don't want to spoil who is in the film, but if you had access to Toho's entire stable, no licensing issues, is there any Kaiju/Titan you would have loved to have included in **Godzilla vs. Kong**?*

*Adam Wingard: Well I kind of lucked out because the hand I was dealt had exactly the ones I wanted to use. My second favorite **Godzilla** film right after the original (you have to go with the original because it's the best one) but my second favorite one is **Godzilla vs. The Smog Monster** [aka Godzilla vs. Hedorah]. I love the Smog Monster! He's an ugly, awful creature but I love the psychedelic vibe of that film. It's kind of the **Easy Rider** of **Godzilla** movies. So, in terms of the original series, that's the main one I reference in my head and wish we could have somehow had some sort of homage at least to the Smog Monster because he really gave Godzilla a run for his money in that film. He's not the best design; he looks like a trash bag. But he's really a bad-ass monster. He's just pollution basically and has one big evil eye and he's kind of unstoppable. I like unstoppable villains, they're the best.*

Check out the trailer and synopsis for ***Godzilla vs. The Smog Monster*** (released in 1971) below.

Synopsis:

From Earth's pollution, a new monster is spawned. Hedorah, the smog monster, destroys Japan and fights Godzilla while spewing his poisonous gas to further the damage.

Godzilla vs. The Smog Monster is directed by Yoshimitsu Banno and stars Akira Yamauchi, Toshie Kimura, and Hiroyuki Kawase.

The Simple Reason

WHY THE CURSE OF LA LLORONA IS NOT PART OF THE CONJURING UNIVERSE

Method: *Junket*

Originally Published: June 7, 2021

Have you ever noticed how *The Curse of La Llorona* is treated like the red-headed stepchild of *The Conjuring* Universe? There's a very simple reason why. During my exclusive interview with the film's director, Michael Chaves, in advance of *The Conjuring: The Devil Made Me Do It* (which he also directed), I asked just that–and I got a surprisingly definitive response.

Despite what you might have heard, *The Curse of La Llorona* is not part of *The Conjuring* Universe like *Annabelle* and *The Nun*. That's right, even though the character Father Perez (played by Tony Amendola) appeared in both 2014's *Annabelle* and 2019's *La Llorona*, and even though we see a flash of the Annabelle doll in the film, *The Curse* still isn't part of the franchise. The reason why is simple.

The Curse of La Llorona **Synopsis**: *In 1970s Los Angeles, the legendary ghost La Llorona is stalking the night — and the children. Ignoring the eerie warning of a troubled mother, a social worker and her own kids are drawn into a frightening supernatural realm. Their only hope of surviving La Llorona's deadly wrath is a disillusioned priest who practices mysticism to keep evil at bay.*

"The very simple reason [why *La Llorona*] isn't [part of *The Conjuring* Universe is because] it was made without one of the [*Conjuring* franchise] producers, so technically it cannot be fully embraced," Chaves explained. "That's the very simple reason. Originally, there was only supposed to be a playful nod [to *The Conjuring* franchise in *La Llorona*], by putting The Father in and having the Annabelle flash. But it wasn't supposed to be marketed that way. The plan was, you would get into it, and then it's like, 'Oh my God, they're connected!' We weren't, from the beginning, supposed to be doing that. And that's why it has this outsider status. But as [the character] La Llorona is an outsider herself, I think it fits.

"It's a tricky situation, I don't want to give away any trade secrets," Chaves continued. "The idea was just to have a playful connection [to *The Conjuring*] because the myth of La Llorona can stand on its own. But James [Wan] was on as a producer, the conversation got started about an Easter Egg. It just kind of got away from itself. People loved that connection. But *The Conjuring* franchise is created by a team that's been there since the beginning. It's not really right to do an unofficial spinoff without the full team."

So why all the confusion?

"When we premiered it in Austin, it was mistakenly announced as 'The next chapter in *The Conjuring* universe'," Chaves told me. "It sent waves of panic all the way through New Line. We didn't want anyone to be offended. It was supposed to be just a wink and a nod. Not like we're trying to steal your mojo or your brand."

So there you have it, folks. There are only seven, not eight, films in **The Conjuring** universe. They are: **The Conjuring**, **The Conjuring 2**, **Annabelle**, **Annabelle: Creation**, **The Nun**, **Annabelle Comes Home**, and **The Conjuring: The Devil Made Me Do It**. The latter is still playing in theaters nationwide and available to stream on HBO Max.

The Conjuring: The Devil Made Me Do It Synopsis:

A chilling story of terror, murder and unknown evil that shocked even experienced real-life paranormal investigators Ed and Lorraine Warren. One of the most sensational cases from their files, it starts with a fight for the soul of a young boy, then takes them beyond anything they'd ever seen before, to mark the first time in U.S. history that a murder suspect would claim demonic possession as a defense.

Chaves directs **The Conjuring: The Devil Made Me Do It** from a screenplay penned by David Leslie Johnson-McGoldrick; the film stars Vera Farmiga, Patrick Wilson, and Julian Hilliard.

M. Night Shyamalan

Method: *Video Conference*

Reflections: In many ways, it's fitting that my last published interview for Dread Central was with M. Night Shyamalan. Objectively, he's one of the most successful and creative horror practitioners of the 21st Century. Sure, not all of his flicks have been aces, but just like Merrill Hess (played by Joaquin Phoenix) in ***Signs***, M. always swings for the fences. ***Old*** was no different.

A year and a half into the global pandemic, the entertainment industry was no longer waiting it out. Rather, filmmakers and studios began pushing forward, making adjustments for what may very well be the "new normal". The pandemic forced us all to figure out videoconferencing. The technology had already been available for years, but people resisted, insisting in-person was the only real way that work could be done. False!

Just as videoconferencing platforms were being utilized in news broadcasting, they were becoming the main form of connection for entertainment media interviews. No more risky roundtables, no more face-to-face interactions, no more crowded press junkets. So, while technologies and the pandemic were and are continuing to evolve, my interview with M. represents the beginning of a new video age, one that I suspect may signal the end to the long-form interviews, like the ones assembled in this book.

I interviewed M. on Zoom. The studio recorded our session and provided a link to the content. From there, we added our Dread Central bumpers and loaded it onto YouTube. In fact, this final interview wasn't even published with text; just an embedded YouTube video. I've taken the time to transcribe it here because it's worthy of remembering and exploring.

The only frustrating aspects of my interview with M. was just how short it was. Four fucking minutes! There was so much I wanted to ask, and he was an open book. But he was also laid back, mesmerized by my movie posters, and prone to natural digressions. I honestly feel like I could have talked to M. for hours and, whether true or not, it felt like he would have enjoyed a longer conversation as well.

Hey M., if you're reading this, I hope we do get the opportunity to sit down and talk at length, someday. For an interview or just for laughs.

———

ORIGINALLY PUBLISHED: **July 23, 2021**

M. Night Shyamalan's new nightmare *Old* arrives in theaters today, and horror fans are in for a treat! I was lucky enough to sit down with Shyamalan to discuss straddling the line between R-rated and PG-13 horror and the film's twist ending! We even had time to look back (briefly) at *The Happening* (you're welcome, Marcos Codas!).

Check out my exclusive sit-down with M. Night Shyamalan below the synopsis for *Old*!

Synopsis: *This summer, Shyamalan unveils a chilling, mysterious new thriller about a family on a tropical holiday who discover that the secluded beach where they are relaxing for a few hours is somehow causing them to age rapidly … reducing their entire lives into a single day.*

The film stars an impressive international cast including Golden Globe winner Gael García Bernal (Amazon's *Mozart in the Jungle*), Vicky Krieps (*Phantom Thread*), Rufus Sewell (Amazon's *The Man in the High Castle*), Ken Leung (*Star Wars: Episode VII—The Force Awakens*), Nikki Amuka-Bird (*Jupiter Ascending*), Abbey Lee (HBO's *Lovecraft Country*), Aaron Pierre (Syfy's *Krypton*), Alex Wolff (*Hereditary*), Embeth Davidtz (*The Girl with the Dragon Tattoo*), Eliza Scanlen (*Little Women*), Emun Elliott (*Star Wars: Episode VII—The Force Awakens*), Kathleen Chalfant (Showtime's *The Affair*) and Thomasin McKenzie (*Jojo Rabbit*).

Old is a Blinding Edge Pictures production, directed and also produced by M. Night Shyamalan, from his screenplay based on the graphic novel **Sandcastle** by Pierre Oscar Lévy and Frederik Peeters. The film is also produced by Ashwin Rajan (**Glass**, AppleTV+'s **Servant**) and also Marc Bienstock (**Glass**, **Split**). The film's executive producer is Steven Schneider.

Look for **Old** in theaters beginning today, July 23rd.

Dread Central: I'm Josh Millican from Dread Central and I'm here with the one and only M. Night Shyamalan! How are you, Sir?

M. Night Shyamalan: I'm great! Is that a Babadook poster behind you?

DC: It sure is! Do you like it?

MNS: I love it. I love that movie!

DC: Fantastic! Well, let's talk about *Old* because I saw it last night and I was just so impressed. I think you kind of tricked us into thinking we were going to get something on the lighter side of horror, you know, with the PG-13 rating and beautiful setting. I was like, "How intense is this really going to be?" But it really goes to some very dark places. Was it always your intension to make this a PG-13 rated film and did you have to cut anything to get that rating? Tell me a little about that.

*MNS: That's such a fun question. I have always had the same relationship when it comes to the ratings board and my movies. It's always an R rating to begin with and then we calibrate the intensity back [to PG-13]. It's almost always sound-related, believe it or not. Like, in the stabbing scene in **The Village** for example, it was an R, but we calibrated the sound back a bit and made it PG-13. But I'm always arguing [with the MPAA] saying, "Don't penalize me for intensity, for* *executing it in a grounded way. You've really got to be literal with me about this." So, it's always on that fine line of PG-13 and R [when it comes to my movies]. There's that one scene [in **Old**] where a character dies unexpectedly at the hands of another and—that was the tricky one.*

DC: Fantastic. Let's talk about endings because the graphic novel *Old* is based on, *Sandcastle*, doesn't have a concrete ending the way your film does. I understand that *Old* is based on *Sandcastle*, it's not a direct adaptation, but I'm curious: Did you feel pressure to come up with an explanation for it all since you're known for your fantastic twist endings? Did you consider leaving it ambiguous?

*MNS: There are a couple of frames in the graphic novel that I though insinuated an ending. So I took that and went with it. I don't want to point it out but if you go back and look at it, then there's something that's not on the beach. I thought, "Oh, what could that mean?" And I thought of [the ending for **Old**] thinking, "I guess this is what that is," you know? It was my interpretation of those specific images, so the idea for the ending came right away, that feeling of, "This is what the story actually is."*

DC: It's almost torture only getting to speak with you for four minutes, because there are so many things I'd love to ask you. I only have a minute left and it's killing me! I'm giving *Old* a fantastic review, but let's go back in time a bit and talk about *The Happening*! People have been re-evaluating it over the years and there's this really great theory making the rounds in a YouTube video by WhatisAntiLogic?. Have you seen it? It makes a case that there's an alien connection with *Signs* that we all missed. Can you speak to that?

MNS: I haven't seen the video. I'll have to look it up! But one of the great things about making a sequence of films is that people are always looking back and re-examining. It's like when you find an author you like and then you go back and read everything they ever wrote. So, it's a really lovely experience for me as different generations get to watch my films. **But The Happening** *for me came from my love of movies like* **The Birds** *and* **The Blob** *and things like that. Looking at your background, I feel like you and I would have a lot to talk about in terms of the history of horror cinema.*

DC: We're both about the same age, so something I really loved about *Old* was the way it illustrates how you can be 50-years-old overnight.

MNS: I appreciate it, brother. Thank you so much.

Random Snapshots of a Life in Horror

Since many of these interviews were done over the phone, I don't have pictures of everyone in this book. I do, however, have many pictures of the amazing horror celebs I've met along the way!

Here, in no particular order, are photos that have graced my social media feeds over the years. Enjoy!

Linda Blair

Michael Berryman   Eli Roth

Lennea Quigley

Billy Wirth

Gigi Saul Guerrero

Don Coscarelli

A. Michael Baldwin and Kathy Lester

Heather Buckley

Jen and Sylvia Soska

Fantasia Fest

Phantasm Ravager
Director David Hartman

Steven Baldwin from the WM3

Mich Garris and Bill Moseley

The Prodigy Director and Writer:
Nicholas McCarthy and Jeff Buhler

Cleve Hall

Steve Barton

Felissa Rose

Twin Peaks - Kimmy Robertson

Alec Gillis

Winchester Mystery House

Christian Ackerman

David Howard Thornton

Craig J. Flores and Sam Raimi

Jim Jarmusch

Doctor Sleep

Justin Long   Adam Jones from Tool

Wrinkles the Clown

Steven Lang and Joe Begos

Martin Kove and William Sadler

Anastasia and Richard Elfman

Doug Jones   Leonard Maltin

Shane Black

Elilene Detz

Mick Garris

Caroline Williams

Annalyn McCord

Tom Holland and Mick Garris

PRESS

DEEPER THAN HELL

Peter Atkins   Lynn Shaye

Starry Eyes Reunion - Kevin Kölsch and Maria Olsen

Adam Green and Paddy Murphy

Chris Roe

Vanessa Decker

Afterword

If you do the math, you could easily think 2020 and 2021 were slow years for interviews, and you'd probably blame the pandemic. But that isn't the case. I actually did more interviews during the pandemic than at any other time in my career. But you won't find the bulk of them here.

In March of 2020, I was contacted by an ambitious up-and-coming PR agent named Jordan Von Netzer (the founder of Projection PR). He inquired if Dread Central would be interested on collaborating on a live-streaming series he dubbed ***Dissecting Horror***. Jordan would provide the talent and promotional materials; then he would herd the cats, getting everyone assembled on Zoom at showtime. Dread Central would provide the streaming platforms, and I was the go-to host.

Between March 2020 and my retirement from Dread Central, we released dozens of ***Dissecting Horror*** panels, sometimes up to three in a month. Panels would have topics (like Special Effects, Costuming, or Soundtracks) or would promote specific films (like **Hunter Hunter**, **Jakob's Wife**, and **We Need to Do Something**).

While I already considered myself a skilled interviewer, moderating live panels with multiple guests was a new arena. Still, it was something I felt comfortable with and grew to love. Now, I consider myself a top-notch moderator, an organic conversationalist who can put panelists at ease. And I loved that **Dissecting Horror** allowed for audience interactions, as streamers could submit questions on the fly. I'd love to continue moderating in the future, whether online or in-person at conventions. There's something electric and exhilarating about live interactions with multiple personalities, interviewing without a safety net in front of a sizable audience.

In many ways, I feel **Dissecting Horror** represents the future of horror journalism. A shift from transcribed deep-dives in favor of formatted video programming. Everything changes.

In October of 2021, I took a planned three-month hiatus from Dread Central.

On December 6, 2021 I made the following announcement via Facebook and Twitter:

"I will not be returning to Dread Central in January 2022 as previously announced. I love Dread Central with all of my heart. These past two years as Editor-in-Chief have been the best of my life. It's almost like there was no separation between who I am and what I did, and I've never felt more self-actualized. I'll always be proud of my contributions and thankful for the readers who have supported us. The writers I've worked with are amazing. ***It was always me intention to maintain the legacy established by Steve Barton (knowing full well there's no substi-***

tute for Uncle Creepy!). *While still technically on hiatus, I will be exploring new opportunities in 2022. My areas of expertise include horror journalism, film acquisition, and content development. If we've crossed paths during my decade+ in horror, I hope you'll stay in touch—and that our paths will cross again. Continue to follow me for status updates, as well as exciting announcements about new creative endeavors. Humbly, Josh Millican, Editor-in-Chief (2019-2021)."*

Not an hour after posting this, I was contacted by the Editor-in-Chief on another prominent horror outlet who said, essentially: "No one quits their dream job. What gives?"

Is there more to the story? Of course there is! But like I've stated in the intro and throughout, this isn't a tell-all about my time at Dread Central, nor is it a behind-the-scenes expose. But I have no problem revealing that the main reason I took a scheduled leave from Dread is because I became a father.

My son, Leon, was born on October 28th. It would have been so "on brand" for me if he had waited until Halloween, but I digress. Initially, I planned to take three months off from working before getting back into the saddle full time. But fatherhood changes everything, doesn't it? What was important before Leon was born seemed less urgent, past motivators morphed into new goals.

An Editor-in-Chief of a news outlet never really gets time off. I'm not saying they work every minute of every hour, but news doesn't only happen between the hours of 9 to 5. And news doesn't take the weekend off. Plus, "fires" and "emergencies" almost never happen when it's convenient. Things fall out of the sky demanding urgent attention, and it doesn't matter if you're previously engaged or asleep or even on vacation. And, for me personally, the pay wasn't that great.

At the end of the day, it became more important for me to concentrate on being Leon's father than the onslaught of never-ending news or the complex mechanics of managing a team of writers. While I had been invited to continue at Dread in a diminished capacity, it made more sense for me to go out on top. And I'm glad I did.

Were my years at Dread Central perfect? Of course not. But I still consider myself one lucky motherfucker for the opportunities gained, the experiences lived, and the connections made.

Leaving Dread Central didn't mean I was retiring from writing. Nothing, in fact, could be farther from the truth. Leon wasn't three months old before I started planning the next chapter of my life: Books.

Back when Obama was still president, I wrote a crazy, disgusting novel about two drug addicts on a journey into Hell. By the time it was completed and ready to be submitted to publishers, however, I was too deeply invested in my career at Dread Central to push it out. As Editor-in-Chief, especially, I considered it my duty to elevate talented filmmakers, actors, and artists within the horror community. My own creative, personal projects went on the back-burner or on a shelf to collect dust. But stepping away from the daily insanity at Dread allowed me to concentrate on myself again. Returning from journalism to a more creative space felt amazing. ***Deeper Than Hell*** was published by Encyclopocalypse in June of 2021, less than nine months after my departure from Dread.

And now there's this: ***The Dreadful Years***.

I couldn't be prouder of this collection or more thankful to Encyclopocalypse for initiating my transition from journalist to published author.

And, as substantial as this assemblage is, it represents just a fraction of my total output for Dread Central. In addition to interviews, I wrote dozens of lists, scores of editorials, and reams of reviews. Plus, 5-12 news articles every single day—including weekends. I've written literally thousands of articles for Dread Central, including enough tent-pole content for the site to continue earning revenue in perpetuity.

As for the future, I'd love to continue pushing forward into the arenas of fiction and non-fiction simultaneously. To that end, I'm currently working with Richard Elfman on an authorized biography. I'll also be penning a novelization of The *Forbidden Zone*, which will be released by Encyclopocalypse in 2023. And when the dust from these projects settles, I can't wait to write a sequel to *Deeper Than Hell*.

Thank you to everyone who supported me during my career as a journalist and editor, especially during my years at Dread Central.

This is my resume. These are my references.

About the Author

Photo credit: Ama Lea

Over the past decade-plus, Joshua Millican has proven himself to be a horror expert of the highest caliber. After establishing a personal blog in 2011, Millican quickly became one of the genre's premiere journalists, contributing to many websites before ultimately landing at Dread Central in 2016. One of the top horror outlets on the planet, Millican served as Editor-in-Chief from 2019 through 2021.

In addition to writing, Millican has been a member of numerous festival juries, a popular podcast guest, and has even scored a handful of acting gigs. His talk show Chronic Horror (sidelined by the Pandemic) explored the intersection of horror movie fandom and cannabis culture. Now married and a father for the first time, Millican is excited to pen more hardcore horror/sci-fi/fantasy fiction for Encyclopocalypse Publications.

Follow Joshua Millican on Twitter at @josh_millican.

Index

Index

Index

Index

Index

Index

Index

Index

Index

Index

D

Index

Index

Index

Index

Index

Index

Index

Index

Index

Index

Index

Index

Index

Index

Index

Index

Index

Index

Index

Index

Index

Index

Index

Index

Index

Index

Index

Index

Index

Index

315

Index

Index